Teaching Coding through Game Creation

TEACHING CODING THROUGH GAME CREATION

Sarah Kepple

LIBRARIES
UNLIMITED™
An Imprint of ABC-CLIO, LLC
Santa Barbara, California • Denver, Colorado

Library of Congress Cataloging-in-Publication Data

Names: Kepple, Sarah, author.
Title: Teaching coding through game creation / Sarah Kepple.
Description: Santa Barbara : ABC-CLIO, [2018] | Includes bibliographical
    references and index.
Identifiers: LCCN 2018021624 (print) | LCCN 2018026221 (ebook) |
    ISBN 9781440851896 (ebook) | ISBN 9781440851889 (hard copy : alk. paper)
Subjects: LCSH: Computer games—Programming. | Computer programming—
    Study and teaching (Elementary) | Education—Data processing.
Classification: LCC QA76.76.C672 (ebook) | LCC QA76.76.C672 K48 2018
    (print) | DDC 794.8/1525—dc23
LC record available at https://lccn.loc.gov/2018021624

ISBN: 978-1-4408-5188-9 (paperback)
      978-1-4408-5189-6 (ebook)

22 21 20 19 18   1 2 3 4 5

This book is also available as an eBook.

Libraries Unlimited
An Imprint of ABC-CLIO, LLC

ABC-CLIO, LLC
130 Cremona Drive, P.O. Box 1911
Santa Barbara, California 93116-1911
www.abc-clio.com

This book is printed on acid-free paper ∞

Manufactured in the United States of America

For Andy, who thinks I can do anything, and
who encourages me to try.

Contents

Preface

I don't quite remember when my family got our first computer, but I know we had it by the time I was in second grade because I remember having a slumber party that year, during which my friends—none of whom had computers at home—all wanted to play on it until the wee hours of the morning. I certainly didn't mind. I can still remember the text commands we needed to enter to load games from floppy disks onto the Commodore 64 (for those who are curious, it was and is *LOAD "FROGGER", 8, 1*). I felt very fortunate then, but I didn't realize just how impactful having a home computer from such a young age would be on my life.

Having a father who was fascinated by the latest advances in technology meant that we always had a computer keeping up with the times, that I could type, use a mouse and comprehend basic computer mechanics from a young age. We had internet before any of our rural neighbors, and I could type and print my school papers at home rather than wait for shared time on the one Apple IIe in class. Most importantly, it meant that I viewed technology as a tool to be learned and used, not feared.

As I advanced into college and the workforce, I often found myself helping friends and colleagues figure things out. If the organization had a "tech team" I was on it, and in some cases leading it. If I came across a mundane problem I tried to find a technological solution. I never viewed myself as a particularly knowledgeable or passionate about technology, but the longer I worked in libraries, the more I realized that my combination of fearless curiosity, service to others, and interest in education was a particular type of technology expertise.

SCOPE

I am not a professional programmer. I have taken no more than one college-level coding class. What I have done is identify the changing technology needs of library customers and help empower staff to respond to them. If you're trying to figure out how to lead coding classes in libraries, then this is the book for you. I've developed these lessons by leading them more times than I can count in a diverse array of libraries and tweaking them over and over.

I wrote my previous book, *Library Robotics: Technology and English Language Arts Activities For Ages 8–24*, to answer the questions that we had when our little robotics team at Cuyahoga County Public Library was trying to figure out how in the world we were going to get started. At the time, I could find resources on how robots worked or take programming classes, but they were geared toward math, physics, or computer science teachers, not complete newbies, and they didn't take into account the unique realities of educating in libraries. Likewise, there are many coding books available that can help readers build deeper knowledge of the coding languages mentioned within these pages, but I'm not familiar with any other books that are geared specifically toward librarian instructors. This book is intended to help those with little to no experience build confidence and competence, so that they can get started leading coding experiences in their libraries.

HOW TO USE THIS BOOK

Each chapter may be used as a standalone class, though there is more content per chapter than a typical class will learn in a two-hour window. Some chapters include activity sets, groups of smaller lessons that work together toward a larger concept. Each activity in these sets may be an individual class when working with younger students or limited time.

The intent of the book is to provide a librarian with the background and content to be able to lead at least ten coding club sessions. Every library's needs are different, and the Introduction provides some guidance to libraries that are considering how best to get started.

I highly recommend that potential instructors work through at least the first few chapters before beginning a new club. The chapters are written in a voice to help the potential instructor learn how to program *and* think about how to help the class understand the same concepts. Downloadable, printable student handouts are available from the link in the Appendix.

VOCABULARY

Throughout this book the term *program* and its variations are used exclusively in their technological sense, rather than in reference to educational and entertainment events hosted by public libraries. This is done not only to avoid confusion, but also to encourage librarians to use more intentional and accurate language about our educational efforts. Each of these chapters could be a *class*.

The term *librarian* is used broadly, and is welcome to be claimed by any reader employed by a library who is willing to take up the causes of computational thinking, technology literacy, and coding. Thank you for everything you do.

Introduction

Those working in libraries, schools, or any education-related field have probably heard a lot of buzz about coding, but many may feel a little unsure of what exactly it is or how best to approach the subject. This introduction attempts to explain what coding is, how it intersects with the mission of libraries, and offers some considerations for getting started. We'll address both the traditional and the colloquial definitions of coding and examine its role and influence in our society. We'll explore how coding intersects with library priorities and address points to consider before launching a coding initiative.

WHY CODING

For adults with fond memories of classic 1980s movies like *War Games*, *Weird Science*, and *Tron*, coding might seem like something only super geniuses do on custom built computers, but nowadays, not only is coding accessible to most, it's applicable to far more than computers. Mobile phones, tablets, and video game consoles need programs to tell them what to do, and an increasing number of appliances use programming, too. Washing machines and dishwashers arrive programmed with different cycles that determine the agitation level, water temperature, and cycle length. The amount of programming in cars continuously increases, from monitoring speed, temperature, emissions, and service dates to interfacing with smartphones and navigation systems and detecting potential accidents. We interact with multiple programs and programmed devices each and every day and may not even know it.

What Is Coding?

With so much buzz about coding, it can be confusing to pin down what is actually meant by the term. The word *code* most often refers to three types of concepts:

- Laws or regulations, such as Ohio Revised Standard Code
- Ideas or rules governing behavior, such as the Boy Scout Code of Conduct or the Harvard Honor Code
- A system of letters, numbers, symbols, or sounds used to create messages that are accessible only to those who understand the system, such as Morse Code, Navajo Code Talkers, or the Enigma Code

When we create code for a computer, we're touching on all three concepts. When we create a **program**, or *a set of detailed instructions*, we follow certain rules so that the computer can interpret it correctly. The program governs the behavior of the computer, and we write it using a system of letters, numbers, and symbols specific to the programming language. Humans can interpret the coded instructions of the programming language into human languages such as English and computers can interpret the instructions in the programming language into binary code, their base language.

Coding vs. Programming

Among professionals in the field there can be some heated feelings about the difference between coding and programming or being a coder vs. a programmer. Among hobbyists the debate may not be taken quite so seriously, but any library staff member considering a coding initiative should understand a bit about the difference.

Coding *is the term now commonly used to describe playful experimentations with computer programs or creating code.* Professionals, however, might use the term to mean entering code, or translating between one language, say English, to another, for instance Python.

Programming, on the other hand, *refers to the logic, the crafting of the instructions.* A programmer typically needs to be able to write in code, or the appropriate computer language for the task, but she also needs to be able to consider the problem at hand and manipulate the order and structure of the code to bring about a desired result.

Let's compare this to some other real-world examples. If Suzy is technically able to read, write, and speak English and French and can translate between the two, she can likely code and decode messages, so that Bob, who only speaks English, and Renee, who only speaks French, can communicate. In this example, Suzy is coding.

If, on the other hand, Suzy writes coffee machine manuals for an item sold in both English- and French-speaking areas, she will need to figure out how the machine works, the correct sequence to give the instructions, as well as the most logical way to give them. This is creating the program, the set of instructions that Bob and Renee will follow to successfully make coffee. When she creates the instructions in any language, she is programming. For both Bob and Renee to understand them, however, these instructions will need to be translated into both English and French. When she simply translates, she is coding.

For the purposes of describing an introductory club or class, it typically makes the most sense to keep things loose and use the term *coding* in the colloquial modern sense of playing around with computer programming and learning to code. In this context, *programming* should typically be used predominantly to refer to the instructions themselves or the logical act of creating the instructions.

Logic and Algorithms

When we code a program for the computer, we are translating a set of instructions, or an algorithm into a language that the computer understands. Whether we know it or not, we all use algorithms on a regular basis—whether using a recipe to bake cookies, following instructions on a keypad to buy and pump gas, or assembling furniture from written instructions. An **algorithm** is simply *a set of step-by-step instructions to solve a problem or perform a task.* Computer programs are algorithms that tell the computer what to do. Humans following flawed instructions can often fill in the gaps by interpreting implied meaning or past experience. Computers, on the other hand, are purely logical, and will only do exactly as they are told. When designing a computer program, humans must exercise their best logical and precise thinking to make sure that the program, as written, achieves the desired result.

For instance, a human following a cookie recipe written in reverse order would likely be able to discern that the instruction "Bake until golden brown," could not be the first instruction, and could figure out how to adjust the algorithm. In comparison, a robot following the jumbled instructions would follow the instructions in the order written. The robot might leave the oven on forever since the cookies hadn't been prepped and therefore couldn't be tested for brownness, or it would display an error that the object *cookie* hadn't been defined.

In the example program in Figure I-1, a student using LEGO® WeDo® robotics software intended to tell the robot to turn on the motor, play a sound, and then turn the motor on again for 2.0 seconds. Unfortunately, when the student runs this program, he'll find that he never gets to hear the sound because the first motor block actually tells the robot to turn on the motor forever. Logically, if the motor runs forever, it will never advance past the first block to the following sound block. Remember that the computer, or in this case the robot, thinks literally, so it doesn't know that the student meant to only have the robot move for a brief time.

In Figure I-2, the blocks have been rearranged into an order that makes more sense. The robot will now turn on the motor for 2.0 seconds *only*,

FIGURE I-1   Coding Error Example.

FIGURE I-2   Coding Error Corrected.

proceed to the next command which is to play a sound, and *then* turn the motor back on forever. To be able to run all three blocks after the start block, they must be ordered correctly. The program will now succeed because it arranges the instructions in a logical process.

Syntax

Creating the algorithm is the logical design part of programming, the part we can think through in our own native language and map out in words and pictures. The other part of creating the program is translating that algorithm into a programming language, coding it. There are hundreds of known computer programming languages in the world, from visual languages like LEGO® WeDo® to text based languages like Python, JavaScript, C++, and more. As in human languages, each programming language expects particular **syntax**, *the standard arrangement of components in a certain language to create shared meaning.*

In English, a standard order for a sentence would be subject, verb, and then object. An example of this structure would be, "My friend Barb likes books." The syntax also tells us to capitalize the proper noun *Barb* in order to indicate that we mean a person named Barbara who likes books, rather than a barb on a fence wire. These types of rules are important. The sentence, "I already ate Grandma" could give the impression that the writer is a cannibal. A little punctuation will clarify the intended meaning. "I already ate, Grandma." One little comma clarifies that the writer is addressing her grandmother to let her know that she ate before arriving. Of course, in a modern world with poorly punctuated texts using improper syntax, most humans are quite adept at extrapolating the intended meaning. As with the algorithms, computers are quite literal about syntax. Let's take a look at a basic Python statement:

```
print('Hello world!')
```

When the program containing this statement is run, the words *Hello world* will appear on the screen. The following statement would also work:

```
print("Hello world!")
```

Python allows either single quotes or double quotes around the text, however, the syntax does not allow a mix of the two.

```
print("Hello world!')
```

This statement would result in a syntax error because it begins with a double quote and ends with a single quote.

The presence or absence of one little tiny mark can make a big difference. When designing the program algorithm, the human behind it must use creativity, problem solving, and critical thinking while considering the big picture. When writing the code for the program, the human behind it must be extremely focused and detail oriented. Though these jobs might be somewhat separated in professional environments, those following the guides in the following chapters will have an opportunity to try their hand at both aspects necessary to create working programs.

Why Coding in Libraries?

Few of the preschoolers who build early literacy skills while participating in storytime will grow up to be professional authors, but each will benefit tremendously from the ability to read and write. Likewise, not all students who build computer literacy skills while participating in coding club at the library will become professional software developers, yet all will be better poised to thrive in a world increasingly integrated with technology. Libraries themselves reflect this type of integration. Many early childhood librarians now incorporate new media such as apps into storytimes. School librarians teach students, parents and teachers how to use Google classroom, Blackboard, and Progress-Book. Teen librarians host video game tournaments, Minecraft events, robotics clubs, and more, and adult librarians help job searchers find and apply for positions, grow computer skills, and download eBooks to their devices. Library staffers serving every age and institution also help their customers find resources using online catalogs, databases, and the Internet. Technology has become integrated into the fabric of traditional library services. In this section we'll explore how coding potentially augments some of the most common library foci including literacy, career readiness, and computational thinking.

Literacy

In the previous sections, we explored the connections between computer languages and human languages. Both use letters, numbers, symbols, and sounds arranged using specific syntax in order to communicate. Certainly, libraries have experience helping those we serve learn to code and decode language through storytimes, writing workshops, and oral storytelling events, but how often do we focus on what the Common Core State Standards (CCSS) English Language Arts Literacy Anchor Standards refer to as Conventions of Standard English Language? As students grow out of preschool story times and into school-age and teen classes, how can we continue to help them meet these standards?

Demonstrate command of the conventions of standard English grammar and usage when writing or speaking. (CCSS.ELA-LITERACY.CCRA.L.1)

Demonstrate command of the conventions of standard English capitalization, punctuation, and spelling when writing. (CCSS.ELA-LITERACY.CCRA.L.2)

One way to help students build these competencies without boring them to death is to teach coding. Students actually get real-time feedback on their work as they attempt to run their programs and get a syntax error for an improperly spelled variable or lowercase command. One semicolon or period out of place can derail the entire program, but properly followed conventions allow students to create and execute original programs, including video games! This is quite a natural incentive. Coding brings language conventions to life, demonstrating their relevance and importance in a way unachievable by traditional methods.

In addition to the syntax and grammar connection, coding also presents an opportunity to create stories in a different way, particularly when creating video games. Classic tales inspire many of the activities throughout this book, and as students translate these stories into games, they are working through a five-stage story structure that includes setting the scene, rising action, creating a climax, falling action, and resolution. For instance, in Chapter 6 we'll create a game based on Hansel and Gretel. Students will literally set the scene, by creating a forest, a path, the woodcutter's cottage, and witch's house. They'll create tension by giving the player a limited amount of time to navigate the path from one house to the other. The climax will hit as the player's health and time wind down and the player either wins or loses the game. The students will create winning and losing screens to greet players after the climax and to tie up loose ends and resolve the story. Though making video games particularly reveals the connections between coding and storytelling, an astute observer can find them even in the most basic computer program. To create a simple computer program that says hello, asks the user for his or her name, and responds with a greeting, a programmer sets the scene with the first question, builds action and climax waiting for the response, and resolves the tension with the greeting.

This type of translation of story into code representation helps students navigate between human and digital interactions. Our evolving global culture, built on technology, requires students to think about a diverse audience as they communicate online. The CCSS-English Language Arts Anchor Standards for Speaking and Listening include emphasis on Presentation of Knowledge and Ideas.

> Present information, findings, and supporting evidence such that listeners can follow the line of reasoning and the organization, development, and style are appropriate to task, purpose, and audience. (CCSS.ELA-LITERACY.CCRA.SL.4)

> Make strategic use of digital media and visual displays of data to express information and enhance understanding of presentations. (CCSS.ELA-LITERACY.CCRA.SL.5)

> Adapt speech to a variety of contexts and communicative tasks, demonstrating command of formal English when indicated or appropriate. (CCSS.ELA-LITERACY.CCRA.SL.6)

When students have the opportunity to code collaboratively, they must find ways to articulate their end goal, but also to express their ideas for how to reach it. As they test and develop their theories, they'll reach solutions based in evidence. Instructors can further help them achieve CCSS.ELA-LITERACY.

CCRA.SL.4 by asking them to add comments in the code to explain each section. The language used by characters in a game that they code might be informal, designed to be in the particular voice of each of character, but the language used to explain the code to the instructor would need to be formal English, and the language used in the code must be precise in syntax. In this way, students would be building the skills of CCSS.ELA-LITERACY.CCRA.SL.6 while also creating a digital media display (CCSS.ELA-LITERACY.CCRA.SL.5). They would also be addressing CCSS-ELA Anchor Standards for Writing, such as number 6: "Use technology, including the Internet, to produce and publish writing and to interact and collaborate with others."

The connections between coding and literacy are vast, not least because of the inherent cross-curricular learning happening. The CCSS Anchor Standards for Reading include a note on the range and content of reading, "By reading texts in history/social studies, science, and other disciplines, students build a foundation of knowledge in these fields that will also give them the background to be better readers in all content areas." The CCSS encourage all of us to be reading teachers. To push students to read complex texts, such as books on coding, to help them gain context and vocabulary that will serve them in every area of study.

Career Readiness

In response to the CCSS and demands from future employers, schools increasingly assign students cross-curricular assignments that require students to think critically, problem-solve, communicate, and collaborate all while creating with technology. After all, few jobs or tasks require employees to only use reading or only do math. Students may be asked to create an animation to summarize the main points of a text. Science fair participants might learn how to program a microprocessor with a sensor to track sunlight levels received by plants. A math class might manipulate vector graphics to create a mural. Students who are able to address problems with coding solutions become highly marketable job seekers who can contribute creativity and increase productivity.

The Bureau of Labor and Statistics predicts that between 2016 and 2026 the job outlook for computer and information technology positions will grow by 13%, faster than the average for all occupations (BLS, 2017). The median annual wage for these positions was $82,860 as of May, 2016, more than twice as much as the median wage for all jobs occupations. Yet, though computer science is a rapidly growing and lucrative field, dedicated computer science classes are offered in just over half of American schools according to a 2015 Gallup report commissioned by Google, and of those, only about half teach programming and coding. These numbers drop for lower income students despite 75% of lower income parents believing that computer science should be mandatory. Librarians, particularly in lower income areas, know that even if a student has a computer at home it may not have high-speed Internet access; the student's time on it may be limited, and if they come from one of the 75% of schools that don't teach coding, they might not know where to begin if they want to teach themselves. The library can provide access to computers, high-speed Internet, and most importantly, guidance. If nothing else, we can connect students with online and print resources, but we can do even better than that with coding clubs and classes.

Computational Thinking

Even students who will not become computer programmers or pursue information technology occupations will benefit from the experience of coding. Mitch Resnick, one of the minds behind Massachusetts Institute of Technology's popular educational programming language Scratch, argues in his January 2013 Ted Talk that learning to code is as much about coding to learn as learning to read is about reading to learn. In a follow-up article later that year, Resnick explains that while the team behind Scratch originally designed it to make learning to code more accessible, the online Scratch community has taken the tool farther. Users have created "animated stories, virtual tours, science simulations, public-service announcements, multimedia art projects, dress-up games, paint editors, and even interactive tutorials and newsletters." Learning to code with Scratch has given users a new perspective on creating and learning about the world. This is in part because learning to code isn't strictly about learning computer science, it's about learning computational thinking.

Computational thinking *is the logical process of identifying and breaking down problems and analyzing the components to create a solution.* Every major technology education institution—including the International Society for Technology Education (ISTE), Google for Education, the American Library Association (ALA), and Code.org—has its own specific definition of computational thinking, but they all agree that it is a critical skill for 21st Century learners and workers to develop. Most advocates of computational thinking agree on four main components; *decomposition, pattern recognition, abstraction,* and *algorithm creation.*

Decomposition

Let's see how computational thinking might help a computer programmer who is creating an app to order pizza. The programmer might start by decomposing the question, "What needs to happen for a customer to successfully order a pizza?" For instance, the app will need to collect:

The customer's name and address
The customer's payment information
The customer's custom pizza order

Pattern Recognition

We can use pattern recognition to further break down the third subproblem. What elements do all custom pizza orders share?

Size
Crust type
Sauce
Toppings

Abstraction

All pizzas that a user could order have a size, a crust type, a sauce, and topping choices, but each particular combination could be different. For instance, Customer A could order a small, deep dish, red sauce pizza with pepperoni, and Customer could order a large, thin crust, white sauce pizza with mushrooms and olives. To create the app, the programmer will think of the shared characteristics as placeholders to store specific information.

Size _____
Crust type _____
_____Sauce
___, ___, ___, ___, Toppings

Algorithm Creation

Finally, the programmer will create a list of commands that will execute when the user selects a choice to design a custom pizza.

```
Prompt to select pizza size (S, M, L, XL)
Prompt to select pizza sauce (red, white, n/a)
Prompt to select toppings—default to n/a
    pepperoni (yes, n/a)
    sausage (yes, n/a)
    extra cheese (yes, n/a)
    banana peppers (yes, n/a)
    onions (yes, n/a)
    mushrooms (yes, n/a)
    olives (yes, n/a)
```

Interestingly, this type of process would be about the same for a pizza shop owner designing an in-person ordering system, and training new waitstaff with a script. This is what makes computational thinking such a universally useful skill. Coding requires computational thinking in order to think about and solve problems via an algorithm that computers can execute, so students naturally learn how to think logically as they design computer programs, but those thought processes will continue to serve them in many other fields and daily life.

In June of 2017, the Young Adult Library Services Association (YALSA) announced the implementation of Phase III of Libraries Ready to Code, an ongoing collaboration between ALA and Google intended "to ensure library staff are prepared to develop and deliver programming that promotes computer science (CS) and computational thinking (CT) among youth, two skills that will be required for challenges and jobs of the future." YALSA, in partnership with ALA's Office for Information Technology Policy, the American Association of School Librarians (AASL), and the Association for Library Service for Children (ALSC) will oversee funding to school and public libraries for the purpose of furthering computational thinking and computer science learning opportunities. This funding opportunity comes after a year-long research effort summarized in a final report, *Ready to Code: Connecting Youth to CS Opportunities through Libraries*. In the report, authors Linda Braun and Marijke Visser argue that libraries are particularly suited to help youth build computational thinking skills because they are located in the communities they serve, are open during out-of-school time hours, and have resources such as computers, meeting rooms, staff with youth development background to serve as role models, and connections to community members and organizations with expertise.

Though not every librarian possesses knowledge in computer programming, all regularly use computational thinking as they serve their communities. When addressing a research question, librarians decompose larger questions into manageable chunks, identify patterns in how they have found answers to such questions in the past, abstract broader subjects to identify potential sources, and finally use this information to create a search algorithm. School librarians are uniquely situated as experts, not in a particular academic subject, but as cross-curricular guides who teach students less about what to think and more about how to think, how to research, and how to learn independently. Computational thinking supports this intersectional approach.

PREPARING TO LAUNCH

If we believe that there is a place in the library for coding initiatives, the next question becomes, how do we do this? Libraries have several options in terms of structure and staffing.

Who Can Lead Coding Classes?

There is no one-size-fits-all solution for libraries that want to offer coding education. Some libraries are ready and willing to embrace ALA's Ready to Code initiative and prepare library staff members to lead public coding classes themselves. Other libraries will need outside assistance or will want to look for alternative solutions.

Librarians

Librarians or library staff members are the obvious choice to champion the coding initiative. They're already there, they're already getting paid, and there is a growing contingent of library professionals who see computer science work as part of their jobs. Of course, there are also plenty of librarians who are intimidated, uninterested, or simply overwhelmed. There are strategies to suit all, however, so let's look at a few different types of librarian leadership.

Librarian as Host

If your community has some folks who are already into coding, you may be able to serve as a referral source and host. The library can provide the meeting room space, computers, and high-speed Internet. Depending on the library, you may also be able to provide publicity, such as flyers, posting on the library's online calendar, and sharing out through the library's email, mailing, or text alerts. This strategy can work well for adults and teens. To get started, the librarian will need to research about any existing clubs or classes in the community, connect with potential stakeholders, and meet periodically with the club to assess how things are going and what they need. This can also be an opportunity for an interested librarian to learn alongside the club members.

Librarian as Coding Resource Mentor

Adding on to the host approach, this strategy still places the responsibility for knowledge about coding predominantly on the members who will teach each other, however, it takes advantage of and highlights the importance of information professionals. The librarian attends the community-led club and listens in or takes requests for further information about particular topics, programming languages, or self-education sites and resources. She might also bring and share interesting articles, books, and breaking news in the world of coding. She would certainly share any additional or related offerings the library or other community partners plan to provide.

Librarian as Coding Coach

With librarians around the country teaching folks how to use 3D printers, laser cutters, robotics, and more, it follows that some brave souls among us are ready to take the plunge into directly coaching a coding club. For those who are, there are numerous resources available designed to help educators of all ages with this task, including this book! The librarian need not go it alone either. If planning a children's coding club, she might recruit some tech-smart teens to help. If planning a teen or adult club, she could reach out to local businesses or solicit some guidance from the library's IT department. She might also consider advertising for assistance through the library's usual channels such as local newspapers, seasonal flyers, bulletin boards, or newsletters. If she's going to go it alone, however, she can use not only the lessons in this book, but also those created by the Ready to Code Phase III cohorts, and the many print and online resources listed in the resources link in the Appendix.

Community Volunteers and Partners

Of course, as we discussed, librarians don't have to necessarily go it alone at first or ever. Let's look at some potential community volunteers and partners.

Professional Programmers

Why not start with the professionals? If your community doesn't have an obvious supporting industry like a software development firm, try reaching out to any major corporation, large government office, or service firm. Most likely if the organization is a large employer, someone on their staff has at least some basic knowledge of coding. If you really don't have anyone close to your vicinity, you may want to try connecting to experts virtually. You may be able to post a volunteer request on SocialCoding4Good.org, VolunteerMatch.org, or similar sites. Also, put the word out to friends and colleagues that you're looking for experts. Even if your neighbor's programmer son lives on the other side of the country, he may be able to provide guidance to your coding club via online video or chat.

Hobbyists

As we discussed when talking about the librarian as host model, coding enthusiasts are found in many communities. For teen and adult clubs you may not need a particular leader, but for children and tween clubs, you'll likely want someone in charge who knows what she's doing. Do be aware, however, that the volunteer might have coding skill, but not youth development knowledge. The same holds true for a professional programmer, so if you bring in either, you will want to make sure to have a youth-oriented volunteer or staff member engaged with the club to both help guide expectations and develop relationships.

Community Organizations

Some libraries are fortunate enough to have nearby colleges, science centers, or museums. Often such institutions are looking for ways to connect with the greater community outside of the confines of their walls or campuses. The library can serve as a hub for just such activity. Funders also typically love to see multiple community organizations collaborating, so the library may be able to be a co-recipient of a grant to fund a coding club. Colleges and universities are rich not only with knowledgeable staff, but also students, many of whom may be looking for résumé-building activities. There are a number of academic fraternities and sororities focused on engineering and technology whose current and alumni members may be able to help: Alpha Sigma Kappa, Alpha Omega Epsilon, Kappa Eta Kappa, Phi Sigma Rho, Sigma Phi Delta, and Theta Tau.

Technology Educators

Of course, you might also be able to tap your local computer science teacher or another interested professional technology educator. In larger cities and many towns there are businesses and non-profits that travel to schools, libraries and community centers to teach technology classes. Be aware, however, that unlike computer programmers who might find volunteering to teach to be a fun community service project, community educators do this for a living. That is not to say that they don't also find it fun or won't volunteer for the library, but be prepared for an honest discussion about their reimbursement needs. The library may find paying an external presenter a worthwhile investment considering the staff time saved, the lack of ongoing salary or benefits paid, and the presenter's expertise at leading this type of event for the targeted age group. This can also be a great way to introduce or test coding clubs in your library. For instance, Cuyahoga County Public Library began their coding club initiative by hiring in Gigalearn, LLC, to lead clubs at two branches for 3 months. At the end of the time, the Gigalearn classes were moved to two other branches, and the branch staff that had been hosting the external presenter continued on with the momentum from the club.

How to Structure Coding Classes

We've been talking about coding club, which is a common model for bringing coding into the library, but it's not the only model. Let's look at some others.

Standalone Classes and Events

Hour of Code is a national initiative that first launched in 2013 from the founders of Code.org. With the support of major technology players such as Apple, Microsoft, and Amazon, and Facebook founder Mark Zuckerberg, the idea quickly went viral. The Hour of Code website hosts a number of introductory tutorials designed to get people, particularly youth, to try coding for at least an hour. The tutorials are always available, but it is particularly promoted during Computer Science Education Week in December. Libraries can certainly make use of any of the resources on the Hour of Code or Code.org websites to host a one-time event. The library might also host a standalone coding event as part of a STEAM or career fair, or in conjunction with a visiting tech author event.

In the following chapters we'll look at some popular software, tools, and languages available to use in coding classes. Each has its own strengths and limitations, but with most, participants are able get a basic introduction and create some code within a single 1.5- to 2–hour time slot. The activities in Chapters 1, 2, 3, 5, 7, and 9 would all work as standalone classes, though the later chapters require students to have keyboarding and mouse skills and are typically more suitable for tweens, teens, or adults.

Camps

Many public libraries have begun offering day camps, particularly during the summer, to keep students productively engaged during out-of-school time and to ward off summer slide—the loss of knowledge and skills that happens when students' brains are left idling for three months. Camps are also a possibility for spring or winter breaks, or day camps may be offered by public libraries on NEOEA Day or other out-of-school times.

A camp may be focused on one particular programming tool, language, or problem. Alternatively, a camp might focus on a particular type of programming such as app development or video game creation, or a camp might include an exploration of a number of different types of coding. Chapters one through four contain appropriate content for a school-age or tween introductory coding camp. Chapters 3 through 6 would serve as great exploratory coding camp for tweens, teens, or adults.

Camps are often designed for youth during out-of-school times, but there are also coding camp options for adults. Civic coding organizations schedule events to bring together professional and hobbyist programmers and coders to solve community issues through code. For instance CodeForAmerica.org connects coding volunteers to opportunities, and it also supports local "brigades." One such local brigade, <OpenCleveland/> currently has several projects including making city council meetings minutes searchable, indexing vacant lots available through the Cleveland Land Bank development program, and creating a map of snow ban parking restrictions (Open Cleveland, 2017). Such groups sometimes have focused projects, set up as lock-ins, hack-a-thons, or, more or less, camps. The library can play host to such an event, but as a public serving non-profit institution it might also be a potential client. For instance, in 2016, Code for San Jose created an app to help their local library coordinate free summer meals according to Michelle Thong's aptly titled blog post, "Hack Nights are a Civic Good."

Clubs

Like the Civic coding groups, library clubs can meet weekly, monthly, or even quarterly. Computer science clubs have been around long before they were well known in popular culture. One of the most famous is the Homebrew Computer Club, where in 1976 Steve Wozniak demonstrated the Apple I computer prototype to supportive peers including Steve Jobs who eventually helped him sell the first Apple personal computer (Computer History Museum, 2015). Wozniak developed the prototype in solitude, but he experienced his lightbulb, "aha" moment of how to do it because of conversation with others in the club. This is the benefit of the ongoing experience of a club, participants, who may be introverts like "Woz," have the time to become comfortable in the group and build social, personal learning networks.

Participants can share and build on each others' ideas. For instance Wozniak famously gave away the schematics for the Apple I to his friends in the Homebrew Computer Club, many of whom went on to develop their own influential products. When asked about the open source movement and social coding, Wozniak says, "It makes me hopeful because young, talented people have a chance to do more than stand by and watch and be paid a salary."

What institution could be better positioned to promote such a democratic exchange of ideas than a library? Of course, some libraries might be particularly interested in helping folks get paid a salary or start their own business. If so, a coding club can help provide the social and technical support needed, but libraries might also reach out to local incubators: organizations that help launch or grow businesses. Incubators can have a variety of foci, but many are particularly technology start-up driven. Be aware, however, that some may be looking to solicit clients.

We've been discussing clubs as meet-ups for like-minded people to collaborate and share in a loose environment. In this type of model, the library might provide the space, computers, Internet, publicity, and even a resource librarian or guest presenters. Clubs may also, however, be structured more formerly as regular classes. A slightly more formal agenda works well for attendees who don't know what they want to know. For instance, the first session of a new teen coding club at Cuyahoga County Public Library typically starts with an icebreaker and meet and greet. Initially, we wanted the clubs to be entirely driven by youth voice, but after several iterations and locations, we discovered a trend that many teens and their parents believe that coding is important, and teens want to do it, but they don't really know what it is. Of course, there are some exceptions. So, instead of asking what languages they want to learn, we begin by discussing what types of things they want to do or like to do on computers, what problems they want to solve, or what apps they like to use or wish they could invent. Then we lead an introductory class on a popular topic like video game creation. In the ensuing meetings we follow up on the interests expressed initially and diverge from our original plan as the group needs change. This strategy works well if the same participants plan to attend all or most meetings. Because we often shift gears each session, it can also work for participants to come in and out. We just have to be careful to adjust registration methods to single-event registration rather than full-quarter registration.

Of course libraries without one particular leader well versed in many things might offer coding clubs that feature a different guest presenter, presenting on a different topic or language each session. Potential participants can come to the sessions that apply to their interests and skip others. Because not all participants will necessarily attend all sessions, a single event registration or no registration strategy will probably work best to provide maximum *access*. For maximum *learning*, it is typically best for participants to attend all sessions, the content of each building on the last. As you work through the activities in this book, notice how cumulative understanding grows with each chapter. It is possible to jump to the introductory lesson with Python, but readers will comprehend more if they've also completed the earlier lesson in Scratch. The same is true for coding club participants. As librarians, we have to be flexible and responsive to the needs and realities of our communities. So if a club can be cumulative, great; otherwise, roll with it. Consider having volunteers to help participants catch up when they miss a session.

Selecting a Strategy

Which if any of these structural options will work for your library? There are several points to consider.

Library Goals

What does the library hope to achieve with a coding initiative? If the library wants to experiment and gauge interest in the topic, then a standalone event may be a perfect choice. If the library hopes to engage students during out of school time or target adults for a particular time frame or project, then a camp may be the right choice. Either of these shorter-term strategies can also help the library gather the necessary data to apply for funding for a long-term strategy like a club or multiple camps. If the library wants to create or support a thriving coding community, help participants build deeper understanding of computer programming and develop as computational thinkers, then a club is likely the best solution.

Age Level

What age participants does your library want or need to target? Any of the strategies, standalone events, camps, or clubs will work for just about any age group, but the parameters will likely shift. Adults and older teens might be up for an all-day camp or event, but early elementary students will likely tap out after 45 minutes to an hour, mid-elementary students might go 90 minutes, and tweens, teens, and adults are usually best served by two-hour sessions. Coding can be intense, detailed work, and programming takes a lot of mental stamina, so typically, even with reoccurring events like camps or clubs, individual sessions should be kept relatively short. Two hours generally provides the balance between having time to get invested, but not too much to get burned out. If the goal is to create a community solution in an intense period of time, then an all-day or overnight hack-a-thon for adults or teens might work.

Participant Knowledge and Expertise

You'll also want to do some research about the expertise level of your potential participants. How many members of your target community have had any experience coding in computer science class, work life, or at home? If you're working with partners to recruit or lead the initiative, they may be able to provide you with some guidance. If not, you may simply want to casually poll folks as they register, or do a community survey as part of your planning. There is a downloadable Coding Participant Survey available from the link in the Appendix. Any of the models—standalone, camp, or club—will potentially work for any experience level, but the content will need to shift. If you find you have a lot of newbies and at least a handful of experts, you might find that the experienced folks are willing to lead an entry-level class, and you can concentrate on finding support for the advanced classes.

Participant Goals

The library may have particular community-focused goals for the coding initiative, but if the people who show up don't share those goals, they won't come long. When surveying potential participants about their current knowledge, also consider asking about their motivations and interests as indicated in the Coding Participant Survey. We've all seen library innovations fail because, though they might be based on the statistics of an overall community, the folks who come to the library don't need, want, or understand that service. Learning about the goals of the potential participants can help you design and market it. If responses indicate that participants are interested in achieving a particular finite project such as coding websites for their small businesses, then a stand-alone or camp solution might be best. If participants respond that they'd like to create their own original video games, then a multisession club, using the activities in this book will work perfectly! Often, participants need some exposure to coding before they begin to understand what may be possible. The activities in this book are designed to give beginners exposure to a variety of languages and types of programming to help them identify and articulate their interests to instructors.

1

Welcome to Coding

The activities in this chapter introduce participants to broad concepts of coding and would be perfectly suited for the first session of a multiple-part coding club or camp series. This is a great place to start for those who are brand new to coding as well as those with some experience. Often, even if students have experience writing code, they may not understand the principles behind what they are doing, particularly if they are simply regurgitating examples from video tutorials or books. In these activities, we'll take a step back and look at some of the core concepts of coding. These activities may also be used altogether as a standalone event or in part as introductory exercises for subsequent activity sets.

ACTIVITY 1A: AMAZING ALGORITHMS

As we discussed in the introduction, a computer program is, at its heart, an *algorithm*, or set of instructions, written in certain syntax and designed for the completion of a task or set of tasks. In this first activity, we'll introduce students to the challenge of creating an algorithm logically, and precisely enough that an interpreter as literal as a computer can follow it.

Amazing Algorithms: Materials Needed and Set-up

For this challenge each student will need five or six Lego®, Tinkertoy®, or K'nex® pieces (or something similar). It is helpful to have a plastic bag or shoebox for each student's pieces. Each student will also need paper and pencil. It will be helpful to have a camera for each student. Students may possess personal devices such as mobile phones that can serve this purpose. If not, one or more digital cameras may be shared. Tablets or laptops with cameras will also work.

The class will be divided into two even groups for this activity. It is often easiest if students are paired into partnerships. Partner A will sit in the Group A area and partner B in Group B. The groups should be arranged in such a way that each is blind to the activity of the other. For instance, the students can be seated in two rows with their backs facing each other. In a school setting, the two groups might actually be two different classes.

Amazing Algorithms: Outcomes

Participants gain skills by creating instructional texts.
Participants develop ability to think through and express a logical process.

Amazing Algorithms: Guide

Typically, at least a few students will have experimented with coding either independently or in school. Often a few students feel confident in their coding ability and appreciate it when their expertise is recognized. Simultaneously, many students feel nervous and intimidated. We'll use this first activity to create a fun, inviting atmosphere while simultaneously providing the extra challenge that more confident students crave.

As students gather, ask each about his or her coding experience. Reassure newbies that this class is designed to start at the very beginning. Ask those with some experience how they would rate their coding expertise and confidence on a scale of one to five, with one being the lowest. Make note of each student's answer. Pair up students with similar numbers. For instance, a student who self-identified as a level-three coder would be a reasonable partner for a level-five student if another level-three student is unavailable. Send one partner to the Group A area and the other to the Group B area.

Distribute five building pieces to each student. Give experienced students one additional piece for each level of experience they possess. For instance, a level four student would receive nine total pieces. Each student will also need a pencil and paper.

Amazing Algorithms Step 1

Explain to students that when we talk about coding, we're really talking about two main actions. The first is to create the **algorithm,** *a set of step-by-step instructions to solve a problem or perform a task,* the list of commands that we want the computer to follow. Just like computers, humans use algorithms all the time! Each time we follow instructions in a recipe, on a worksheet, or to assemble furniture or to play a game, we're following a set of step-by-step instructions to solve a problem or perform a task. When we create computer programs, we need to be careful to be clear, precise and thorough. If a human comes across a recipe missing one instruction—for instance, how long to bake the cookies—he would likely be able to make an educated guess and complete the recipe, but a computer following an algorithm missing an instruction would likely return an error message and freeze up.

After this explanation, ask partners to separate into their two groups. Give students five to ten minutes to create a sculpture from the pieces that they've been given. It may be representative. For instance, it could, when finished, resemble an animal, or it could be abstract or randomly constructed. Students should keep their sculptures secret from their partners.

Amazing Algorithms Step 2

At the end of the construction period, have students take a photo of their creations. If cameras aren't available, have them draw it to the best of their ability. The completed sculptures represent the end goal of a computer program, what we want the computer to accomplish. The next step is to create the algorithm or set of instructions for the computer, which, for the game, will be represented by each partner's counterpart. Using words and/or drawings have students create step-by-step instructions that their partners will follow to recreate their sculpture. The winning team will be the partners whose algorithms most successfully instruct each other into producing exact replicas of the each other's sculpture.

Remind students as they create their instructions that their partners will be interpreting them like a computer. So, if they leave something out, or give an instruction that isn't clear, their partners may get stuck on the error. After answering any questions, give students a time limit to create the instructions, and set a timer. About fifteen minutes is typically sufficient.

Amazing Algorithms Step 3

Depending on the age, expertise, and focus level of the students, more time may be needed for Step 2. Once you have called time, make sure that each student has saved a photograph of his or her sculpture. Students will dismantle their sculptures and exchange components and algorithms with their partners. Before the "computers" begin their work following the instructions, remind them that they are to think logically and literally like a computer. Give students about 10 to 15 minutes to try to construct the sculptures from the algorithms. If both members of a team finish early, they may submit themselves for judging. The instructor will compare the completed sculptures to the pictures. It is very likely that multiple teams will complete the sculptures correctly, and multiple teams won't. It's okay to have a tie.

Amazing Algorithms Post-Activity Discussion

After the teams have finished their reconstruction attempts, gather everyone together for a brief group discussion using the following questions.

How many of you preferred being the programmer, writing the instructions? Why? How many of you preferred being the computer, following the algorithm? Why?

Make note of students' choices. It can be helpful to partner one student who prefers building with another student who prefers programming for future activities.

You had a choice of using just words, just drawings or a combination of both. Which do you think worked the best?

Programming languages can be visual, created using images and blocks representing chunks of code. They can also be text only, or they can be a hybrid. We'll explore all three types as we move through the activities.

How would you approach this game differently if we were to play again?

One of the challenges with which students struggle when learning to code is wanting to do too much too fast. For instance, in this activity a student wants to impress everyone with her fantastically complicated sculpture, but then struggles to detail every component in the instructions. The same thing happens in coding on the computer. Students, particularly those with experience, want to impress the others and end up frustrated when their big plans don't work out. Instructors must balance students' ambitious plans with the realities of available time and support. If a student who had never cooked before in her life chose a complicated soufflé for her first attempt, it is possible that she could achieve it, but it is more likely that she would not, and depending on her temperament, it could lead her to believe that she's hopeless at cooking. Alternatively, if her cooking instructor were to hear her long-term goal of soufflé making, and guide her toward recipes that would build up the skills needed, she will be better able to achieve her goal and understand how to troubleshoot problems along the way. One of the goals of this exercise and question is to plant seeds of self-awareness, planning, and time management within the students without discouraging their ambitions. To be successful programmers, students will need to be able to learn and grow from mistakes.

ACTIVITY 1B: SYNTAX SAYS!

As we discussed in Chapter 1, every programming language employs **syntax**, *the standard arrangement of components in a certain language to create shared meaning*. In the Amazing Algorithms activity, partners were able to experience some modicum of success because they share understanding of the syntax of the English language in a broad sense. In this activity, we'll practice paring that language down into code-like commands.

Syntax Says: Materials Needed

One Syntax Says card may be printed out per student, or the contents of the card may be written on a board or projected for all to see. The cards are available to print from the link in the Appendix. Instructors may choose to offer prizes. A whiteboard or chalkboard would be helpful for both the syntax says game and the following read-aloud activity.

An open space large enough for students to gather in a line and move forward is preferable, but students can also simply stand behind their desks if necessary. If this is required, make sure to clarify to students that the Forward and Backward commands should be in place, or simply replace them with other commands such as Right Foot Hop (# of Hops) or Left Foot Hop (# of Hops).

Syntax Says: Outcomes

Participants will build attention to detail.
Participants will increase ability to discern between intended and literal
   meaning.

Syntax Says: Guide

This game is based on the classic game Simon Says in which participants follow the commands of the designated "Simon" as long as he begins the phrase with "Simon Says."

Syntax Says: Level 1 Rules

In our game, we'll change the rules slightly. Simon will now represent a programmer using specific commands understood by the computer participants. Those commands are:

Forward (# of steps)
Backward (# of steps)
March In Place (# of seconds)
Duck Waddle (# of seconds)
Air Guitar (# of seconds)
Monkey Around (# of seconds)

If the programmer says, "Forward Three," all of the computer students should walk forward three steps. If the programmer says, "walk forward." The computers should stay still because they don't understand the command *walk* and no number was given following the word *forward*. Instructors may also choose to allow computers to say "Error" when they don't understand a command.

Computer students who move when the command is given improperly will be eliminated from the round and may sit down. The game may continue until only one student remains, or instructors may set a time limit to give each student the opportunity to be the programmer.

Introduce some creativity, and allow each programmer to add one original command to the list by announcing it before the round begins. For instance, the programmer of the second round might add *Pat Your Head*. The programmer of the third round might introduce *Rub Your Belly*.

Once students get a handle on the game, try introducing a few new terms. You may also choose to come back to these additions when we address these concepts in future activities.

Repeat Until Clap

Instead of using time to determine how long the computer students duck waddle or play air guitar, a programmer might use another event to trigger them to stop. If the programmer uses the command, "Syntax Says, Repeat March in Place Until Clap" the computer students should keep marching away until the programmer claps her hands. When creating a video game, a programmer might use a loop like this to trigger the end of the game, for instance, repeat counting down the time until it reaches the trigger point of 0.

While (# of Seconds)

This command tells the computer students to do something while another condition is true. For instance, if the programmer uses the command, "Syntax Says, Air Guitar, While March in Place 10," then as long as the students are marching in place, they should also be playing air guitar. Game programmers might use a "while" command to continuously loop a command. For instance, "While Time Is Greater than 20 Seconds, Play Happy Music."

Syntax Says: Read and Connect

After finishing as many rounds as appropriate for the class, gather the group together and read aloud from the 2006 picture book *Eats, Shoots & Leaves: Why, Commas Really Do Make a Difference!* written by Lynne Truss and illustrated by Bonnie Timmons. Examples from a similarly titled book by the same author, *Eats, Shoots & Leaves: The Zero Tolerance Approach to Punctuation* may also work with some adaptation, but is intended for an adult audience and is not illustrated.

While reading through the examples, discuss why the comma placement changes the meaning of the sentence. Helpfully, Truss and Timmons include a guide at the end of the book that explains each instance. Compare the comma's impact to how parentheses affect the order of operations in math. Write the following examples on the board.

$$2 + 1 * 3 = 5$$
$$(2 + 1) * 3 = 9$$

In the first example, we get the answer five, because in the normal order of operations multiplication and division always come before addition or subtraction, so one multiplied by three is three. Two plus three equals five. In the second example, the order is interrupted by parentheses around the addition, which tells us to do that operation first. Two plus one is three, which multiplied by three equals nine. Similarly computer programs typically run the commands in the order given, from top to bottom and from left to right, but placing multiple commands inside of a loop or block can affect the program's outcome.

ACTIVITY 1C: TINKER WITH COMPUTER CODING

In the previous activity, we practiced ordering steps in a series of instructions to achieve a specific result with our human computer stand-ins. Now, we'll put that practice to work using actual computers.

Tinker with Computer Coding:
Materials Needed and Set-up

This activity requires enough computers for all participants to work individually or in teams of two. If not enough computers are available from your institution; students may be divided into two or more groups and rotate through the activities in this chapter with the assistance of additional instructors or volunteers. Another option is to invite participants to bring their own laptops. A projector for the instructor's laptop may be helpful, but is not required.

This activity also requires that each computer be connected to the Internet. The free online software in this activity, Tynker™, requires the use of one of the following browsers: Chrome, Firefox, or Safari. It is always good to test websites prior to the date of the class to ensure that any firewall or other safety settings won't prevent access. According to the 2017 Tynker™ website parents' page, the only devices on which Tynker™ is supported are laptops, desktops, and Chromebook computers, so students will not be able to use other personal devices such as tablets and smart phones.

Tynker™ offers a variety of tools for parents and teachers, many of which come with a paid subscription. For this activity, however, students will use the openly available tutorial games in the Free Play (https://www.tynker.com/free

-play/) or Hour of Code (https://www.tynker.com/hour-of-code/) sections of the website. No subscription or account is necessary to access these games. If more than one student uses the same laptop, be sure to clear cookies from the browser between students to reset the levels available.

Instructors may wish to have students sit facing a projector screen in order to demonstrate aspects of particular games, but otherwise, each student only needs a place to sit with his or her laptop in range of a solid Internet connection.

Tinker with Computer Coding: Outcomes

Students will increase ability to decompose large tasks into smaller commands.

Students will gain familiarity building algorithms in a visual language environment.

Tinker with Computer Coding: Guide

There are numerous free games on the Tynker™ website that can help provide an introduction to computer coding. Though some are designed for students as young as kindergarteners, all offer valuable practice in logical thinking and develop skills upon which the activities in the next chapters will build. These activities also offer instructors who are new to coding an opportunity to learn, so if you've never programmed before, be sure to play through a few games.

Tinker with Computer Coding Step 1

Whether the club participants are seven or seventy years old, the Tynker™ game *Candy Quest* offers the perfect introduction to coding. In this game, participants use blocks of code to guide a little monster toward candy pieces. The program guides users through the meaning of various blocks and how to connect them. This technique as well as the incorporated concepts of repeat loops will come in handy when students begin working with Scratch in future activities.

Tinker with Computer Coding Step 2

After completing all of the free levels of *Candy Quest*, have students try *Lost in Space*. The initial levels of this game resemble those of *Candy Quest*, but it advances more rapidly into intermediate concepts including repeat loops, repeat until loops and if/then statements.

Tinker with Computer Coding Step 3

Finally, have students put everything together in *Dragon Dash*. This game employs similar blocks to the first two games, yet the puzzles increase in difficulty, requiring more complex thinking.

In this first activity set, students learned about the two foundational parts to a computer program, creating the algorithm (or set of instructions) and translating (or coding) those instructions into the correct syntax. Students played games that encouraged them to be precise with instructions and language, and think logically. We put these skills into action by playing coding games that required computational thinking skills. They needed to define the problem at hand, express a solution, and analyze the results, adjusting as necessary. In the next chapter, students will build on these experiences as they begin to create scripts in Scratch.

2

Intro to Scratch

Scratch is an incredible resource created and supported by the Lifelong Kindergarten Group at the Massachusetts Institute of Technology (MIT) Media Laboratory. Like Tynker™, Scratch uses blocks representing simple scripts that snap together to form snippets of code. With Scratch, users can create animations and video games and program via the online or downloadable interface. The offline version is very convenient for libraries doing outreach to areas that may not have a reliable Internet connection. Users may also create a free online account that allows them to create, edit, and post projects for others to watch, play, embed in their websites, and "remix." The Scratch team encourages remixing, or taking and building on others' good ideas, which is a central tenet of open-source, social coding. For instance, one student might create a game in which the player controls a spaceship and earns a point for every planet visited. Another student might remix this game by adding a health component in which the player loses health each time the ship is hit by an asteroid. A third student might then remix the game to earn a point each time the player shoots an asteroid, and the player can gain health back by collecting certain elements from each planet.

Within the Scratch framework there are built-in lessons to launch new users into quick understanding of how to code and give ideas about what's possible. Users can create their own **sprites**, *standalone graphical elements that can move or be manipulated among other graphical elements*, or they can pick from a number of preloaded sprites. They can also upload sprites and sounds created by others. This is a great opportunity for librarians to help participants understand copyright, fair use, and the difference between possessing the ability to do something versus the permission to do it. Yes, you could technically upload your favorite Beyoncé song as the background music to your animation, but when you upload that to the Internet you will also be technically violating her copyright, even if you're not making any money from it.

Scratch works well with children as young as seven, but also provides a rich enough spectrum of tools and extensions to continue to entice teens and adults. Users can build impressive animations and games, and they'll develop computational thinking while they're at it.

ACTIVITY 2A: SCRATCHING THE SURFACE

Designed with beginners in mind, Scratch provides a clean and simple interface, yet some preliminary overview may help new users navigate better. In this activity we'll explore and explain coordinates, sprites, costumes, stages, and events.

Scratching the Surface: Materials Needed

For this activity it is helpful to have a projector for the instructor and copies of the handout, printable from the activity resources link in the Appendix, and it is necessary to have computers, ideally one per participant. As of April 2018, Scratch 2 is the most current version and it is only available for desktop and laptop computers; however, the Scratch team members are currently working on options for tablets. Most participants find it useful to have a mouse, but laptop trackpads will work in a pinch.

Prior to the class, seriously consider installing the Scratch Offline Editor, available for Mac OS, Windows, and Linux, from https://scratch.mit.edu/scratch 2download. The software may be freely installed on as many computers as desired, and will allow participants to create and save projects locally without an Internet connection. Instructors who choose this option should instruct participants to bring a flash drive to save their projects. Projects may also be transferred via an online file sharing service like Dropbox, but are typically too large for emailing as an attachment. To play or edit their projects at home, participants will need to install the Scratch Offline Editor on their personal computers. A sample letter explaining this process is available from the downloadable resources link in the Appendix. Note that in order for the offline editor to run successfully, additional free software called Adobe Air may need to be installed. Both the instructions online and linked in the Appendix explain this step.

Alternatively, participants may create projects using the online editor https:// scratch.mit.edu in any major web browser. Projects created online may be saved to the online community or downloaded to the local computer. Be aware that projects downloaded to the local computer will not run unless the offline editor is installed. To save to the online community, each participant will need to create a free account. Depending on the coding club host organization's policies, parent permission may be required to help students create accounts. Asking participants to create accounts prior to class potentially alleviates this concern and reduces the time spent dealing with accounts during class; however, typically some participants will not be able or willing to create an account in advance. Creating accounts during class typically proves problematic for some students, so it is often wise to have a few instructor-created accounts available for general use. If possible, it is often the best option to install the

Scratch Offline Editor for the class and send the projects home either on a flash drive or through an online file transfer service like Dropbox.

Scratching the Surface: Setup

Often computer labs are set up with the presenter station at the front of the room, but it is much more efficient to place the instructor station at the back of the room, so that the instructor can see the participants' screens. Participants tend to look at their own screens rather than at the instructor, and with the instructor keeping an eye on things, she can quickly monitor each student's progress, help those who are struggling, and redirect those who are off track. If possible, arrange the student stations so that they are facing the projected screen of the instructor who will stand behind them with her own computer.

Open Scratch on each computer prior to the beginning of class as it may take a few moments to open and this will reduce wasted class time. If the computers have an Internet connection, the Offline Editor will search for updates as it opens. There may be prompts to update Scratch or Adobe Air. These prompts may be cancelled and installed after the class, to prevent unanticipated changes to the software from disrupting the class.

If it is possible to print a handout for each participant, consider the audience before distributing them. It tends to be helpful for adult audiences to have the handout as a reference point from the beginning. Adults, particularly older adults, tend to take notes, and prefer to do so on the handout. It is also sometimes helpful for those with visual impairments to have the handout for a closer view of the code. Some adults, teens, and children often ignore the handout until directed to refer to it, but some with more confidence will often plow ahead, missing the important *whys* of the instruction process that will enable them to be self sufficient in Scratch and build the fundamental knowledge needed to code in more advanced languages. Consider waiting to distribute handouts to younger groups until after making explanations. Then, each individual can use the handout to work at his or her own pace.

Scratching the Surface: Outcomes

Participants understand the mathematical concepts of axes on a plane and their use in computer coding.
Participants know how to trigger actions using event blocks.
Participants understand rotation styles and direction.
Participants effectively create an animation effect using costumes.
Participants know how to change stage backgrounds.

Scratching the Surface: Guide

In this activity we'll make a simple user-controlled animation in which the Scratch Cat will walk along the x and y axes when the user presses the appropriate keys.

FIGURE 2-1   Scratch Stage.

FIGURE 2-2   Scratch xy-Grid Selection.

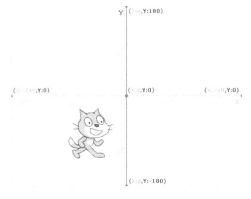

FIGURE 2-3   Scratch Stage Panel.

Scratching the Surface Step One: Set the Stage

Opening Scratch creates a new file, blank with the exception of the preloaded Scratch Cat sprite. From the main screen, go to the bottom left corner and select the white square representing the **Stage** options, as shown in Figure 2-1. Hover your mouse over the icon on the far left below the Stage icon that resembles a mountain scene. The descriptor **Choose Backdrop from Library** should appear on hover. Select this option.

Scratch comes preloaded with a library of possible backgrounds. These are listed alphabetically in the library. Scroll to the bottom and choose the **xy-Grid Backdrop**, as shown in Figure 2-2. Click **OK**.

The **xy-Grid Backdrop** should now fill the **Stage Panel**, the top left quadrant of the main screen. Note that the Scratch Cat appears in front of the backdrop, as shown in Figure 2-3. That is because the stage, and whatever backdrop is on it, always appears at the lowest level.

Understanding the Grid

The **xy-Grid Backdrop** illustrates what is happening behind the scenes when we make an animation or game. Scratch determines where to display sprites based on their coordinates using the Cartesian Coordinate System (which adults and older students will likely recognize from math class). In this system, each point on a plane has two values, one x and one y, to describe its exact position.

Explain to the students that a computer screen is a flat, two-dimensional surface. Though some images might look three-dimensional, everything we see on our screen is actually two-dimensional. For instance, the tail of the Scratch Cat is not sticking out of the back of the computer monitor because it has no discernable depth. The cat image does, however, have width and height, as does the stage in which he'll move. Let's move the Scratch Cat so that his toe is touching where the red and blue lines cross, the (0,0) position, as shown in Figure 2-4.

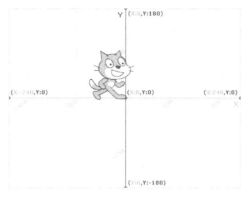

FIGURE 2-4   Scratch Cat on (0,0).

This will make it appear as though the Scratch Cat is ready to walk a tightrope. That horizontal-line tightrope is called the **x-axis**, and it is a reference tool to help us measure location values. Each pixel along the line has a value. For instance, the number 100 to the right of the cat indicates the 100th point in the line. Right now, the Scratch Cat's front toe is at the pixel assigned to the zero location on the x-axis. If the Scratch Cat were to move to the right on the x-axis until he reaches the 100th pixel, as shown in Figure 2-5, his front toe's **x-coordinate** would become 100, and his toe's **y-Coordinate** would still be 0.

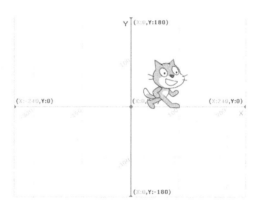

FIGURE 2-5   Scratch Cat on (100,0).

The **y-axis** works the same way, but measures vertical pixels. The middle of the line is considered the zero co-ordinate, and the top of the y-axis is the 180th pixel. Let's move the cat back to the center, with his toe touching the (0,0) position. Have students click and drag the cat straight up the y-axis so that his toe has a y position of 100, as shown in Figure 2-6.

The cat's toe is now at the position (0,100). His x position is 0 because he is still centered horizontally in

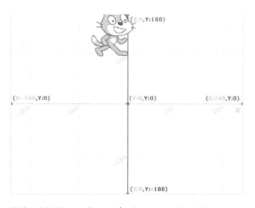

FIGURE 2-6   Scratch Cat on (0,100).

the screen, and his y position is 100 because he has moved 100 pixels up the y-axis. Note that when written, the convention is to place the x value first, followed by the y.

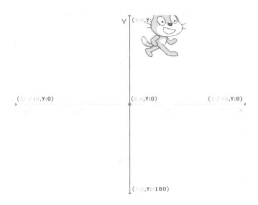

FIGURE 2-7   Scratch Cat on (100,100).

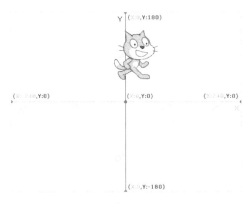

FIGURE 2-8   Scratch Cat on (50,50).

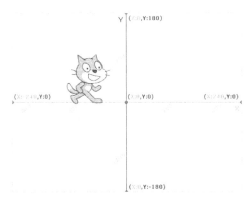

FIGURE 2-9   Scratch Cat on (−50,0).

Practicing with Position

Challenge students to move the cat to x position 100 and y position 100 or (100,100), as shown in Figure 2-7. Review how they did, and explain any needed adjustments.

Explain to students that the marked pixels such as 100 and 200 are only some of the pixels along the line. Challenge them to place the cat at approximately (50,50), as shown in Figure 2-8.

Negative Coordinates

At this point, the students have only worked with positive numbers. For younger students, the concept of negative numbers will be new. Use the challenges below to introduce the concept. Skip to the explanation for older students.

Have students move the cat back to (0,0). Explain to them that if we want to move our cat to the left, we need to use negative numbers. Have them pretend that the x-axis is a thermometer, and the cat represents the temperature. Tell them to imagine that it is a hot summer day, and it is 100 degrees outside, and have them move their cats to (100,0).

In the fall the weather starts to cool down, and it gets 50 degrees cooler. Have the students move their cats to the new temperature, (50,0).

Then, in the winter, it gets 50 degrees colder than that. What would the temperature be? (They should move the cat to (0,0).) Finally, if you lived in Antarctica it might get 50 degrees colder. Ask them to place their cat 50 degrees less than zero, as shown in Figure 2-9.

Their cat thermometer should land on (-50,0). Explain that the minus symbol represents how far below zero our number is. The farther the number is below zero, the smaller it is. Ask students which direction we would move the cat if it got 50 degrees colder. Wait for responses, and then move the cat to (–100,0). What if it got 50 degrees warmer? Wait for responses, and then move the cat to (–50,0).

Clarify with students that the y-axis works the same way, just like a vertical thermometer. Challenge them to place the cat on (0,–100), as shown in Figure 2-10. If students are struggling, practice a few more negative y values on the center x-axis.

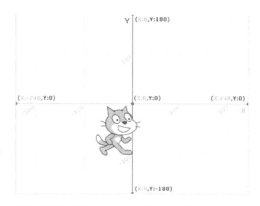

FIGURE 2-10   Scratch Cat on (0,–100).

If they seem to be grasping the concept, challenge them to combine two negative values by placing the cat's toe on (–200,–100), as shown in Figure 2-11. Finally, challenge them to combine a negative coordinate with a positive coordinate by asking them to move the cat to (–100,100), as shown in Figure 2-12.

Great job! Now that we understand the grid, it's time to make our cat walk along it.

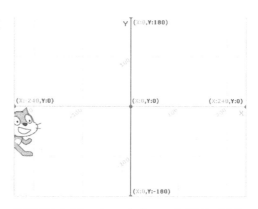

FIGURE 2-11   Scratch Cat on (–200,–100).

Scratching the Surface
Step 2: Basic Sprite Scripts

The **Sprite Pane** is located in the bottom left quadrant of the screen and *shows all of the sprites currently in our project.* As we can see in Figure 2-13 we only have one, the cat.

Understanding Sprites

Point out to students that the cat is labeled **Sprite 1**, and ask them what they think the term *sprite* means?

Typically at least one student will have an idea. Discuss as a group that the noun *sprite* has at least three meanings.

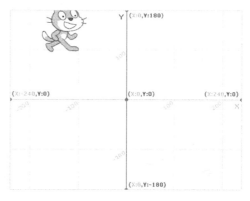

FIGURE 2-12   Scratch Cat on (–100,100).

1. a small magical creature, like an elf or fairy
2. a standalone two-dimensional computer graphic that can be manipulated as part of a larger scene
3. a reddish-orange flash caused by electrical discharge above thunderstorms

There is, of course, also a proper-noun version of the word that refers to a copyrighted carbonated beverage. In Scratch **Sprites** *are visual elements that we can program and control.* Each of our sprites has its own scripting area where we tell it what to do. Make sure that you and the students have the cat selected so that there is a blue square around it, as shown in Figure 2-14. We're going to give it some scripts.

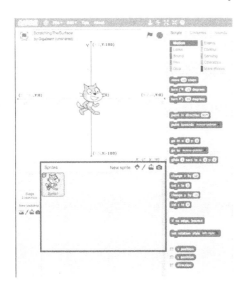

FIGURE 2-13   Sprite Pane.

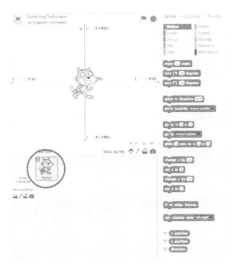

FIGURE 2-14   Scratch Cat Sprite Icon.

Event Scripts

We've been moving the cat around by dragging it with our mouse. When we start making video games, we'll want to be able to control it with keys on the keyboard. To do this, we need to create an event that tells the cat sprite when and how to move.

Figure 2-15 shows the block palette, located in the middle of the Scratch window. The **Block Palette** *contains bits of code that snap together to form scripts.* Make sure that **Scripts** is selected at the top, and then select the brown **Events** tab. **Events** *trigger scripts to begin.* We'll use a key to start our cat moving, so select the second block, **When Space Key Pressed**, and click and drag it to the right, into the grey **Scripts Area**. As shown in Figure 2-16, click the dropdown arrow to select the key that will activate the script. Since this script will make the cat to move to the right, we'll choose **Right Arrow**.

Change X by ()

When the right arrow is pressed, we want the cat to move, so, not surprisingly, we'll find our next block in the

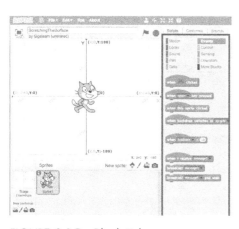

FIGURE 2-15   Block Palette.

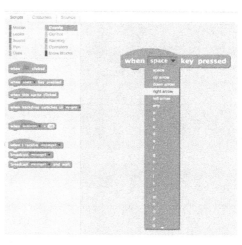

FIGURE 2-16   Events Palette When (Right Arrow) Key Pressed.

blue Motion Palette, shown in Figure 2-17. Select **Change X by (10)** and snap it onto the previous block. This block increases the Scratch Cat's x position by 10 pixels, which we know will move it to the right on the x-axis. Now, each time we push the right arrow, the cat should move 10 pixels to the right. Try it!

Have students add another **When Key Pressed** event block, but this time change the key to the **Left Arrow**. Ask the students what block they think should be added to make the cat move to the left. (They will click in the white circle to change the value to **–10**.) They should now be able to move the cat to the left and to the right using the arrows.

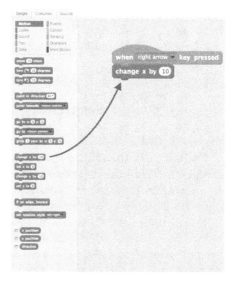

FIGURE 2-17   Motion Palette Change x by (10).

Change Y By ()

Have students add two more **When Key Pressed** event blocks, and change them to **Up Arrow** and **Down Arrow** respectively. So far, our cat has been walking along the x-axis tightrope. Ask the students which blue motion block we should use to make the Scratch Cat move vertically. Give them a few moments to respond individually or as a group and try to solve the blocks and settings themselves. If needed, guide them through, or ask a successful student to explain it to his peers.

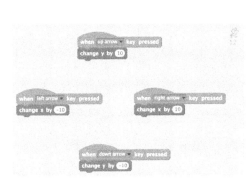

FIGURE 2-19
Save Now.

FIGURE 2-20
Save As.

FIGURE 2-18   Change Y by (10) and (–10).

As indicated in Figure 2-18, we'll snap a **Change Y by (10)** block onto each of the new **When Key Pressed** blocks. To move the cat up, we want to increase the cat's y-position, so under the When Up Arrow Key Pressed event we will change y by positive 10. To move the cat down, we need to decrease the cat's y position. To subtract 10 pixels from its current position we'll use the Change y by Block, but change the value to –10. Once students have added these blocks, have them test it again. They should be able to move the cat left, right, up, and down using the arrows.

Scratching the Surface Step 3:
Saving Your Project

If working in the Online Editor, students will login to their accounts to save then go to **File** and then **Save Now**, as shown in Figure 2-19. Students without accounts may select **Download to Your Computer** and save their work onto the desktop or a flash drive.

If working in the Offline Editor, students will select **File** and then **Save As**, shown in Figure 2-20, which will prompt a pop-up window. Students may then select the location on which to save, such as a personal flash drive, desktop, or server folder, and then name the file. It is helpful to each student include her name in the file name, so that the file can be easily located and identified if needed.

Scratching the Surface Step 4: Costumes

At this point, the cat moves in response to the trigger keys, but it does not yet appear as though the cat is walking. Let's help students learn to animate sprites using the **Costumes** tab and purple **Looks** palette. Make sure that the cat is selected in the sprite pane so that a blue square appears around him, and then select **Costumes** from the top middle of the window, as shown in Figure 2-21.

Each sprite may have multiple costumes, or alternate appearance frames. The default costume for the sprite is indicated by the blue highlight square around that costume. We can change the default costume for the sprite by clicking on a different costume. Try this by clicking on **Costume2**. Notice that the cat on the stage changes in response. Return the default costume to **Costume1**.

To make our cat appear to walk, we'll switch between costumes as he moves. Click on the **Scripts** tab to return to the cat's scripts. Choose the purple **Looks** palette. Add a **Next Costume** block to each of the four event scripts, as shown in Figure 2-22. Save and then test. Each time an arrow is pressed, the cat costume should change giving an illusion of animation similar to a flip book.

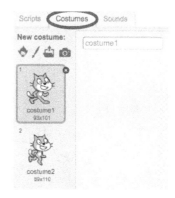

FIGURE 2-21   Costumes Tab.

Scratching the Surface
Step 5: Direction and
Rotation Style

At this point the cat appears to be moonwalking when he walks backward and floating when he walks up and down. To turn our cat to face the direction that he's walking, we need to use two of the sprite's parameters from the blue motion palette.

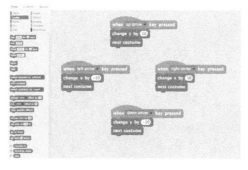

FIGURE 2-22   Looks Palette Next Costume.

Set Rotation Style ()

First, we'll set the sprite's rotation style for each event. Let's start with the **Left Arrow** event. Add a **Set Rotation Style ()** block. From the drop down menu choose **Left–Right**. Repeat this for the right arrow block. The left–right rotation style tells the sprite that it can only rotate on its vertical axis. It can flip to face the left or flip to face the right, but it cannot flip up or down.

Add **Set Rotation Style ()** blocks to the **Up and Down** events. To make the cat face up or face down, we'll need to change the rotation style to **All Around**. This allows the cat to rotate 360 degrees if necessary. In our case, we only need the cat to flip on its horizontal axis, to face up or face down. If you choose to have students test at this point, they'll probably be disappointed in the results. That's because we've told the cat how he *may* rotate, but not to go ahead and *do* it. We'll add that next.

Point in Direction ()

Add a **Point in Direction** block to the left and right arrow events. Set the **Left** direction to **–90** and the **Right** direction to **90**. Save and test. The cat should

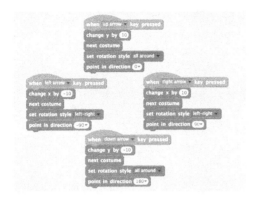

FIGURE 2-23   Set Rotation Style() and Point in Direction().

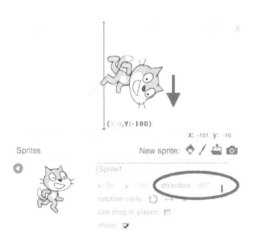

FIGURE 2-24   Sprite Info Pane Direction Indicator.

FIGURE 2-25   Go to x () y ().

turn in the direction he's moving now when walking along the x-axis. To get the cat to look as though he is walking along the vertical axis, we'll repeat these steps for the up and down events, but make some alternations. For the up event, **Change the Point in Direction Setting to 0**. For the down event, **Change the Point in Direction Setting to 180**. Save and test. The cat should now face whichever boundary wall he is walking toward. Figure 2-23 demonstrates the completed directional scripts.

In the sprite pane, click on blue circle with the letter I in the top left of the cat sprite icon. This will open the **Sprite Info Pane** for the cat sprite. Test each of the arrows again while noticing how the settings in the sprite info pane change with each different arrow. The bar in the direction circle indicates the direction that the cat is facing with each arrow key. Click on the blue arrow in the top left corner of the Sprite Info Pane to close the info pane.

Scratching the Surface
Step 6: Go to x () and y ()

Now that our cat can wander around, it would be nice to be able to re-center him easily. Have students return to the brown **Events** palette, and drag another **When Key Pressed** block into the scripting pane. Students may select any key not currently in use as the trigger. Using the zero key makes sense as the purpose of this script is to return the cat sprite to (0,0).

Have students return to the blue **Motion** palette and attach a **Go to x () y ()** block, as shown in Figure 2-25. The coordinates in the block are initially set to the associated sprite's current coordinates. Have students change both values to zero. Save and test. Now when the associated key is pressed, the cat should return to the intersection of the two axes.

ACTIVITY 2B: SHAPE SHIFTERS

Although some extremely enthusiastic students could sit and program all day long, many will crave a break. Kinesthetic learners will particularly benefit from the opportunity to experience concepts physically. The following activity is a team game designed to reinforce how to use the Cartesian Coordinate System to locate and place elements.

Shape Shifters: Materials Needed and Set-up

This activity requires masking, duct, or gaffer's tape, something visible that can stick reasonably well to the floor. If possible, it is helpful to have three different colors of tape. Print and cut out one set of Coordinate Shapes per team, making sure to have at least one shape per student. Laminate them for repeated use. Print out two Shape Shifter Coordinate Sheets. Consider attaching tape or sticky tack to the shapes to help them hold their positions. Print off the appropriate Shape Shifter Answer Sheet for the instructor. It is also fun if there is a buzzer or bell for students to ring when their team is finished.

Prior to student arrival, complete the following tasks. Use the tape to map out one grid for each team. Refer to the Scratch xy-grid as a template. If possible, choose one color of tape for the x-axis and one color tape for the y-axis, with another color for the remaining grid lines.

Shape Shifters: Guide

This activity is inspired by geocaching, a treasure hunt type of activity in which participants search for and locate items using GPS coordinates and clues. Our version uses this concept in reverse. Each team will use their Shape Shifters Coordinate Sheet to place the appropriate shape at the corresponding coordinate point on their grid.

When one team places all of the shapes, they will ring the bell or announce to the instructor. The other team will then be required to pause while the instructor checks the finished team's responses. If all shapes are placed on the correct coordinates, that team wins. If there are errors, the paused team may resume, and the team with errors may work as a group to rearrange their board appropriately. The first team with all of the shapes placed correctly wins. There are multiple Shape Shifter Coordinate Sheets so that the game may be repeated. Instructors may choose to allow rematches or to redistribute team members.

ACTIVITY 2C: CAT GOT YOUR NUMBER?

The first Scratch activity introduced students to the foundational components of Scratch, sprites, stage backgrounds, costumes, and scripts. Now, let's dig a little deeper into coding scripts to make our first game. This activity simply requires computers with Scratch preinstalled or accessible via the Online Editor.

Cat Got Your Number? Outcomes

Participants grasp mathematical concepts such as variables, greater than, less than, and random numbers.

Participants gain awareness of conditional statements and their importance in coding.

Participants build understanding of loops and interruptions.

Participants grow skill decomposing problems into smaller questions.

Cat Got Your Number? Guide

In this game, the cat will ask players to guess a random number between 1 and 20. Start a new Scratch project. If Scratch is already open, go to **File** and then **New**. Once again, we'll use the Scratch Cat for this project.

Cat Got Your Number? Step 1: Greeting the Player

In our Scratching the Surface animation, the Scratch Cat is triggered to move by specific keystrokes. Each key launches a different script. This time, we'll use one main event to put our game into motion.

When Green Flag Clicked

From the block palette, select the brown **Events** tab. Click and drag the **When Green Flag Clicked** block to the right in the cat's grey **Scripts Area**. Game players will begin the game by clicking the green flag above the stage panel.

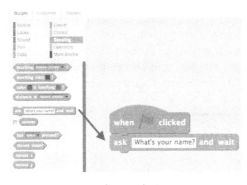

FIGURE 2-26   Ask () and Wait.

Ask () and Wait

Once the game launches, the cat will ask the player for his or her name. As shown in Figure 2-26, go to the turquoise **Sensing** menu, and add an **Ask () and Wait** block, which *gives the user a prompt and launches an input box*. For our game, the cat will ask the default question, "What's your name?" Type this question into the block.

Answer

The player's input is stored in the **Answer** block, also on the turquoise Sensing menu. Let's go ahead and grab that, but just set it aside in the scripting area, rather than attaching it to the rest of the script. The **Answer** block *is a sensing block, in that it can absorb information and a reporting block because it stores that information for potential use in other parts of the script.* If, at the prompt, the player typed in "Joe," *answer* now equals *Joe.* We'll use the answer block to address the player by name.

Say () for () Secs

From the purple **Looks** palette, add a **Say (Hello) for (2) Secs** block to the script. This block *adds a speech bubble to the sprite with the designated text for the indicated amount of time.* Save the game after adding this block, and then test it by clicking the green flag. The cat should ask for the player's name. Once text is entered, using the return key or clicking the checkmark, the cat should say, "hello."

Join ()()

Currently, the cat greets the player, but not by name. To do this, we'll go to the green **Operators** palette and add a **Join ()()** block to the scripting area, but we won't attach it yet. The **Join ()()** block *concatenates, or merges, two values together.* Remember that computers are literal, so joining (Hello)(World) would report out "HelloWorld." A space must be added within one of the input squares for the concatenated result to contain a space, so (Hello)(World) would result in "Hello World."

As shown in Figure 2-27, type a greeting into the first square, and then drag **Answer** into the second square. Drag this merged block into the input square of the **Say () for (2) Secs** block, to replace "hello." Save, and test again. This time, the cat should greet the player by name. Each time the player clicks the green flag, the value of answer is wiped out,

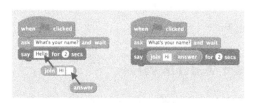

FIGURE 2-27   Say (Join (Answer)()) for () Secs.png.

so if the user hits enter without typing a name, the cat will leave the second part of the greeting blank. Try it.

We need to give our player some guidance if we want them to play. Add a **Say () for () Secs** block, and input text such as "I'm thinking of a number between 1 and 20."

Cat Got Your Number Step 2: Variables

A **variable** is *a changeable value assigned to a letter, word or symbol.* Any game that uses a score to determine the winner uses a variable. Ask students what the score of a basketball game would be when it first starts, and then what it would be after one team makes a regular basket. The variable we call *score* changes from zero to zero at tipoff to zero to two or zero to three, etc. . . . The value assigned to the variable called score keeps changing until the game is over. For our game we'll need to set two variables, **Number** and **Guesses Taken**.

Make Variables

Go to the orange **Data** tab, as indicated in Figure 2-28. Select **Make a Variable** to create a new variable. Enter a name for the variable in the pop-up box

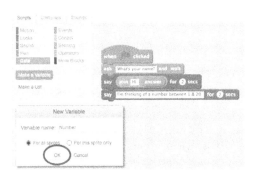

FIGURE 2-28   Make a Variable.

that appears. Although the variable could be named just about anything, for the sake of clarity in this first experience, encourage the students to name it **Number**. Leave **For All Sprites** selected. This ensures that Number will be a **Global Variable**, so that *it can be read and changed by any sprite.* Click **OK** to create the variable. After the variable is created, blocks for that variable will appear. We'll use those shortly. For now, follow the previous process to create a variable for **Guesses Taken**.

Notice that after each variable is created, a corresponding indicator appears on the stage. Students may click and drag these to a different area of the stage if desired.

Set Variable Values

We've created the variables in the same way that one might build a box to hold a gift, but currently our boxes are empty. We need to place a value inside

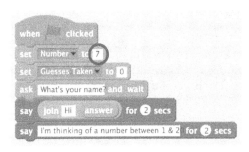

FIGURE 2-29   Set Variable Values.

each variable, like a present in each box. As the game continues the values assigned to the variable will change, just as we might keep reusing the boxes to hold different presents. To set the initial value of the score, select the first block in the orange **Data** menu, and select **Number** from the drop down. Place **Set Number to (0)** below When Green Flag Clicked. This will ensure that each time the game begins, the score will reset to zero. Follow the same steps to set **Guesses Taken** to 0. As shown in Figure 2-29, enter a value inside the Set Number to () block. This will be the number that the player tries to guess, so make sure it is between 1 and 20.

Cat Got Your Number Step 3: Test Variables

We need to prompt the player to take a guess. From the turquoise Sensing palette, add an **Ask () and Wait** block. Use the text square to prompt the player to "Take a Guess." When the player enters a number in the input box, that value becomes the new value of Answer. The player will need to know if her answer is too high or too low. Grab three **Answer** blocks and set them aside in the scripting area.

() is Greater Than/Less Than/Equal to ()

Go to the green **Operators** palette. From here grab one each of the **() is Greater Than ()**, **() is Less Than ()**, and **() is Equal to ()** blocks, and set them, unattached to anything, into the scripting area. These three blocks are Boolean blocks. A **Boolean** *presents a condition that can either be true or false.* We'll use these to test whether the number the player guessed is higher in value, lower in value, or exactly equal to the secret number. Place one **Answer** block in each left-side box. The secret number is represented by the variable called Number, so return to the orange Data palette, and place one **Number** block into each of the right-hand boxes, as shown in Figure 2-30.

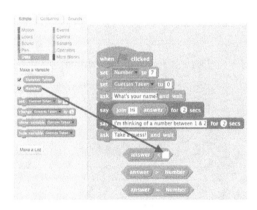

FIGURE 2-30   Compare Variable Values.

These combination blocks represent Boolean statements, each can only be true or false. For instance, in our example, the value of Number is set to 7, so the first Boolean statement, "Answer is greater than Number" would be true if the player guessed anything above 7. It would be false, if the player guessed seven or anything below. We'll use each true or false result to trigger different responses.

If () Then

Returning to the block palette, select the yellow **Control** tab. Select the fourth option down, the **If () Then** block. Attach three of these, stacked one on top of the other onto the script. The If () Then block checks a Boolean condition, and if it is true, runs the script placed inside of its C shape. If the condition is false, the script continues to the next block.

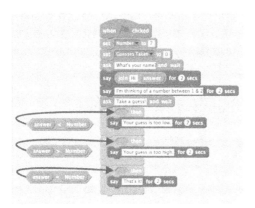

FIGURE 2-31   If (Condition Is True) Then Say ().

Place a **Say () for () Secs** block inside of each If () Then block, as shown in Figure 2-31. The first Say () for () Secs block should indicate that the guess was too low, the second was too high, and the third was just right. Drag the Boolean statement into the condition area of each If () Then. Students sometimes struggle with this step. It helps to think of placing the condition into the empty space like a jewel into a crown. It also works best to align the left edge of the block with the left edge of the space.

Save, and test. Currently, the player can see the "secret" number in the variable box on the stage. We'll remove this later, but right now it's useful for testing. Run the game once, entering a value that is lower than Number. Does the cat respond with the appropriate message? Run the program at least two more times to test the message received when the value is too high and then when it is equal to Number.

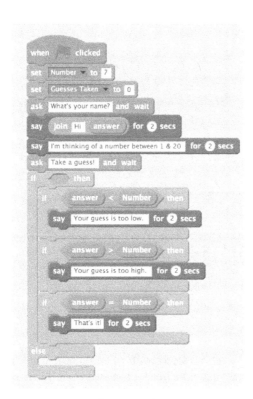

FIGURE 2-32   If () Then, Else ().

Cat Got Your Number? Step 4: Limit Guesses

After testing the game, ask students to think about remaining problems. What still needs to happen? What could improve our game? They'll have a variety of answers. Make note of them for later. One problem that we'll address next is that the player can guess as many times as he wants. Another is that the player has to click the green flag for each guess.

If () Then, () Else

From the yellow control menu, place an **If () Then, Else** block into the scripting area. It *checks its Boolean condition, and if it is true, it activates the code held inside the first C, but if the condition is false, it activates the code inside the second C.* As shown in Figure 2-32, drag the three If () Then blocks into the top section of this new block, and then reattach it to the script. The If () Then, Else block functions similarly to the If () Then block which checks for a condition, and if true it executes the code inside its C. If it is false it ignores the code in the C and moves on.

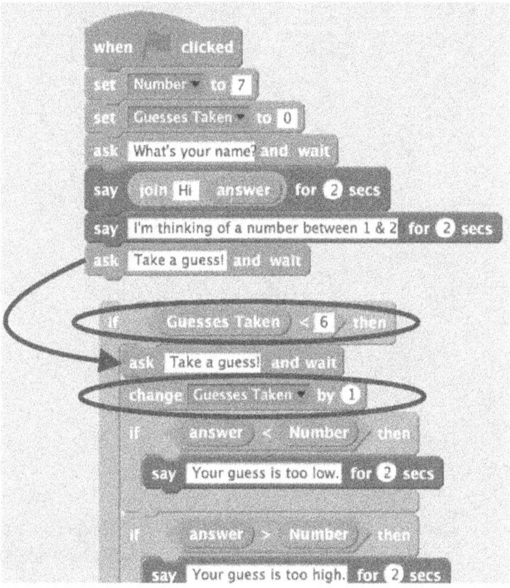

Go to the green **Operators** palette. Drag a **() is Less Than ()** block into the condition area of the If () Then, Else block. From the orange **Data** palette, drag **Guesses Taken** into the left side of the statement. Decide how many guesses players should get, and enter this value on the right side. The top C of the If () Then, Else block, testing the number, will only run now if the player still has guesses remaining.

FIGURE 2-33   If (Guesses Taken Is Less Than 6) Then.

As shown in Figure 2-33, detach the **If () Then Else** Script temporarily to move the **Ask (Take a Guess!) and Wait** block into the top part of the **If () Then, Else** block. This will give the player the opportunity to respond again after each guess, if they have not reached their limit.

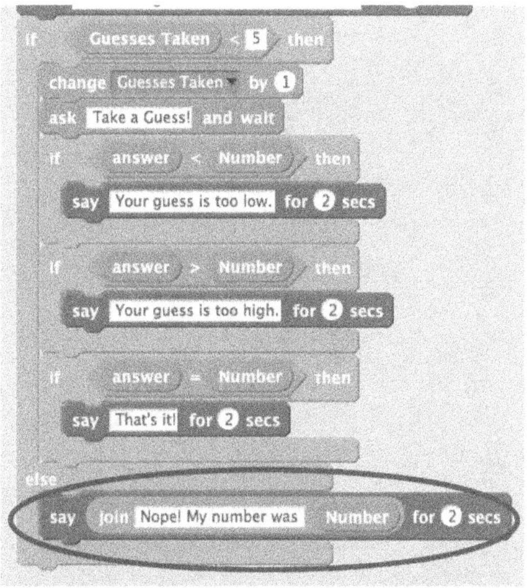

Add a **Change (Guesses Taken) by (1)** block into the top of the If () Then, Else block. This will increase the value of the variable Guesses Taken each time the player takes a guess. Eventually, the value of Guesses Taken will be greater than the conditional statement in the If () Then, Else statement, causing the Else part of the statement in the bottom C to run instead of the top C.

FIGURE 2-34   Else Reveal Number.

Add a **Say () for () Secs** block into the Else section. We'll use this to inform the player that he is out of guesses and to share the correct value for the secret number. To do this, we'll place a **Join ()()** block inside of the Say block, as shown in Figure 2-34. Place a **Number** block in the second input box. In the first, enter a message such as, "Nope! My number was. . . ."

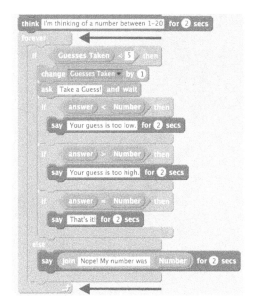

FIGURE 2-35   Forever Loop.

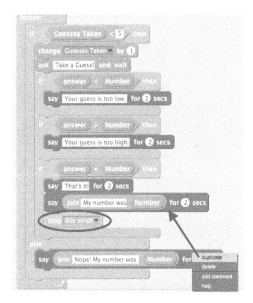

FIGURE 2-36   Interrupt Loop.

Forever

From yellow control, grab a Forever block. Place this C block around the entire If () Then, Else script, as shown in Figure 2-35. The Forever block *causes the blocks it contains to loop continuously from the time the program starts until the time it ends or the script is interrupted.*

Cat Got Your Number? Step 5: Forever Interrupted

Have students save and test their games. The cat should now ask for another guess after each unsuccessful guess, but he also does it for accurate guesses. Why does he do that? Well, currently our loop has him continue to ask for guesses as long as there are guesses remaining, so if the player guesses correctly on guess three, there would still be two guesses remaining, so the loop would run two more times asking for guesses before sending players to the Else section when guesses run out. Let's fix this by interrupting the forever loop when the guess is correct. From the yellow Control palette, place a **Stop ()** block under the Say (That's It!) for 2 Secs block in the If ((Answer) equals (Number)). From the dropdown list select **This Script**. Save, and test. Now, when the player guesses the correct number, the loop will end after the cat says, "That's it."

The winning player may not remember the last number he guessed. Right-click on **Say (Join (Nope! My number was (Number)) for (2) Secs,** and select **Duplicate**. Drag the block before Stop (This Script), and update the message to reflect the win. For example, in Figure 2-36, simply removing "Nope!" from the beginning of the message works. Save, and test again. An alert message and then one informing him of the correct number should now greet a winning player.

Cat Got Your Number?
Step 6: Random

While working on our game we left the Number displayed on the stage while playing, so that as we tested we could confirm that the number guessed was indeed too high, too low, or correct. We've also used the same value for Number each time. To finish our game, we'll ask Scratch to choose a random number each time the game is played and to hide the Number variable from the stage.

From the green Operators menu, select the fifth option down, **Pick Random () to ()**. Click and drag this reporter block into the white parameter oval of the Wait () Secs block, as shown in Figure 2-37. Though the numbers generated by the Pick Random () to () block are not truly random, they are unpredictable. The default values in the block are (1) and (10). Let's change the second parameter to **20**. Save, and then test, noting that a different value should appear in the Number display on the stage each time the green flag is clicked.

FIGURE 2-37   Randomize and Hide Number.

Finally, we want to hide the Number variable from the stage, so that players can't see the number that they are to guess. To do this, go to the orange Data palette. As highlighted in Figure 2-37, uncheck the box next to Number. Save and test. The value of Number should now be hidden from the player, and it should change randomly with each click of the green flag.

Congratulations! You and your students have just completed your first video game! Figure 2-38 reveals the full, final script for the Cat Got Your Number? game. In our next game, we'll build on the lessons, vocabulary, and logical processes of this experience. Before moving on, however, consider inviting students to customize their games, attempt to solve the remaining questions on the class list, or test their comprehension by giving challenges that can be solved with the blocks and concepts covered in this lesson. For instance, what block(s) would we add,

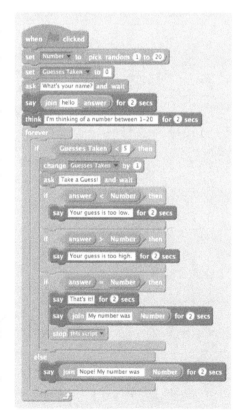

FIGURE 2-38   Cat Got Your Number? Full Script.

if we wanted to offer a personalized greeting to a player who shares the programmer's name? How could we redirect a player and not count a guess that was outside of the stated parameters, for instance, a guess of 25. Need help solving these yourself? Possible solutions to these challenges are posted on the website listed in the Appendix, but try to figure it out first.

3

Into the Jungle with Scratch

In the previous chapter we explored some of the basic elements found in Scratch such as coordinates, sprites, costumes, stages, and events. In this chapter, we'll dig into more concepts of coding while creating our first playable video game using intermediate features in Scratch. Participants will learn how to trigger scripts with conditional statements, work with loops to repeat scripts, define variables, and create clones. This activity set provides more than enough content for a two-hour session, and the activities in Chapter 4 build on what we'll create here. If you plan to use this activity set as a standalone class, consider skipping Step 12: Add Butterfly.

INTO THE JUNGLE: PREPARATION

In these activities, we'll create a game based on Rudyard Kipling's classic work *The Jungle Book,* specifically the third chapter "Kaa's Hunting."

Into the Jungle Materials Needed and Set-up

Computers, ideally one per participant, are required for this activity. Either Scratch 2 will need to be installed on the computers, or participants will need to be able to access the Scratch Online Editor. Refer to Scratching the Surface: Materials Needed section in the previous chapter for details about these two options. It is helpful to have a computer and projector for the instructor and to print each student a copy of the handout from the activity resources link in the Appendix. In the first step of the activity, it will be useful to have a method to scribe student responses such as a chalkboard, whiteboard, or large paper and markers.

Additionally, it may be valuable to provide copies of *The Jungle Book* for class discussion and checkout. Public domain copies of the original text are available to print and read in a browser from World Book Online Reference Center. Project Gutenberg also offers the original text to be read online and on devices that accept ePub and Kindle editions.

Instructors might also wish to read aloud from an abridged version such as the 2014 offering from Cider Mill Press, illustrated by Don Daily and truncated by Elizabeth Encarnacion, which contains a condensed version of the "Kaa's Hunting" story.

Set-up for this activity simply requires a computer lab or set up of laptops and an instructor projector. As mentioned in the previous chapter, it is preferable to set up the student stations so that the instructor can see their screens. This typically places the instructor behind the students who are facing the instructor's projected screen.

Into the Jungle Outcomes

Participants increase understanding of loop types and how to use them.
Participants build awareness of objects and instances as it relates to clones.
Participants augment knowledge of conditional statements and Boolean operators.
Participants recognize patterns in sprite behaviors and use abstraction to replicate them.

INTO THE JUNGLE: GUIDE

The storyline of this game mimics that of "Kaa's Hunting" which begins a few years after the wolfpack adopts Mowgli. He is now a young boy, often guided by Baloo the Bear and Baheera the Black Panther. Baloo teaches Mowgli the Master Words so that he can communicate with all of the different animals of the jungle. This comes in handy when the monkeys later kidnap him. As the monkeys carry him through the trees, Mowgli asks Rann the Kite to track his path and report his location back to Baloo and Bagheera. In our game, we'll guide Rann as he flies to get help. We'll use keys to navigate him away from monkeys and toward friendly animals. When he connects with a monkey, we'll lose points. When he connects with a friendly animal, such as an elephant, we'll gain points.

Into the Jungle Step 1: Decompose Game

Help students decompose the game storyline into smaller projects. As a class, discuss the types of things that they'll need to address as programmers to create the game. Write down their answers, and collaboratively group these into categories, such as those listed next. Your students' answers may vary, and that's perfectly okay. One of the great freedoms of coding is that there are many possible solutions. As you work through this activity, return to the list that your class creates to track progress.

Navigate Rann
Generate Friendly Beasts
Move Friendly Beasts
Animate Friendly Beasts
Manage Game Statistics (Score, Time, Health)

Into the Jungle Step 2: Sprite Library

Open a new Scratch project. This project will not use the Scratch Cat sprite that comes preloaded on a new file. Right-click on the Scratch Cat icon in the sprite panel. As shown in Figure 3-1, select **Delete**.

The Scratch Project Editor comes preloaded with a **Sprite Library**, a *collection of sprites including some with multiple costumes*. To open the sprite library, click on the sprite icon beside the words "New Sprite" above the sprite panel, as shown in Figure 3-2. The Sprite Library may take a moment to load, and may freeze briefly before users can scroll through the numerous offerings.

FIGURE 3-1
Delete Sprite.

Note that users can filter the sprites by category or theme. For instance, in this case, we know that we are looking for a bird, so under category, select **Animals** to limit the displayed options accordingly. As shown in Figure 3-3, the sprites appear alphabetically. Use the scroll bar on the right-hand side to browse all of the available animal sprites.

Though Rann is described as a kite, that particular type of bird is not available from the sprite library. Instead, we'll choose another type of bird that is native to India, which is the setting of the Jungle Book. Scroll down and select one of the two available **Parrot** sprites, and then click **OK**.

FIGURE 3-2   Choose Sprite from Library.

Into the Jungle Step 3: Change Sprite Name

FIGURE 3-3   Sprite Library.

Each sprite is assigned a default name. In this case, our sprite is simply called *Parrot*. This could get confusing if we add in more parrots. Let's name our sprite specifically for the story. Click on the blue *i* in a circle on the

parrot's icon in the Sprite Panel. Rename the sprite in the text box. Click the blue circle with the triangle to go back. The parrot should now be labeled **Rann**, as shown in Figure 3-4.

FIGURE 3-4   Change Sprite Name.

Into the Jungle Step 4: Key Controls

Players will navigate Rann using keys on the keyboard. Rann will need to be able to move left, right, up, and down. In the previous chapter, we accomplished this goal by creating four separate **When Key Pressed** events for the Sprite cat. This time, we'll use only one event and combine it with a **Forever** loop and multiple **If/Then** statements.

From the block palette, select the brown **Events** tab. Click and drag the **When Green Flag Clicked** block to the right in the grey **Scripts Area**. From yellow **Control**, add an **If () Then** block.

Select the blue Motion tab from the block palette. In the fourth grouping of blue blocks, find **Change Y by ().** Click and drag this block into the mouth of the If () Then block. We know from the last chapter, that the y position of a sprite indicates that sprite's placement on the vertical axis of the stage panel. Our current script indicates that if a certain condition is met, then the position of the parrot should change by 10 pixels. In other words, it should move upward. For our game, the condition will be if a certain key is pressed.

Key () Pressed

From the turquoise **Sensing** tab in the block palette, find and select the seventh choice down. It will initially read **Key <Space> Pressed**. Click the black dropdown arrow on the block to select a key that makes more sense, such as the up arrow. Some students may prefer to control the game using the left side of the keyboard with WASD. If so, the student would choose **W** rather than **Up Arrow**. After selecting the trigger key, drag the **Key <Up Arrow>**

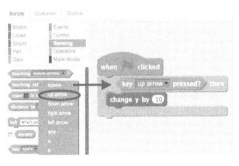

Pressed block into the empty polygon area of the **If () Then** block, as shown in Figure 3-5. Once this task is completed, have students save their projects.

Have students test their games by clicking the green flag above the Stage Panel. Does the parrot move up when the up arrow is pushed? Why not? Ask students for their thoughts before continuing. The reason nothing appears to happen is because

FIGURE 3-5   If (Key Pressed) Then.

our current script is a conditional statement but not a loop, so that the condition is only checked once, at the moment the green flag is clicked. We need to add another element to make sure that the condition is constantly checked while the game is running. Can your students guess what that block will be?

From the yellow **Control** tab, select the third block down, the **Forever** block, and drag it under the **When Green Flag Clicked** block in the

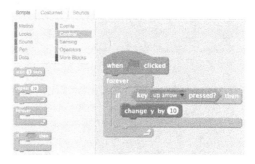

FIGURE 3-6 Forever Loop.

scripts area. It should automatically wrap around the **If () Then** block, as shown in Figure 3-6. The key state will now be constantly checked, over and over from the moment the game starts until the user stops the game by clicking the red **Stop** icon. Save and test.

Complete Key Controls

We'll follow the same process that we used for the up arrow to complete the other directions, so that we can move the parrot up, down, left, and right. Click and drag three more **If () Then** blocks into the **Forever Loop**. Stack them one after the other. Return to the turquoise **Sensing** tab in the block palette. Click and drag a key pressed block into the condition polygon of each of the **If () Then** blocks. Click on the black arrow in each to name them **Down, Left,** and **Right**—or **S, A,** and **D,** respectively—as shown in Figure 3-7.

Finally, return to the blue **Motion** tab in the block palette. Click and drag a **Change Y by ()** block into the **If (Down Arrow) Pressed** block. Change the value to –10. As we learned in the previous activity, a sprite's horizontal location is measured on the x-axis. Click and drag a **Change X by (10)** block into the **If (Left Arrow) Pressed** block. Make sure to change the value to –10. Do the same thing for the right arrow block, but keep the value positive. Save and test again. After clicking the green flag, students should be able to move the parrot up, down, left, and right.

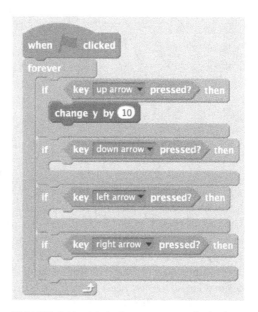

FIGURE 3-7 Multiple Key Pressed Blocks.

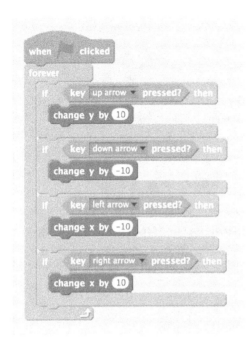

FIGURE 3-8   Completed Key Controls.

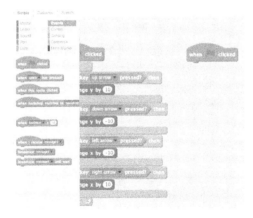

FIGURE 3-9   Start Second Rann Script.

Into the Jungle
Step 5: Appearance

Now that we can control Rann, let's think about how he appears. Currently, he takes up a significant percentage of the stage. Also, since we're able to move him now, we might accidentally move him off stage, and not be able to find him when the game starts again. Finally, though he moves on command, he doesn't appear to be flying because his wings remain still. Let's address all of these issues.

Begin a new script by returning to the block palette and selecting the brown **Events** tab. Click and drag another **When Green Flag Clicked** block into the grey Scripts Area. Leave it separate from the previous script, as shown in Figure 3-9.

Resize Sprite

Return to the block palette and select the purple **Looks** tab. The **Set Size to ()%** block *shrinks or grows the sprite from its original size depending on the number indicated.* Add one under the new **When Green Flag Clicked** block. Click on the numbers in the white circle of the block to change the size to 50%. Save and test. Now, when the green flag is clicked, Rann should shrink to 50%, or half, of his original size.

Ask the students what they think will happen when the game stops. Will Rann return to his original size or not? Why or why not? After some discussion have students test by clicking the red octagon to stop the game. Rann remains the same size because there is no script that tells him to do otherwise. When we work with a **Forever Loop,** the scripts repeat so long as the game is running. In this case, the resize block happens once, but the setting remains unless we adjust the program otherwise. If we wanted to restore Rann to full size, we would need to change the number in **the Set Size to ()** block to 100% and then click the green flag to trigger the game to start and the change to take effect.

Set Starting Position

Now that we have Rann a more reasonable size, let's give him a starting position. Return to the block palette and select the blue **Motion** tab. Look for the **Go to X: () Y: ()** block, but do not move it into the scripting area yet. We used this block in the Scratching the Surface activity to reset the cat to the center of the screen by giving him the coordinates x:0 y:0. Now, we'll use it to give Rann a starting position. Each time we begin the game by clicking the green flag, he'll return to this position.

Drag Rann to a suitable starting position. He'll be flying left to right across our screen, so it makes sense to move him to the upper left side. Notice that as you move him, the coordinates automatically adjust at the bottom of the stage panel and in the **Go to X:() Y:()** block, as shown in Figure 3-10. This is why we wait to attach the block to the script. Once it is attached, the coordinates no longer automatically adjust, which is good, because we want Rann to have a fixed starting position regardless of where he finished the previous game. Once Rann is positioned, click and drag the **Go to X:() Y:()** block under the **Set Size to 50%** block.

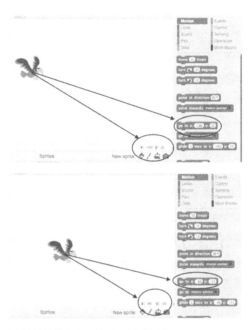

FIGURE 3-10   Go to X () Y ().

Next Costume Loop

In our Scratching the Surface program, we used the **Next Costume** block to animate the cat each time we pushed a button. In this game, we want Rann to always appear as though he's flying. Ask students which blocks they think we might combine to create this animated effect. As always with coding, there are often multiple correct solutions. One possibility is to use the **Next Costume** block in a **Forever** loop. Notice in Figure 3-11 that a **Wait** block has been added into the loop. This slows the animation to more realistic pace. Have students update, save, and test their games.

FIGURE 3-11
Next Costume Loop.

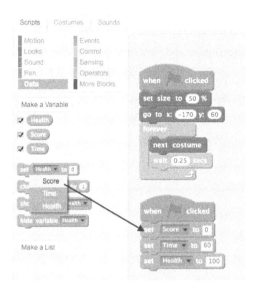

FIGURE 3-12   Set Score, Time, and Health.

Into the Jungle
Step 6: Variables

As we discussed in the Cat Got Your Number? activity in the previous chapter, variables store values that can change. Follow the same process we used in that activity to create a few global variables for our game: **Health**, **Score,** and **Time**.

Start a new script by dragging a **When Green Flag Clicked** block from brown **Events** into Rann's scripts area. To set the initial value of the score, select the first block in the orange **Data** menu, and select **Score** from the drop down. Drag **Set Score to (0)** below the new **When Green Flag Clicked**. This will ensure that each time the game begins, the score will reset to 0. Follow the same steps to set the **Time** to **60** and the **Health** to **100**, so that the finished script resembles that in Figure 3-12.

Have students save and test their games. Invariably at least one will notice that values of each variable remain constant. Ask them why they think they aren't changing. Ask them how they think we could change the value of **Time**, so that it ticks down one second at a time. In the next section, we'll look at one possible solution.

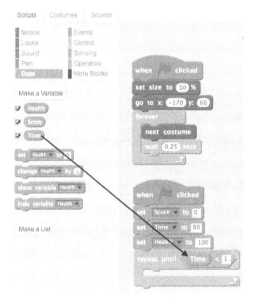

FIGURE 3-13   (Time) Is Less Than (1).

Change Variable Value

To use the variable **Time** to create a count down clock for our game, first go to the yellow **Control** palette. Select the seventh option down, the **Repeat Until ()** block, under our new variables script. Just as in our **If ()** **Then** blocks that control Rann, the **Repeat Until ()** block includes a hexagonal area to be filled with a Boolean block. In this case, we want to check to see if the value of **Time** is less than 1. From the green **Operators** palette, select **() Is Less Than ()**. Click and drag it into the condition gap on the **Repeat Until ()** block. Next, we need to add the values to compare. Return to the orange **Data** palette. Place the variable block for **Time** to the left side of the **() is Less Than ()** block. We want the blocks that we'll put in the **Repeat Until ()** block to continue to loop until the value of **Time** is less than 1 second, so click in the white box to the right of the comparison to type the number 1, as shown in Figure 3-13.

Finally, we need to fill in what we want to repeat until **Time** is less than one. Stay on the orange **Data** palette. **Select Change () by ()** and drag it into the mouth of **Repeat () Until.** Make sure that **Time** is selected as the variable to change. We want to reduce the value of **Time** each second, so click in the white circle and change the number 1 to –1.

FIGURE 3-14   Completed Game Clock.

Save and test. Notice that the value of **Time** appears to instantly drop down to zero. Ask students why they think that is and how they think we could fix it. One possible solution is in Figure 3-14.

Into the Jungle Step 7: Edit Elephant Sprite

In Rudyard Kipling's original story, we don't hear about Rann's flight from the kidnapped Mowgli back to Baloo and Basheera, but in our game, we'll take a flight of fancy, and assume that he would ask friendly creatures to help him on the way. The Scratch library includes a few animals that are native to India. Let's start with elephants, a species specifically mentioned in *The Jungle Book,* particularly their leader, Hathi. Follow the same steps we used to load the parrot representing Rann. Open the **Sprite Library** to select the elephant, and then click **OK.**

Flip Costume

Because Rann is flying from left to right, it will feel more natural for him to encounter animals as they approach from the opposite direction. To make this feel natural, we need to change the orientation of the elephant costumes. With the **Elephant** sprite selected, choose the **Costumes** tab above the **Block Palette**. Select the **Elephant-A** costume. Click the **Flip Left–Right** button in the top right-hand corner, as shown in Figure 3-15. Repeat for the **Elephant-B** costume.

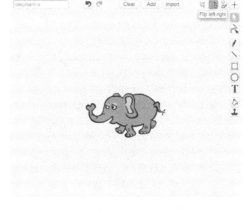

FIGURE 3-15   Flip Costume Left–Right.

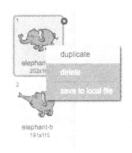

Duplicate and Customize Costume

FIGURE 3-16
Duplicate Costume.

We were able to create an animation effect with Rann because the parrot sprite that we used had two costumes that we could alternate to make his wings appear to flap up and down. The elephant has a trumpeting costume, but not an alternative costume to make him appear to be walking. Let's fix that! Right-click on the **Elephant-A** costume and select **Duplicate,** as shown in Figure 3-16. Drag the duplicated costume, **Elephant-A 2,** under **Elephant-A**.

To create the illusion that the elephant is walking, we need to reposition each of his legs in the **Elephant-A 2** sprite. Fortunately, the elephant sprite allows users to edit certain segments. Click on the first leg. A transformation box will appear around the leg. Use the top handle to rotate the leg to a slightly different position, as shown in Figure 3-17. Repeat for all of the legs. Click back and forth between **Costume A** and **A 2** to see how the animation will look and adjust legs as needed.

FIGURE 3-17   Rotate Sprite Segment.

Into the Jungle Step 8: Parent Script

Cloning is a useful feature for creating multiple iterations of a parent sprite. Clones inherit the parent clone's scripts and costumes; so numerous instances can be created quickly from one previously coded sprite. We'll clone our elephant to make it appear as though numerous elephants are passing through the jungle. Make sure that the **Elephant** sprite is selected in the **Sprite Panel** then click the **Scripts** tab. The scripts area for the **Elephant** should be empty, but don't worry. The scripts we created for Rann are still there. You can click on Rann's sprite to confirm, just make sure to click back on the **Elephant** to start his script.

Begin the **Elephant** parent script by dragging a **When Green Flag Clicked** block from the brown **Events** menu into the **Scripts Area**. From the blue **Motion** palette, click and drag a **Go to X: () Y: ()**. We want the **Elephant** sprite and its clones to begin on the right edge of the stage, so for the X value we'll enter **240**. We also want him to appear at the bottom of the stage, so enter a Y value of **–120**. Save and test by clicking the green flag. The **Elephant** sprite should appear in the bottom right-hand corner of the stage.

Next we'll create a conditional loop to create clones. Go to the yellow **Control** tab. Click and drag a **Forever** loop under the **Go to X: () Y: ()** block. We'll place an **If () Then** loop inside of the **Forever** block. In this case, we want to check if there are positive values for **Time** and **Health**. If so, we want to create an elephant clone. If not, the blocks to create the clone will be skipped.

() And ()

Now, let's move to the green **Operators** palette to select our Boolean and reporter blocks. For the **If () Then** statement, we'll add an **() And ()** block into the hexagonal area to *check that two conditions are both true*. The **() And ()** block is a Boolean block, which means it can only be true or false. For it to report back as true, both statements must be true. For instance if Jordan is 11 years old and 4 feet, 8 inches tall, the statement ((Jordan) is Greater Than (10)) and ((Jordan) is Greater Than (5 feet)) would be false because Jordan only meets one of those two conditions.

() Is Greater Than ()

For our game, we'll also use **Greater Than** to check to see if the value currently assigned to our variable is higher than a stated minimum. Drag a **() Is Greater Than ()** block into each of the hexagonal spaces of the **() And ()**, as shown in Figure 3-18. Students new to the greater than (>) and less than (<) symbols sometimes get confused about which is which. A helpful visual is to think of the symbol as an alligator mouth that always opens toward the larger amount of food.

Return to the orange **Data** menu. Add **Health** and **Time** variables into the left side of each **() Is Greater Than ()** block, as shown in Figure 3-19. Enter the number **1** for the **Health** Boolean block and the number **2** for the **Time** Boolean block. Why are we using a higher number for **Time**? Remember that the friendly beasts' clones will generate on the right-hand side of the stage and then move across to the left side. This action takes time. If we set the Boolean to **(Time) is Greater Than (1)**, an **Elephant** clone could still be walking across the stage after the game is over. By checking that **(Time) is Greater Than (2)**, we'll make sure that the **Elephant** clone will be able to complete its journey before it is generated.

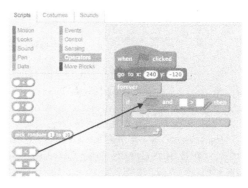

FIGURE 3-18   (Is Greater) and (Is Greater).

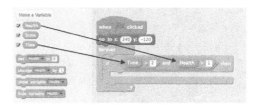

FIGURE 3-19   ((Time) Is Greater Than (2) and ((Health) Is Greater Than (1)).

Create Clone of ()

Return to the yellow **Control** palette, drag a **Wait (1) Second** block into the **If () Then** block. Then drag a **Create Clone of (Myself)** block after it. The **Create Clone of ()** block *may be used to create a copy of the sprite in which it*

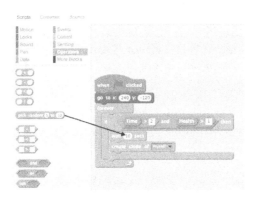

is located or it may create a copy of a different sprite. The available options appear in the drop down menu in the block. In this case, we want the **Elephant** parent to create more elephant clones, so leave the selection on **Myself** or **Elephant**.

Our current parent script would generate one new **Elephant** clone per second. This will make it very predictable and thus easy for players to time their interactions with the **Elephants**. To create a more difficult game and natural feel, let's schedule clone generation at random inter-vals. To do this, return to the green

FIGURE 3-20   Wait Random then Create Clone of (Myself).

Operators palette, and grab a **Pick Random () to ()** block. Change the default numbers to **(5)** and **(10)** and place it in the **Wait () Secs** parameter space, as shown in Figure 3-20. With these parameters set, an **Elephant** clone should generate after 4, 6, 7, 8, 9, or 10 seconds pass.

Add Comment

At this point we already have three scripts for Rann and we'll soon have even more for the **Elephant.** A great way to keep things from getting too con-fusing is to add **Comments** into our **Scripts Areas. Comments** *do not affect the functionality of the code and are used by programmers to explain sections or keep track of progress.* Let's use a comment to label the parent script. Right-click on **When Green Flag Clicked**. Scroll down to **Add Comment**, as shown in Figure 3-21. In the pop-up text box that appears, type in **Elephant Parent Script**. Click the dropdown arrow to minimize the box.

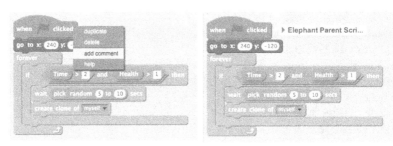

FIGURE 3-21   Add Comment.

Into the Jungle Step 9: Clone Movement

We need to tell the clones what to do once they're born. Let's create a script that gets our clones moving across the stage.

When I Start as a Clone

To start our new script go to the yellow **Control** palette and choose the third from last block. You may need to scroll down to find it. The **When I Start As A Clone** block *activates each newly created clone*. It is a **Hat** block, *which means that it is intended to start a new script*. Click and drag it into a fresh spot in the **Scripts Area**. It's a good idea to use a **Comment** to label this new script as **Elephant Movement**.

Repeat Until ((X Position) Is Less Than (–240))

We want each new clone to walk across the stage and then disappear off the left-hand side. Click and drag a **Repeat Until ()** block under **When I Start as a Clone.** Since we want the **Elephant** clone to move left, toward the –240 border, we need to decrease its x position. From the blue **Motion** palette select **Change X by ()**, and place it inside the **Repeat Until.** Click in the white circle and type in **–3**. Students may choose to make their elephants move faster or slower.

We want the **Elephant** clones to keep moving left until they hit the left-side stage boundary, located at the –240 coordinate on the x-axis. We'll use the **() Is Less Than ()** Boolean to test to see if the clone has reached this coordinate. From the green Operators palette, drag an **() Is Less Than ()** block into the gap of **Repeat Until ().** Type the number **–240** into the right side box.

X Position

The **X Position** block *reports the current horizontal coordinate of a sprite*. It functions as a built-in variable. Go to the blue **Motion** palette and scroll to the bottom to locate the **X Position** block. Drag it into the left box of the **() Is Less Than ()** block, as shown in Figure 3-22. Save and test. Remember that it may take up to 10 seconds for the first elephant clone to generate. The elephant clone will start moving to the left, and then remain in place once it reaches the left border. We want it to disappear as though it has walked out of the scene. Let's take care of that next.

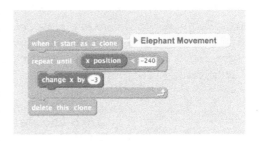

FIGURE 3-22   Elephant Clone Movement Script.

Delete Clone

There are many reasons why one might wish to delete a particular clone. In our case, we want to remove clones that have finished walking across the stage. In some cases, we may want to delete clones that have been effectively targeted. Another good reason to delete clones that are no longer in play is to reduce potential lag time. Scratch limits the number of clones per project to 300, and staying well below that is good practice. There's no reason to keep each of our individual clones once they've moved off screen, so let's delete them. Go to the yellow **Control** menu. Scroll down to the last block, and drag **Delete Clone** under the **Repeat Until** block in our latest script. Save and test again. The elephant clones should now disappear at the left border.

Into the Jungle Step 10: Show and Hide

After our last test, students may have noticed that the original elephant stays grounded on the right side of the stage. There are a few ways to fix this, but one of the easiest is to use the **Hide** block. The hide block does exactly what one might think, it *renders the sprite invisible to the viewer without deleting it.* This is perfect because we want the parent Elephant to remain in the game so that it can continue to call clones, but we don't want to see it standing awkwardly to the side.

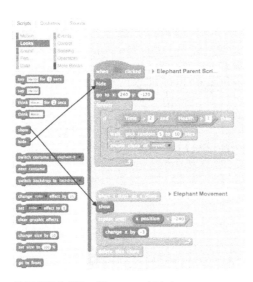

FIGURE 3-23   Show and Hide.

Go to the purple **Looks** palette. Drag a **Hide** block under the **When Green Flag Clicked** block of the **Elephant Parent Script**. Save and test. Oh no! We solved the problem of the parent Elephant remaining still, but now our clones are invisible. This is because our clones inherit their parents' scripts, including the **Hide** block. Luckily, there is an easy fix. The **Show** block, not surprisingly, *renders the sprite visible to the viewer.* Drag a **Show** block under the **When I Start as a Clone** in the **Elephant Movement** script as shown in Figure 3-23. Save and test again. The elephant clones should once again march across the screen.

Into the Jungle Step 11: Elephant Animation and Reaction

Our elephants now move across the stage, but they don't look quite natural. In this step we'll use costumes to create an animated appearance and program the **Elephants** to react when they intersect with Rann. Go to the yellow **Control** menu. Start the script with a **When I Start as a Clone** block, and use a comment to label the script *Elephant Animation*. Add a **Forever** block. Place an **If () Then Else** block inside of the **Forever** loop.

Touching ()

The **Touching ()** block *is a Sensing block that detects if a sprite's boundaries are overlapping with those of another element and reports back a Boolean value of true or false.* We'll use this block to check if the **Elephant** clone is touching Rann. If so, the **Elephant** will react; if not, it will appear to walk.

Go to the light blue **Sensing** menu. Find the first block. Notice that it defaults to **Touching (Mouse-Pointer)**. This is a helpful setting when making games in which the player clicks on objects. For our needs, however, we need to use the dropdown to select Rann, and then drag the block into the gap of the **If () Then** block, as shown in Figure 3-24.

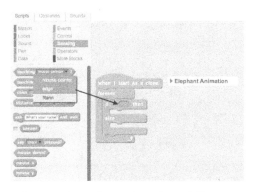

FIGURE 3-24 If (Touching (Rann)) Then.

Switch Costume to ()

We used the **Next Costume** block in our Scratching the Surface activity to make the Scratch Cat appear to walk by alternating between its two costumes. The **Switch Costume to ()** block *is used to jump to a specific costume rather than the next one in consecutive order.* We'll use this block to make the **Elephant** clone appear to trumpet when Rann touches him.

Go to the purple **Looks** palette. Select the sixth block down, **Switch Costume to ()**, and drag it into the first C of **If () Then Else**. Use the dropdown triangle to select the **Elephant-B** costume. If Rann is not touching the **Elephant** clone, we want the **Elephant** to appear to walk, so we'll add **Switch Costume to (Elephant A)** and **Switch Costume to (Elephant A 2)** into the **Else C**. Save and test.

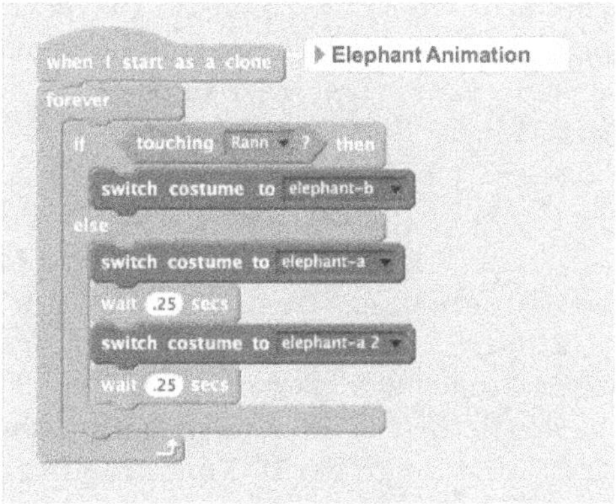

At this point, our script does make the **Elephant** appear to trumpet when touching Rann, but the walking animation doesn't appear to work. This is because as long as

FIGURE 3-25 Else Switch Costumes.

the Elephant is touching Rann, it will hold the trumpeting costume, but we left out a set amount of time for it to hold each of the walking costumes. We've used a block that would help. Ask students to suggest how we might fix this. Figure 3-25 shows one possible solution.

Play Sound ()

Let's jazz up our game by having the **Elephant** clone trumpet when Rann intercepts him. The **Play Sound ()** block *will play the selected audio while the remaining script continues to run.* The **Play Sound () Until Done** block *will pause the remaining subsequent script blocks until the audio file finishes playing.* We want our other scripts to continue while the trumpet sound is playing, so go to the violet **Sound** palette and drag the first block, **Play Sound ()**, directly under **If () Then**. Save and test.

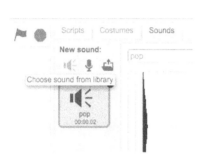

FIGURE 3-26   Choose Sound from Library.

The **Elephant** should play the default sound, *Pop,* when touched by Rann. Let's find a more appropriate sound. Go to the **Sounds** tab above the **Palette Menu**. Select the speaker icon to **Choose Sound from Library,** as shown in Figure 3-26. The **Sound Library** contains numerous audio files. Students often enjoy testing out a few, so it can be helpful to give a selection time limit. They can always go back and change it later. Unfortunately, there is no realistic elephant trumpet sound; however, at the bottom of the library there are trumpet and trombone sounds that will serve. Make a selection and click **OK**. The new sound will appear in the **Sounds** tab. Return to the **Scripts** tab to update the selection in the **Play Sound ()** block. Save and test.

The sound may come out in a stuttered manner. This is because the **Play Sound ()** block is triggered each time that the condition **If (Touching (Rann))** is true. When Rann touches the **Elephant**'s trunk it's true, then when he touches his eyeball, body, and tail. The **Play Sound ()** block is constantly triggered the whole time that the two sprites overlap. Luckily we can fix this with our handy **Wait () Secs** block. It takes about two seconds for the elephant to pass by Rann if he stays in place, so try entering the number **2** into the white oval.

Change (Score) by ()

Finally, because the point of the game is for Rann to alert the other animals, we want to assign the player points each time Rann touches a friendly beast. Return to the orange **Data** palette. Add a **Change (Score) by ()** block in the C directly under **If (Touching (Rann)).** Enter an easy to test number such as **10**. Save and test.

The score should increase by ten each time Rann intersects with an **Elephant** clone. Sometimes the player will be awarded points twice for one effort because Rann's intersection with an **Elephant** clone lasts longer than the **Wait () Secs** block, so the loop begins again. There are a few ways to fix this. Invite students to try to problem-solve. Figure 3-27 shows one solution in the completed **Elephant Animation** script.

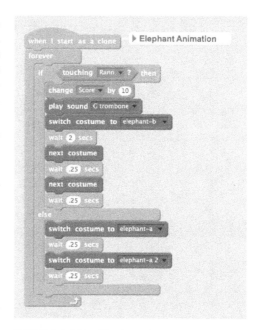

FIGURE 3-27   Elephant Animation Script.

Into the Jungle
Step 12: Add Butterfly

Note that if you are leading this activity set as a standalone class, you may wish to consider skipping this step in the interests of time. If you choose to add the **Butterfly** sprite, click on the **Choose a Sprite From Library** icon, and add **Butterfly 1**.

Pattern Recognition

Discuss with students which Elephant scripts would be applicable to the Butterfly. What behaviors will they share? Which attributes will be different? For instance, both friendly beasts will move from right to left across the stage. Both will increase the score when they collide with Rann. Both have a **Speed** attribute and a **Points Scored** attribute, but we may want these values to be different. For instance, the **Elephant** may move slower than the **Butterfly** and thus be worth fewer points.

Copy Script to New Sprite

Because the two sprites share so many behaviors, we can save time by copying and updating scripts. Click on the **Elephant** sprite. Click on the first block of the **Elephant Parent Script**, and drag the whole script down to the **Butterfly** in the **Sprite Panel**, as shown in Figure 3-28, and then let go. The **Elephant Parent Script** should remain in the **Elephant Scripts** area, but a copy should now also be in the **Butterfly's Scripts Area**. Click on the **Butterfly** to make sure. Copy over the Elephant's **Elephant Movement Script** and the **Elephant Animation Script**. With duplicate copies of each script, things can start to get confusing. Add a **Comment** to label each of the **Butterfly's** scripts, as shown in Figure 3-29.

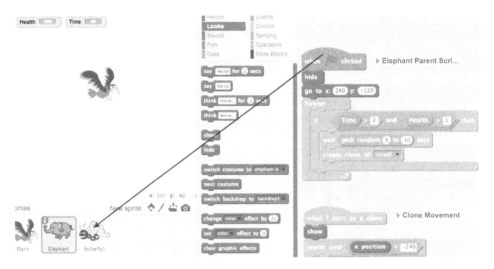

FIGURE 3-28   Copy Script to New Sprite.

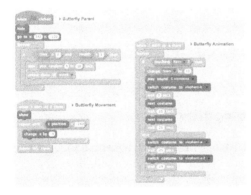

FIGURE 3-29   Butterfly Copied Scripts.

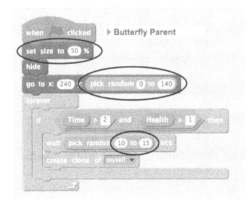

FIGURE 3-30   Updated Butterfly Parent Script.

Update Butterfly Parent Script

Most of the **Elephant Parent Script** remains appropriate for the **Butterfly Parent Script**, but we may wish to change the value of some attribute values such as size, height, and clone creation pace, as shown in Figure 3-30. First, to make our game feel more natural, it makes sense to shrink the butterfly to a size smaller than Rann. Add a **Set Size to (50)%** block. Second, to make the game more challenging for players, we can also change the height at which each Butterfly appears by switching placing a **Pick Random () to ()** block into the Y value of the **Go to X: () Y: ()** block. A nice range for the **Butterfly** is **0**, the middle of the stage, to **140**, the top of the stage. Third, since the **Butterfly** clones will be more difficult, and therefore more valuable to catch, consider making them appear less often by raising the numbers to **10** and **15**.

Update Butterfly Movement Script

Again, players will earn more points for catching the **Butterfly** clones, so it's appropriate to make them more challenging to catch by increasing the speed at which they fly. Adjusting to **Change X by (–6)**, as indicated in Figure 3-31, will make the **Butterfly** twice as fast as the **Elephant**. Try this or your own number. Save and test.

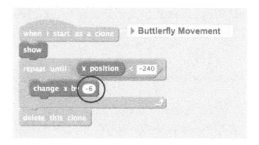

FIGURE 3-31   Updated Butterfly Movement Script.

Update Butterfly Animation

Since the Butterfly is now faster, let's increase the number of points awarded by changing the number in the **Change (Score) by ()** to **20**.

Change Sound

It doesn't make a great deal of sense for a butterfly to make an elephant noise, although that doesn't mean that some students might not like to keep it that way. To change it, follow the same steps that we used in **Step 11: Elephant Animation and Reaction** to choose the **Cricket, Bird,** or other appropriate sound.

Delete Block

To update the **Butterfly Animation** script, we need to remove a block. In Scratch, deleting one block also deletes any blocks attached below it. To avoid this, pull out the **Switch Costume to (Elephant B)** block. The blocks attached below it will also come along for the ride, as shown in Figure 3-32. Pull the **Wait (2) Secs** block down. This will detach the remaining script from the **Switch Costume to (Elephant B)** block. Right-click on the **Switch Costume**

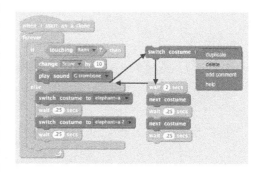

FIGURE 3-32   Remove Block and Return Remaining Script.

to **Elephant B** block and select **Delete**. Drag the remaining script back under the **Play Sound ()** block.

Else Switch Costume to (Butterfly)

Finally, use the dropdown to change the alternating costumes in the **Else C** section from **Elephant A** and **Elephant B** to **Butterfly 1A** and **Butterfly 1B**. Save and test. Butterflies should appear at regular intervals, at varying heights, and 20 points should be awarded for each intersection with Rann. The fully updated **Butterfly** scripts are displayed in Figure 3-33.

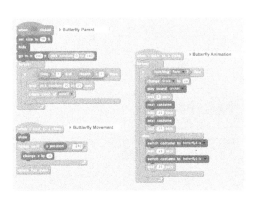

FIGURE 3-33   All Updated Butterfly Scripts.

This is a good stopping point for the game, as we have animated animals, a way to score points, and time ticking down. As you close the session, review the decomposition list. Which groups have we addressed in full? Which problems do we still need to solve? In the next chapter we'll tackle managing **Health**, generating opponents, expanding visual effects, and more.

4

Deeper Into the Jungle with Scratch

In the previous chapter we set up the basics of our game. The player of our game can score points by interacting with Butterflies and Elephants. To take our game to the next level, we need to create a way for players to win or lose, add additional challenges, and create a scrolling background.

DEEPER INTO THE JUNGLE: PREPARATION

In these activities, we'll continue creating a game based on Rudyard Kipling's short story "Kaa's Hunting" in *The Jungle Book*. Participants will need to complete Activity Set 3 prior to attempting the activities in this chapter.

Deeper Into the Jungle Materials and Set-up

Just as with Activity Set 3, this set requires computers with Scratch installed or available through the online editor. Additionally, students will need access to the following files:

Jungle Background.png
RunningMonkey.sprite2
SwingingMonkey.sprite2

The instructor will likely want a computer, a projector, and the handouts from the activity resources link in the Appendix.

Finally, it may be worthwhile to provide copies of *The Jungle Book* for class discussion and checkout. Refer to the Materials Needed section in Chapter 3 for information about acquiring free access to this public domain work.

Setup for this activity is identical to Activity Set 3. Procure a computer lab or setup of laptops and a projector. If possible, set up the student stations so that you can see their screens. This typically places the instructor behind the students who are facing the instructor's projected screen.

Deeper Into the Jungle Outcomes

Participants know how to upload and work with backdrops.
Participants understand how to use sprites to create a scrolling effect.
Participants increase ability to custom design games using audio and
  visual effects.
Participants gain insight into creating projectiles.

DEEPER INTO THE JUNGLE: GUIDE

Prior to starting to program, review the list that the class created in Step 1 of Chapter 3. Which categories remain incomplete? Are there more to be added? Discuss and write down these ideas, and check them off as they are accomplished. Note that students may have visions of functionality beyond the scope of this lesson. That's great! Encourage them to attempt to solve these questions. Here are some tasks that this chapter will address.

Generate opponents
Move opponents
Animate opponents
Respond to variable changes (Time, Health, Score) to end game
Animate background

Deeper Into the Jungle Step 1: Running Monkeys

So far in our game we have a way to score, but no way to lose health. In Kaa's Hunting, the Monkey-People, or Bandar-Log, kidnap Mowgli and try to hold him captive. In our game, monkeys will try to prevent Rann from contacting help. Unfortunately, neither of the monkeys included in the Scratch Sprite Library have costumes that would be easy to adapt to create a running animation as we did with the Elephant. Luckily, a customized monkey sprite, **MonkeyRunning.sprite2,** may be downloaded from the link in the Appendix. Click on the **Upload Sprite from File** icon shown in Figure 4-1. Navigate to the sprite's location, and then click **Open**.

FIGURE 4-1   Upload Sprite from File.

Running Monkey Parent and Movement Scripts

Once again, we can duplicate the algorithms from the Elephant because the behavior of the two animal sprites follows the same pattern. Drag the **Elephant Parent** and **Elephant Movement** scripts into the Running Monkey sprite. Adjust the parameter values of three blocks as shown in Figure 4-2. Change the Running Monkey's starting **Y Position** to **–140** because the monkey is smaller than the elephant. Adjust the frequency at which clones will generate by changing the numbers in the **Pick Random () to ()** block. Finally, change the speed at which the monkeys will run by adjusting the number in the **Change X by ()** block in the **Monkey Movement** script.

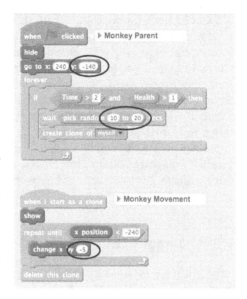

FIGURE 4-2   Updated Monkey Parent and Movement Scripts.

Running Monkey Animation Script

Because the Running Monkey uses more costumes than the other sprites in our project, we'll approach its animation separately from the reaction script, but the components should look familiar. Begin a new script with a **When I Start as a Clone** block. Connect a **Forever** block directly underneath. Ask students which two blocks they think should be placed inside to make the monkey appear to run. As shown in Figure 4-3, place a **Wait () Secs** block inside the Forever C and assign it a value of **.25**. Finally, add a **Next Costume** block under the Wait (.25) Secs block.

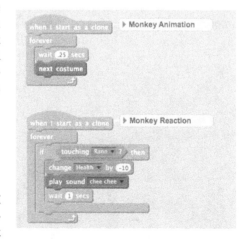

Running Monkey Reaction Script

Begin again with a fresh **When I Start as a Clone** block. Attach a **Forever** block. Place an **If () Then** block inside of the **Forever** block. From the light blue sensing menu, click and drag

FIGURE 4-3   Running Monkey Animation and Reaction Scripts.

a **Touching ()** block into the **If () Then** gap. Ask students for expertise in how to finish the script. What should happen if Rann touches the Running Monkey? Once you've created a list as group, ask students which blocks would address each item. Most likely, the list will include reducing Health and playing a sound. Possibly some students will remember to add a **Wait ()** **Secs** block to make sure that Health isn't deducted twice as Rann and the Running Monkey continually intersect. Other options may be added, but one solution to this list is indicated in Figure 4-3.

Save and test the project thus far. The game should award points, deduct Health, and count down Time, but it does not yet stop when Time or Health run out, indicate that the player has won or lost, or feel particularly atmospheric. In the next step we'll increase the visual interest.

Deeper Into the Jungle Step 2: Setting the Scene

Though we know that the story takes place in the jungle, currently our animals exist only in a field of white. Let's create a scrolling background.

FIGURE 4-4
Upload Backdrop
from File.

Upload Backdrop from File

In our *Scratching the Surface* activity we chose the **XY Grid** backdrop from the library. Now we'll follow similar steps to upload a custom backdrop. Be sure to create a path from each student computer to the file **JungleBackground.png** prior to the beginning of class. Under the **Stage** icon in the bottom left corner, select the folder icon, indicated in Figure 4-4, to **Upload Backdrop from File**. Navigate to the file and select **Open**. Save and test. We have a background now, but the visual effect is a little off. To make it appear that Rann is flying through the jungle, encountering different animals along the way, we'll want the background to move in the opposite direction of Rann to create the illusion of movement.

FIGURE 4-5   Delete Backdrop.

Delete Backdrop

To avoid confusion as we move on, it will be helpful to delete the Jungle Background from our Stage. Click on the **Stage** icon, and then navigate to the **Backdrops** tab. Click the x above the Jungle Backdrop to delete it, as shown in Figure 4-5. Don't worry. We'll bring it back better than ever in the next step.

Scrolling Background

With the Stage icon selected, click on the **Scripts** tab. Click through a few of the palettes. Notice that some of the palettes contain roughly the same collection of blocks as their sprite counterparts, yet others contain different blocks or, in the case of the Motion palette, none at all. Though the stage can have some scripts, there are restrictions. To create the illusion of motion, we'll need to use our Jungle Background as a Sprite rather than a Backdrop. Use the **Upload Sprite from File** icon to create a Jungle Background sprite, following the steps we used for the Running Monkey sprite in Step 1.

Go Back () Layers

Since our background is now a Sprite, it behaves like any other sprite. As sprites are added to a project they automatically move in front of the sprites already placed in the project. We want our background to sit behind the other sprites, the animals that we've already placed into the project. Go to the Jungle Background sprite's Scripts Area. Grab a **When Green Flag Clicked** from the brown **Events** palette, and then navigate to the purple **Looks** palette. Scroll to the bottom to find the fourth block up, **Go Back () Layers**, and attach it. Enter **100** in the white circle of the block. Save and test. The Jungle Background sprite should now appear behind all of the animal sprites.

The **Go Back () Layers** block *changes the assigned depth value of a sprite.* We are telling the layer how many steps back it should take. For instance, since the Running Monkey was the last sprite we added prior to the Jungle Background, it appears at the front of the stage. When a Running Monkey clone overlaps with an Elephant clone, the Running Monkey clone will therefore appear to be in front, just as the Elephant would be in front of the Butterfly, which flies in front of Rann. Rann is, therefore, three steps back from Running Monkey. We told the Jungle Background to go 100 steps back, so even if we placed 96 more sprites into the project, it would still appear behind them. The only thing behind our Jungle Background at this point is the Stage, which is always the backmost layer.

Animate Background

Create a starting position for the **Jungle Background** sprite by attaching a blue **Go to X: () Y: ()** block onto the current script. Since this block places the sprite based on its center, and the Jungle Background sprite is 480×360 pixels, assigning it to **(0,0)** will assign the sprite to cover the entire stage. Add a **Forever** loop from the yellow **Control** palette to continuously restart the animation. From the blue **Motion** palette, add a **Change X by ()** block into the Forever loop. Save and test. The background sprite should start by fully covering the stage, and then it should begin moving to the left. Allow the program to continue to run until the background script reaches the far-left stage boundary. Notice that it freezes prior to fully leaving the stage. This is because the Scratch environment

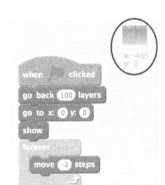

FIGURE 4-6 Current X,Y Position of Sprite.

includes built-in parameters to keep sprites on the stage. A sprite may not fully exit the stage while visible. We'll fix this in the next step. For now, test the program again. This time, make sure that the Jungle Background sprite is selected, and watch the readings in the upper right corner of its scripts area (highlighted in Figure 4-6). The Y position reading will remain constant at 0 because the sprite does not move up or down, but the X position reading changes until it freezes at −465. When the center of the background sprite reaches this coordinate, it stops, due to the Scratch parameter that requires the sprite to leave 15 pixels on the stage.

If the center of the Jungle Sprite, its X Position, were at the −480 position, half of the sprite, 240 pixels, would be on either side, so its left border would be at −720 and its right at −240, the left stage boundary. These coordinates would place it completely off the stage to the left. We would then reassign it to 480 (to the right of the stage), and it would start sliding left again, then off of the stage. If we had two of the same sprites back to back, the center part, the stage, would always be covered, as illustrated in Figure 4-7. Since Scratch won't let us take our background sprite completely off of the stage, we'll apply the same principles, but shift the starting coordinates of each background sprite slightly to the left. Change the starting value of X to **−15**, so that the third block in this script reads **Go to X: (−15) Y: (0)**.

From the yellow **Control** menu, add an **If () Then** block. Add an **() Is Less Than ()** block from the green palette as the condition. Move an **X Position** block from the blue **Motion** tab into the left oval. If the X Position of the background sprite is less than −464, than we want to shift the sprite to the far right by reassigning its coordinates with a **Go to X: (464) Y: (0)**. Figure 4-8 shows the completed script for the Jungle Background sprite. Update the script, and then save and test.

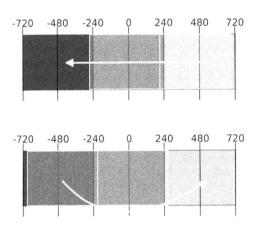

FIGURE 4-7 Scrolling Using X coordinates.

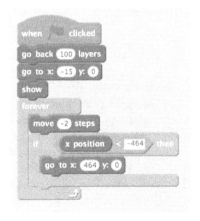

FIGURE 4-8 Scrolling Background Sprite 1.

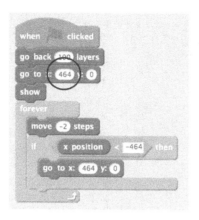

FIGURE 4-9
Duplicate Sprite.

FIGURE 4-10   Scrolling Background Sprite 2.

FIGURE 4-11   Paint New Backdrop.

Notice during the test that once the sprite clears the −264 coordinate, it jumps to the positive 464 coordinate, leaving significant white space between the disappearing end and the reappearing end. We'll fix this by adding an additional background sprite. Right-click on the Jungle Background sprite, and then scroll to **Duplicate,** as shown in Figure 4-9.

A duplicated sprite retains the original's scripts, so we only need to update them. Change the starting x value to **464** as shown in Figure 4-8. Save and test.

The two background sprites should now create a scrolling effect with only a minor seam. Note that the illusion works in large part because of the particular image used for the background sprites. It was designed with this purpose in mind, so the image edges are relatively free of overlapping elements, and the terrain patterns remain at the same height on each side. Not all images will create an effective scrolling background.

Deeper Into the Jungle Step 3: Win or Lose

In the previous chapter we created variables for Time, Health and Score, all of the ways to measure a player's rate of success with the game. Now, we'll use these measures to end the game.

Create Custom Backdrops

When the game ends, the scrolling background sprites will hide, so that we can see backdrops indicating if the player won or lost. Let's create those backdrops now. Click on the **Stage** icon in the bottom left corner. Choose the **Backdrops** tab. Click the paintbrush icon, as shown in Figure 4-11, and choose **Paint New Backdrop**. An additional backdrop will appear.

Select the paint bucket icon, as shown in Figure 4-12, to **Fill with Color**. Choose a color for the win backdrop from the **Color Palette** at the bottom of the **Paint Editor**. Click on the backdrop in the editor to fill the backdrop with the selected color.

FIGURE 4-12   Fill with Color.

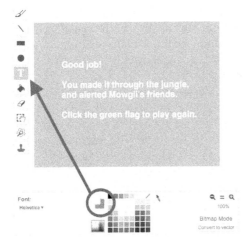

FIGURE 4-13   Add Text to Backdrop.

FIGURE 4-14   Rename Backdrops.

Use the color palette again to select a different color for the text. Click on the **Text** icon, shown in Figure 4-13. Click on the backdrop to insert a text box. When the cursor appears, begin typing a greeting for winning players. When the message is complete, click outside of the text box. Note that you will no longer be able to edit the text box after clicking outside of it. Handles to move or resize the text box will appear. Again, after clicking outside the text box, you will no longer be able to move or resize the text. To change the win screen, use the **Undo** arrow at the top of the Paint Editor or use the **Clear** button to start over completely.

Select the other backdrop icon. Follow the same steps to create a backdrop to greet losing players at the end of the game. Rename each backdrop appropriately, as shown in Figure 4-14.

Create Backdrop Scripts

The backdrops now exist on the stage behind the scrolling background sprites. When the game ends we'll hide these sprites and display the appropriate win or lose backdrop. Click on **Jungle Background Sprite 1,** and then select the **Scripts** tab. Start a new script with a **When Green Flag Clicked** block. This script will continually monitor the value of Time and Health, so we'll need to add a **Forever** block. Stack two **If () Then** blocks inside of the Forever loop. The first will check to see if the player won, and the second will check to see if the player lost.

From the green **Operators** menu, drag an **() and ()** block into the condition space of the first If () Then block. The player will win if she still has Health remaining when Time runs out, so we'll need to add a **() Is Less Than ()** block into each side of the () and () block. The bottom If () Then block will activate if Health is less than one, regardless of time remaining, so add another () Is Less Than () block into the condition area of the bottom If () Then block. The script so far should mirror Figure 4-15.

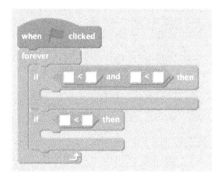

Now we need to add the variables into the conditional statements. From the orange **Data** palette, drag **Time** into the left square of the first () Is Less Than () block, and drag **Health** into the right square of the second () Is Less Than () block. Drag another Health into the left square of the bottom () Is Less Than () block. Type the number **1** into each of the three squares. Point out to students that the phrase (1) Is Less Than (Health) equates to (Health) Is Greater Than (1). The statement is simply flipped. As long as the open-mouth side of the inequality symbol faces Health, it indicates that the Health variable contains a higher value than that on the other side of the symbol.

FIGURE 4-15   If (Less Than) and (Less Than).

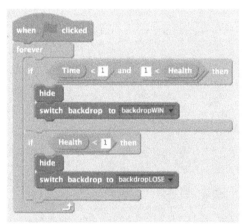

Finally, add the blocks to indicate what should happen if the conditions are met. From the purple **Looks** palette, add a **Hide** and a **Switch Backdrop to ()** into each If () Then block. Switch the top block to **back-dropWin** and the bottom to **back-dropLose**. Figure 4-16 shows the completed script. Copy this script into **JungleBackground Sprite 2**. Save and test.

FIGURE 4-16   Completed Win/Lose Script.

Hide Sprites When Game Ends

At this point, our win or lose screens appear at the end of the game, yet, Score and Health may continue to change because the animal sprites continue to move across the screen and intersect with Rann. Let's fix this. Select the **Elephant** from the sprite panel. Begin a new script with a **When I Start as Clone** block. This script will need to run continuously, so add a **Forever** block. Insert an **If ()** **Then** block inside to check for a condition. We want the clone to **Hide** if either **Time** or **Health** has run out, so from the green **Operators** palette, move an **() or ()** block into the condition area of the If () Then and add a **() Is Less Than ()** into each hexagonal area. Finally, add Time and Health to the left square of each side and the number **1** into the right side. Figure 4-17 shows the completed script.

Copy this full script into the Butterfly and Monkey sprites. Drag the Forever block into Rann, and attach onto the bottom of the Score, Time, and Health

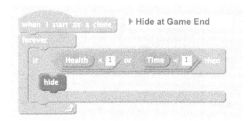

FIGURE 4-17   Hide Clone at Game End.

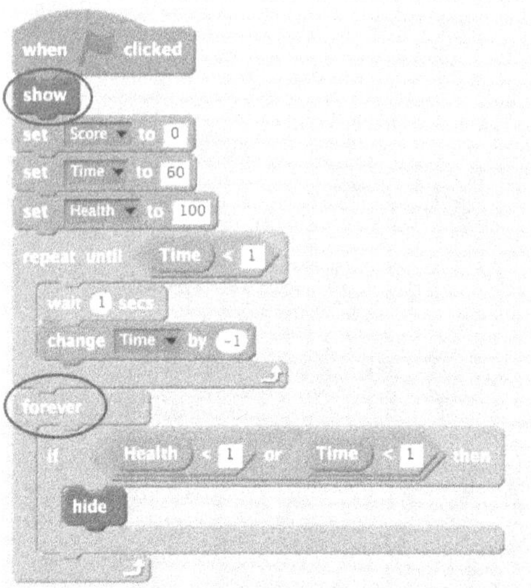

script. Save and test. The sprites should all disappear now at the end of the game, which is good, but there's a problem. When a new game is started, Rann remains hidden! Ask the students how they might fix this. One possible solution is to add a Show to the top of the Rann script, as indicated in Figure 4-18.

Deeper Into the Jungle Step 4: Swinging Monkeys

FIGURE 4-18   Hide Rann at Game End.

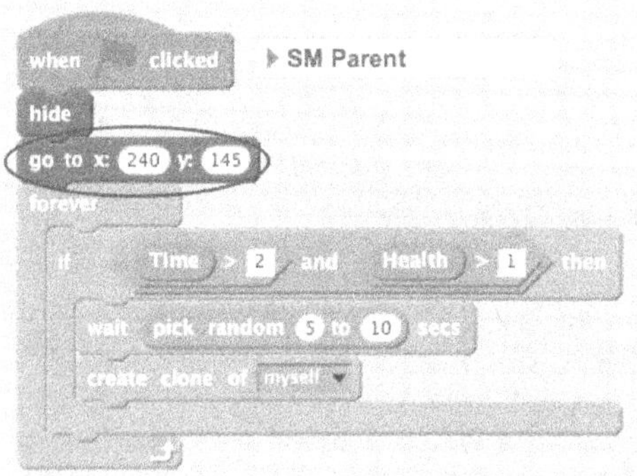

We've completed all of the necessary elements of the game. If class time is limited, you may choose to skip the remaining activities. If, however, students would like an additional level of difficulty, continue on with this activity, which adds monkeys to the upper half of the screen, making it more challenging for players to avoid colliding with monkeys.

Click on the folder icon above the sprite panel to **Upload Sprite from File**. Navigate to **SwingingMonkey. sprite2** and click **Open**. We'll use the same cloning technique that we used for the Elephant, Butterfly, and Running Monkey sprites. In fact, we can simply drag the **Elephant Parent Script** onto the Swinging Monkey sprite icon to copy it. Update the coordinates in the third block to **Go to X: (240) Y: (145),** so that the Swinging Monkey starts at the right stage boundary in the upper part of the screen. Refer to Figure 4-19 for the complete Swinging Monkey Parent Script.

FIGURE 4-19   Swinging Monkey Parent Script.

We'll also duplicate the **Clone Movement** script from the Elephant sprite into the Swinging Monkey. We want the Swinging Monkey to continue to move down and to the left until it reaches the middle of the stage, so update the third block to **Repeat Until ((X Position) Is Less Than (1))**. To make the Swinging Monkey move down the stage, we'll need to add a **Change Y by ()** block and give it a negative value, for instance **–1**. Save and test.

Notice that the Swinging Monkey moves across the stage, but it doesn't appear to swing, rather it glides. To create the arc like motion needed, return to the blue Motion palette, and add a clockwise **Turn () Degrees** block inside the loop. The Turn () Degrees block *rotates the sprite the specified amount and direction around its center*. Save and test again. The monkey now appears to swing in, but it stops at the halfway point. To fix this, **Duplicate** the **Repeat Until ((X Position) Is Less Than (–1))** block and place it under the original. We need to update this block's values so

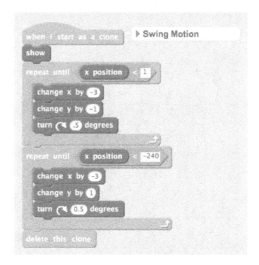

FIGURE 4-20   Swinging Monkey Clone Motion.

that the Swinging Monkey moves back up toward the top stage boundary until it reaches the left boundary at **–240**. Switch the Change Y By block value to a positive value such as **1**. Compare your script with Figure 4-20, which shows the completed Swinging Monkey Clone Motion script.

Duplicate the **Elephant Hide at Game End** script into the Swinging Monkey to hide clones when the game ends. Finally, copy the **Monkey Reaction** script from the Running Monkey sprite into the Swinging Monkey sprite, so that the player loses points when Rann collides with a Swinging Monkey clone. Note that although this script includes a Play Sound (Chee Chee) block, that sound is not yet loaded into the Swinging Monkey sprite. With the Swinging Monkey sprite selected, click on the **Sounds** tab and **Choose Sound from Library** to upload the **Chee Chee** sound to the Swinging Monkey. Refer to Figure 4-21 to see all four Swinging Monkey scripts.

Deeper Into the Jungle Step 5: Projectiles

Projectiles are commonly found in video games, whether the protagonist is throwing an object or an opponent is shooting. In this section we'll explore methods to add projectiles to a Scratch game.

Opponent Projectiles

In a single-player game, the opponents are computer controlled, and thus need automated shooting. For our game, we'll use the Running Monkey clones as our opponents, and they will throw bananas at us. This same technique may be used for spaceships shooting laser blasts, or any other variant.

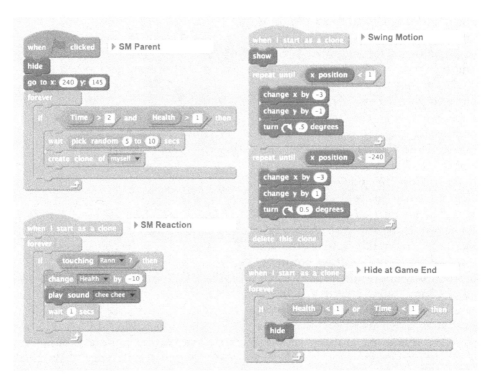

FIGURE 4-21   All Swinging Monkey Scripts.

Create Projectiles

Begin by choosing **Bananas** from the **Sprite Library**. We'll create a clone of the Bananas each time a new Running Monkey clone spawns. Select the **Running Monkey** sprite to use it as a trigger, and start a new script with a **When I Start as a Clone** block. Underneath, add a **Create Clone of (Bananas)** block. We want the newly created Bananas clone to find the newly created Running Monkey clone, so we'll add a **Forever** block to begin a locator loop.

We know that we can use the X Position and Y Position blocks to check or assign a sprite's location, but in order to assign one sprite's coordinates to a different sprite, we need to create variables to hold those values. Go to the orange **Data** tab. Create two new variables for all sprites called **BananaX** and **BananaY**. Add a **Set (BananaX) to ()** block and a **Set (BananaY) to ()** block inside of Forever. Return to the blue Motion tab to add **X Position** and **Y Position** blocks as indicated in Figure 4-22. Now the variables BananaX and BananaY will constantly update to the Running Monkey clones X and Y coordinates.

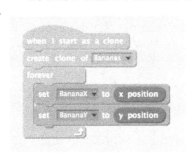

FIGURE 4-22   Create   Banana Clones.

Projectile Behavior

We've now created the projectiles, but we haven't told them what to do when created. Select the **Bananas** sprite to code its behavior. Start the first script with a **When Green Flag Clicked** block. The Bananas are a bit large for our animals, so let's resize them with a **Set Size to ()** block from the purple **Looks** palette. Finally, as with the other sprites we've cloned, we'll hide the parent, so add a **Hide** block.

Next, we need to tell the Banana clones how to behave. Start a new script with a **When I Start as a Clone** block. Since the parent Bananas were hidden, we'll need to add a **Show** block. Next, we'll set the starting location for the bananas, using our new variables. From the blue Motion palette, select **Go to X: () Y: ()**, and add it under show. Fill in the assigned values with the **BananaX** and **BananaY** variables. The newest Bananas clone will now go to the newest Running Monkey clone. In the orange **Data** palette, uncheck the BananaX and BananaY boxes to hide the variables from the stage.

The **Point Towards ()** block from the blue Motion palette *aims its sprites center at that of the target, changing the host sprite's direction and rotation.* Add this block next, and select Rann as the target. Once the Bananas are aimed, we need to launch them. Add a **Repeat Until** block. From the green **Operators** palette add a **() Is Less Than ()** block into the hexagonal space. We want the Bananas to continue to move toward Rann until they either intersect with him or go off the stage, so add an **X Position** on the left side of the condition and **–240** on the right side. Inside the loop, add a **Move (10) Steps** block. Once the condition is true, the Bananas will be off the stage, or almost off, due to the Scratch parameters, so we'll want to add a **Delete This Clone block** under the loop. Save and test. The Running Monkeys should now appear to throw bananas at Rann as they enter the stage.

Finally, we want Rann to lose health when hit by bananas. Add an **If () Then** block inside of the Repeat Until block in the Banana Motion script. From the turquoise Sensing palette, add a **Touching (Rann)** into the condition area. Add a Change (Health) by () block and set the value to deduct. Add a **Delete This Clone** inside the loop, so that if the bananas hit Rann, they will disappear rather than continuing off the stage. View both of the completed scripts in Figure 4-23.

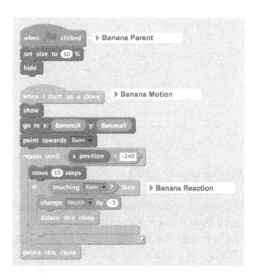

FIGURE 4-23   Bananas Parent and Clone Scripts.

Shooting Projectiles

Though not strictly necessary for our game, in many games the protagonist needs to be able to shoot. This requires a different coding strategy because unlike the computer-controlled opponents that shoot automatically, the protagonist is controlled by the player and needs to shoot on demand.

Set Projectile Position

Begin by choosing a projectile. Since oranges have long been cultivated in India, we'll use the **Orange** from the **Sprite Library** for our example. We'll want Rann to appear to hold the Orange, just as we had the Running Monkeys hold the Bananas, so select Rann, and start a new script with a **When Green Flag Clicked** block. Go to the orange Data palette and create two new variables for all sprites, Rann ClawX and Rann ClawY. Place a **Set (Rann ClawX) to ()** block and a **Set (Rann ClawY) to ()** block in the new script. Add an **X Position** and a **Y Position** to the right side of each, respectively.

Our current script would send the Orange to Rann's center, his X and Y position. The Orange would look more natural in his claws, a bit to the right and down from his center. From the green Operators palette, replace the X Position with a **() Plus ()** block and the Y Position with a **() Minus ()** block. Move the **X Position** and **Y Position** blocks back onto the left side of each operator.

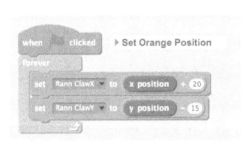

FIGURE 4-24   Set Orange Position.

Since we want the Orange to move right of Rann's center, we'll **Set Rann ClawX to (X Position + 20)**. To move the Orange down from Rann's center we'll **Set Rann ClawY to (Y Position –15)**. Finally, add a **Forever** loop around the two set blocks to continuously check for Rann's updated location. Figure 4-24 shows the completed script to set the Orange location.

Projectile Motion

We've created the variables to set the starting location of the Orange. Now we need to tell the Orange to go there, and when and how it should launch. Select the **Orange** sprite. Start the first script with a **When Green Flag Clicked**. The Orange is a little big for Rann to grip, so add a **Set Size to (50)%** block from the purple Looks palette. Add a **Forever** loop underneath. Place two **Repeat Until ()** blocks inside of the Forever loop, stacked on top of each other.

We'll use the first Repeat Until () block to keep the Orange with Rann until the player pulls the figurative trigger, in this case, clicking the mouse. From the turquoise **Sensing** palette, grab a **Mouse Down?** block and place it in the hexagonal space of the first Repeat Until (). Inside, place a **Go to X: () Y: ()**

block, and fill the spaces with Rann ClawX and Rann ClawY respectively. Unless the player is depressing the mouse button, the Orange should stay at the same coordinates as Rann.

If the player is depressing the mouse button, then the script moves on to the next block outside of the Repeat Until () loop. Use a **Point Towards (Mouse-Pointer)** block to aim the Orange to the cursor's location on the stage.

Return to the Sensing palette to get a **Touching (Edge)** block for the second Repeat Until () condition.

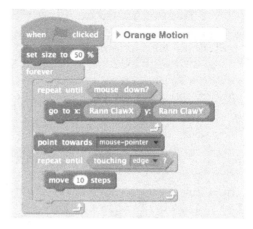

FIGURE 4-25   Orange Motion Script.

Inside, place a **Move (10) Steps** block to tell the Orange to continue moving in the direction that it's been pointed until it reaches the edge of the stage. Once the condition is true that it is touching the edge, the Forever loop will redirect the Orange back to Rann to throw again. Figure 4-25 demonstrates the completed Orange Motion Script. Save and test.

Projectile Scoring

Rann should now appear to throw Oranges wherever the player aims with the mouse, but nothing happens with the score yet. Also the Orange remains floating after the game ends. Copy the **Hide at Game End** script from the Elephant, Butterfly, Running Monkey, or Swinging Monkey. Back inside the Orange scripts area, detach the script from the When I Start as Clone, and remove that block. Start the script with a **When Green Flag Clicked** script instead. The orange will now hide at the end of the game.

To add points when the player hits a monkey, add an additional **If () Then** inside the Forever loop on this second script. From the green Operators palette, add an **() or ()** into the hexagonal area. From the turquoise Sensing palette, place **Touching (Swinging Monkey)** on one side and **Touching (Running Monkey)** on the other. Inside the loop, place a **Change Score by (5)** block to gain points each time the player hits either monkey type with an Orange. Figure 4-26 demonstrates how the hide and score components have been combined into one script. Save and test. Note that clicking around the stage may jar the scrolling backdrop. To avoid this, change the **Mouse Down?** block command to **Key (Space) Pressed**.

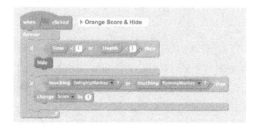

FIGURE 4-26   Orange Score and Hide Script.

Deeper Into the Jungle Step 6: Background Music

Students tend to love adding music and sounds to their projects; these can be a great way to personalize projects with creativity. It often works best, however, to wait until closer to the end of the session to encourage students to add background music so that each test of the game won't create a cacophony in the classroom.

Loop Sound from Library

The simplest way to create background music is to simply loop a sound from the Sound Library, as shown in Figure 4-27. Select a sprite without clones, such

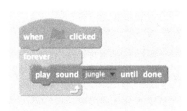

as **Jungle Background 1**. Click the **Sounds** tab and select the **Choose Sound from Library** icon that we used in Activity Set 3. Select a sound, ideally one from the **Music Loops** section, and then click **OK**. Create a new script with a **When Green Flag Clicked** block. Add a **Forever** block to loop the sound. Finally, add **Play Sound () Until Done**. When the sound finishes playing it will restart from the beginning. Save and test.

FIGURE 4-27   Loop Sound Forever.

Finding Music

The Scratch sound library contains mostly sound effects rather than musical tracks. Thankfully, we can upload our own sound files in either MP3 or WAV format. This is a great opportunity to talk with students about copyright and intellectual property. We often assume that it is acceptable to use copyrighted materials in a classroom setting under the fair use doctrine, but a closer look at Section 107 of the Copyright Act indicates that this is not always the case. For instance, it *might* be permissible for a student to use copyrighted music in her Scratch project for the purposes of learning how to program, but it would likely *not* be permissible for the student to then post the project to the Scratch online community; this would be distributing unlicensed music. Additionally, public libraries typically do

not qualify as educational institutions for the purposes of copyright. Luckily, it is easy to avoid copyright infringement by using appropriately licensed music.

One great resource to find music is CreativeCommons.org, a global nonprofit organization that empowers artists of various media to share their works. Visitors to the site can search partner sites such as Jamendo,

FIGURE 4-28   Upload Sound from File.

Sound Cloud, and ccMixter for music with appropriate licenses. Note that some of the music on these sites may be royalty-free for personal use, but may require paid licenses for use in multimedia projects, such as a published video game. Almost all music requires attribution. Be sure to check the individual track's licensing restrictions.

The example in Figure 4-28 uses the track "Genesha's Footprints" by German Mister Thomas, downloaded from SoundCloud. This work is licensed for sharing and adapting under a CreativeCommons Attribution 3.0 unported license, so the user is free to embed it in a Scratch project and post the project to the online community as long as proper attribution is given.

Upload Sound From File

After downloading your chosen track, we need to insert it into the project. In the previous step we used BackgroundJungle1, so we'll return there now. Click on the **Sounds** tab, and then choose the **Upload Sound from File** folder icon. It may take a few moments for Scratch to convert the file. Note that the sound editor provides tools to fade the track in or out, raise or lower the volume, and to trim the clip. Return to the **Scripts** tab to update the sound script to the new file. Save and test. The background music should play on a loop while the game is running.

Record New Sound

Of course, another way to avoid any trouble with copyright is for students to record their own original music. This is a great opportunity to collaborate with local music teachers or musicians, and it also provides a chance for students to connect coding with other interests. If a local expert isn't available, consider researching some Indian music to play for the students to inspire them as they create their own.

Note that the microphone will likely pick up other noises in the room, such as other students creating their tracks. Have students practice their tracks a few times, and then have them record individually, either in the same room while others remain quiet, or in an adjacent room or hallway. Remind them that the track will loop, so they only need a short pattern.

When you are ready to record, return to the **Sounds** tab. As shown in Figure 4-29, select the **Record New Sound** microphone icon to start a new sound file, rather than recording over an existing file. Click the circular **Record** button when ready to begin. Go to the link in the Appendix to hear an example recording created by simply drumming on the desk in front of the computer.

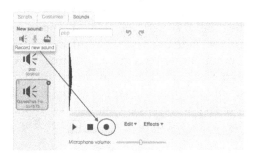

FIGURE 4-29   Record New Sound.

FIGURE 4-30 Paint New Sprite.

FIGURE 4-31 Splash Screen Example.

FIGURE 4-32 Splash Screen Script.

Deeper Into the Jungle Step 7: Splash Screen

A splash screen typically greets visitors while they are waiting for a game to start up. Game designers can use this screen to give game play instructions, attribute content, and promote their brands.

Begin by clicking the **Paint New Sprite** paintbrush icon indicated in Figure 4-30. Use the **Fill with Color** and **Text** tools to create a custom splash screen. If you uploaded a music file, be sure to include an attribution on the splash screen. In the example in Figure 4-31, Rann is included to provide more visual interest. Include stationary sprites by clicking the **Add** button at the top of the Sprite Editor.

Switch over to the Scripts tab. Start a new script with a **When Green Flag Clicked**. Since the game will start upon the click, we won't want the splash screen covering up the action, so add a **Hide** block. When the sprite does appear, we want it in the center of the stage, so add a **Go to X: () Y: ()** block. We want the screen to appear after the game has finished and the player has seen their win or lose screen. Add a **Wait (80) Secs** block. Adjust the time according to how long you've given players for the game. Finally, add a **Show** block, so that the screen appears. View the completed script in Figure 4-32. Save and test. The splash screen will appear at the end of the game, and will remain when the red stop sign is clicked. This will now be the screen a new player sees upon opening the game.

We've explored the most commonly used Scratch blocks and methods. As we continue into other programming languages, you'll see similarities. Though the particular syntax of a language may change, the logical constructs tend to remain the same or overlap. In the next chapter we'll move into GameMaker Studio, a high-powered tool that can take students from visual programming into text-based programming. Scratch remains a great resource, however, and it is wise for younger and less experienced students to continue to build skill and confidence with Scratch before moving on to more complex languages. Encourage students to explore the online Scratch community. Remixing is encouraged, and students can learn a great deal by clicking the **See Inside** button on any given project.

5

Game Maker Grimm

GameMaker: Studio, now distributed by YoYo Games, was originally created by Dutch professor Mark Overmars. The software allows users to work with a drag-and-drop interface, the text-based GameMaker Language, or a hybrid of both. GameMaker: Studio is intended for building 2D games, but it is possible to use 3D graphics in a limited capacity.

As of this writing, GameMaker: Studio 2 cannot be installed on computers using the 32-bit version of Windows. This can be a problem for some users with smaller, less expensive computers, so we'll use GameMaker 1.4.1773 in our activities. This version of GameMaker: Studio is only available for Windows; however GameMaker: Studio 2 is available for Mac. You may find that these activities translate to GameMaker: Studio 2; however, they are untested. A direct link to download GameMaker 1.4.1773 is on the website listed in the Appendix.

YoYo Games offers a free trial version of GameMaker: Studio that may be used indefinitely. This is the version used in all of the GameMaker: Studio activities in this text. YoYo Games also offers licensed versions for one-time or annual fees. These licenses allow users to export games to target platforms such as HTML5, PS4, Xbox One, and more. The free trial version only allows testing, or in our case, learning. Students using the trial version will, however, be able to save their games for play on Windows computers. Schools interested in moving beyond the trial version may wish to explore educational licensing options. These are available from the YoYo Games website, but schools are also permitted to simply use the free trial version.

Please note that the screenshots in this chapter are provided with the permission of YoYo Games, but without endorsement or guarantee. Any questions about or issues arising from the use of the following guide should be directed to the author of this book.

GAME MAKER GRIMM: PREPARATION

In this chapter we'll learn about the basics of GameMaker: Studio by creating a simple game using inspiration from the *Grimm's Fairy Tales* story "The Twelve Huntsmen."

Game Maker Grimm: Materials Needed and Set-up

As with the previous activities, the instructor will want a projector and students will need copies of the handout, printable from the activity resources link in the Appendix. One computer per participant is best if possible, but if necessary, two students can share. Prior to class, make sure to download and install GameMaker: Studio 1.4.1773 onto each computer. A link to the install file is provided on the website listed in the Appendix. The free trial version is sufficient for all activities in this book. Student projects may be saved locally or to portable drives. Due to the size and output type of files, it is typically difficult to transfer files to students electronically using a cloud service, so students who wish to take their games home should bring flash drives.

Students will also need access to the files **Bootprint.png** and **StoneTiles .png**, downloadable from the website in the Appendix.

You may also wish to provide copies of "The Twelve Huntsmen," or you may wish to read the story in class. *Grimm's Fairy Tales* are in the public domain, so free digital access to the story is easily acquired from Project Gutenberg, Apple iBooks, Overdrive, and numerous other digital sources.

Set-up for this activity simply requires a computer lab or set of laptops and an instructor's projector. As mentioned in the previous chapter, it is preferable to set up the student stations so that the instructor can see the student screens. This typically places the instructor behind the students who are facing the instructor's projected screen.

Game Maker Grimm: Outcomes

Participants transfer knowledge between programming environments.
Participants become familiar with concepts of objects and incidents.
Participants know how to create custom sprites using the Sprite Editor.
Participants understand how to use steps to control timing of events.

GAME MAKER GRIMM: GUIDE

In this lesser known tale, a passed-over fiancée plots to woo back her lost prince by gathering eleven identical maidens who then pose as twelve huntsmen to join his entourage. When the prince is tipped off that the huntsmen may actually be huntswomen, he sets various traps to test them. One of those tests is placing peas all over a floor. The idea is that men would smash them, but women would shuffle their feet and roll them around. Our first simple project with GameMaker: Studio will ask players to smash peas as they move around the playing field.

Game Maker Grimm Step 1: Start a New Project

GameMaker: Studio typically takes some time to load, and each click of the icon will open an additional window, slowing down the process. For the first class, it may be helpful to pre-open the program, and leave the welcome window displayed in Figure 5-1 open for students to begin.

FIGURE 5-1   Create New Project.

Select the **New tab** at the top. The **Project Directory** indicates the future location of the new project. Typically it is easiest for students to save to the Desktop if they are saving locally for the duration of the class. If students have portable drives, ask them to plug them in. Use the ... icon, located above the **Create** button, to the far right of the **Project Directory** to select the path to the drive. Once the path is selected, each future save of the project will update the file via the existing path, so students using portable drives must leave them connected throughout class and properly eject them to retain their game updates.

FIGURE 5-2   Resource Tree.

Title the project in the **Project Name** text bar. Students name this project **Twelve Huntsmen** or anything else appropriate. It is typically wise to add the name of the student programmer, particularly if multiple classes use the same computers and the programs are stored locally. Choose **Create** to generate the new project.

Once the new project loads, the **Resource Tree** column will appear, as shown in Figure 5-2. Ask students to point out elements that they recognize from Scratch. These may include **Sprites, Sounds, Backgrounds,** and **Scripts**. The **Resource Tree** is also sometimes called the **File Explorer** or **Resource Explorer**. This is similar to the way most modern operating systems organize files, in folders, with subfolders, etc. . . .

Game Maker Grimm Step 2: Rooms

In Scratch, the prebuilt stage spawns when the user creates a new game. Scratch stages are always 480 pixels by 360 pixels. In GameMaker: Studio,

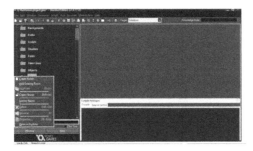

we have a lot more freedom to dictate the size and other characteristics of the play space, so we need to design the room ourselves. Right-click on the **Rooms** folder, and select **Create Room**, or select the white rectangle icon from the top bar as shown in Figure 5-3.

FIGURE 5-3   Create Room.png.

Naming Conventions

The room editor window opens to the **Settings** tab where we can create a unique name for the first room. Scratch forgives extra spaces and special characters in names, but most programming languages and environments, including GameMaker: Studio, do not. Consider that in a text-based environment a space might indicate the second word in a resource name or a completely different resource. Encourage students to get in the habit of using one of the common naming practices used by programmers: camel case or underscore. Camel case, typically styled **CamelCase**, *is the practice of capitalizing the first letter of each new word or abbreviation in a compounded file name.* Each capital letter is like a bump on a camel's back and indicates the start of a new segment. Another popular option is to use an underscore between segments; for instance RoomDragonCave would become Room_dragon_cave. Introduce both options to students, and allow them to choose based on personal preference. Examples moving forward will use the more succinct CamelCase.

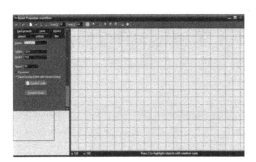

Our first room will represent the floor on which the peas roll. Because each game will involve numerous resources, often with similar names, it is helpful to stick with a standard naming convention that indicates the appropriate type of resource in the name. For instance, this room would be **roomFloor**. Enter a custom name in the area indicated in Figure 5-4.

FIGURE 5-4   Room Settings.

Room Dimensions

Notice the numbers indicated in the left column for **Width** and **Height**. Just as in Scratch, these represent the pixels for each dimension, but unlike in Scratch they may be customized. For now, we can leave these at the default size, 1024 pixels wide by 768 pixels high, but keep this area in mind when working with custom background images or small screens.

Room Backgrounds

Click the Backgrounds tab, and then click the **Color** block as indicated in Figure 5-5. Choose a color to represent the floor from the color palette, and then click **OK**. Save the changes to the room and exit by clicking the **Green Checkmark** in the top left of the window.

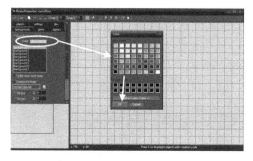

FIGURE 5-5   Background Color.

Game Maker Grimm Step 3: Sprites

Now that we have the floor, we need to create our peas. We'll start by designing how the peas will look. In Scratch, the term **sprite** is used broadly, but in GameMaker: Studio, it is used more strictly in a traditional sense as *a standalone 2D computer graphic that can be manipulated as part of a larger scene*. In Scratch, a sprite may have assigned scripts, but in GameMaker and other more advanced programming environments, a sprite is simply a visual element, similar to a *costume* in Scratch.

From the Resource Tree, right-click on the **Sprites** folder, and then choose **Create Sprite**. Those who prefer icons may reach the same destination by clicking the green PAC MAN–shaped icon in the top toolbar. When the **Sprite Properties** window appears, as shown in Figure 5-6, enter a standard convention **Name** for the pea sprite, such as **spritePea**.

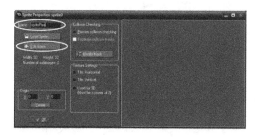

FIGURE 5-6   Sprite Properties.

Sprite Editor

Choose the **Edit Sprite** button to bring up the **Sprite Editor**, shown in Figure 5-7. The **Sprite Editor** may be used to customize the image or images used for a sprite. Select the icon that looks like a blank sheet of paper to **Create a New Sprite**. In the pop-up window, set the dimensions of the new sprite to **Width: 50, Height: 50**, and then click **OK**. Double-click the created canvas, or click the pencil-shaped icon in the toolbar to **Edit the Image.**

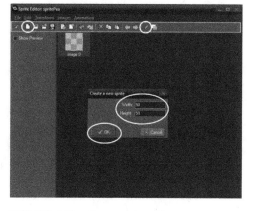

FIGURE 5-7   Create New Sprite.

Image Editor

When the **Image Editor** window opens, select the **Draw an Ellipse** tool. As indicated in Figure 5-8, select the **Filled Only** option to draw a solid shape. Finally, select the fill color from the color palette before clicking and dragging the shape into being. Hold down the shift key while dragging to force the ellipse into a circle. Note the magnifying glass–shaped **Zoom In** tool in the toolbar. It can be helpful to zoom in when drawing a sprite.

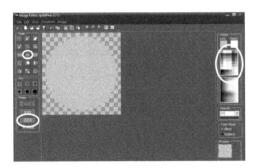

FIGURE 5-8   Draw Sprite.

Select the **Image** tab to see the more advanced image manipulation options. Let's use the **Gradient Fill** tool, shown at the bottom of the list in FIGURE 5-09 to give our image the appearance of depth.

As shown in Figure 5-10, select a base color on the left and a highlight color on the right. Select the radial kind of gradient. This will make the peas appear to be lit from above. Select **OK** to confirm the gradient. Click the **Green Checkmark** on the **Image Editor** to save changes to the image, and then click the **Green Checkmark** of the **Sprite Editor**. Finally click **OK** in the **Sprite Properties** window to save the changes to the sprite.

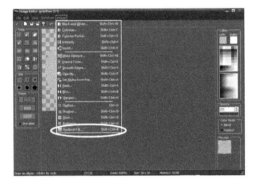

FIGURE 5-9   Gradient Fill.

Game Maker Grimm
Step 4: Objects

In GameMaker: Studio, an **object** *may contain actions and events, be assigned a sprite, and serve as a template for multiple instances of itself.* Think of an object as a cookie-cutter and an instance as an individual cookie. We'll create an objectPea resource and assign it certain characteristics and behaviors. We'll create multiple pea instances from this object that will all inherit those behaviors.

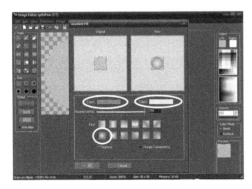

FIGURE 5-10   Gradient Fill Color and Kind.

To create a new object, right-click on the **Objects folder** or click on the green sphere icon in the toolbar. In the **Object Properties** window that opens, name the new object **objectPea**. As indicated in Figure 5-11, assign **sprite-Pea** to the object from the dropdown menu. Leave the Object Properties window open to add events.

Events

Just as we used **Events** in Scratch to trigger scripts to start; in Game-Maker: Studio, we'll create **Events** to trigger certain actions. Click the **Add Event** button, and select **Create**. The **Create** event *triggers its assigned actions as soon as an instance of the object exists in the room.*

Click the **Add Event** button again, and select **Other,** then **Intersect Boundary**. The **Intersect Boundary** event *triggers actions when the sprite overlaps with the edges of the room.*

FIGURE 5-11   Name Object and Assign Sprite.

Actions

Select the **Create** event. We'll use this event to tell objectPea instances to begin to move as soon as they are created. From the **Move** tab on the far right, click and drag the **Move Fixed** icon into the **Actions** area. In the **Move Fixed** window, select all nine of the arrowed directions, as shown in Figure 5-12, and set the speed to **8**. The peas will now begin moving in one of the nine directions as soon as they spawn. Select **OK** to close the window.

Select the **Intersect Boundary** event. From the same **Move** tab, click and drag each of the two U-shaped icons, **Reverse Horizontal Direction** and **Reverse Vertical Direction,** into the actions area, as shown in Figure 5-13. These actions will cause the pea instances to turn around and head back the opposite way when they hit the room edges. Click **OK** to close the objectPea **Properties** window.

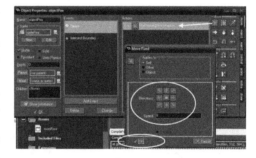

FIGURE 5-12   Create Event and Move Fixed Action.

FIGURE 5-13   Intersect Boundary Event and Reverse Direction Actions.

Add Object to Room

We've created a template for how instances of objectPea should behave when they are created, but we don't yet have an event to cause them to exist. To test our code thus far, let's place an instance in the room. This instance will spawn with the creation of the room.

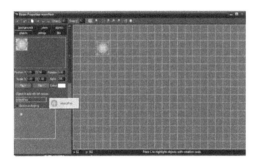

FIGURE 5-14   Add Object to Room.

Double-click on **roomFloor**. Select the **Objects** tab as shown in Figure 5-14. From the dropdown menu below **Objects to Add with Left Mouse,** select **objectPea**. **Left-click** anywhere in the room to create an instance of the object. If you accidentally create more than one, simply right-click on the instance and select **Delete**. Click the **Green Checkmark** in the upper right corner to save changes to the room.

Save and Test

Go to **File** and then **Save** or click the floppy disk icon. Either option will save the project to the same location as initially indicated. To save to a new location, choose **Save As** instead.

To test the game, select **Run** and then **Run Normally** from the main toolbar, or click the sideways green triangle icon. The game will take a few moments to compile, and then a window should open. The window will be the size specified in the **Room Settings**, and the game will be running. A single pea should be bouncing around the room and off of the walls. Close the test window.

Note that the test window will minimize but not close if the user misses the **X** in the upper right corner. The run options will remain unavailable until this window is closed. If this happens, look for the white GameMaker: Studio icon in the taskbar to close it properly.

Create Multiple Instances

Squashing one lone instance of objectPea won't be a particularly difficult game. We need more! Double-click on **objectPea** in the **Resource Tree** to reopen the **Object Properties** window. Select the **Create** event. Since we've placed one instance of objectPea in the room, its **Create** event will happen simultaneously with the creation of the room, similar to a **When Green Flag Clicked** block in Scratch. Any other actions we assign to this event will, therefore, also happen at the start of the game as the room is generated. We want multiple instances of objectPea to appear from the beginning, so we'll place the actions that will lead to that being true in the **Create** event's actions area.

Go to the **Control** tab. Select the **Test Instance Count** action from the **Questions** area and drag it into the **Actions** area below **Start Moving in a Direction**. The **Test Instance Count** question serves as an **If/Then Statement**: If the number of instances of objectPea is less than a designated number, do the next action. Using the first dropdown, select **objectPea** as the instance to count. As shown in Figure 5-15, enter the **number** of desired instances, such as **12** to represent each of the huntsmen. Choose **Smaller Than** as the operation. Click **OK** to close the window.

In Scratch the action to take place if the conditional statement is true goes inside of the C-shaped block. In GameMaker: Studio, the action to follow simply stacks underneath the

FIGURE 5-15   Test Instance Count.

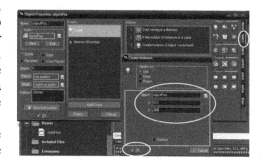

FIGURE 5-16   Create Instance.

test block. Go to the **Main1** tab and select the light bulb icon in the top left of the object section to **Create Instance**. Place this under the **Test Instance Count** block, as shown in Figure 5-16, and in the **Create Instance** window select **objectPea**. For now, let's have the newly created pea instances generate in the middle of the room, so set X to **512** and Y to **384**. Save and test.

At this point you should have multiple instances of objectPea in the room, moving in various directions. You may not, however, have twelve instances. Ask students why they think there are fewer and talk it over logically as a group. With the exception of the instance we placed directly into the room, all of the instances spawn at the exact same coordinates. We gave the instances nine possible directions in which they could move, and they all move at the same speed, so two pea instances that both start at (512,384) and both travel down the right diagonal at a speed of 8 will stack right on top of each other, hiding one of the instances from view.

Assign Random Coordinate

To fix this, and to make the game more challenging, let's have each instance generate at a random location in the room. Close the test window, and return to objectPea. Choose the **Create** event, and then open the **Create Instance** action. We'll now take advantage of GameMaker: Studio's ability to incorporate

FIGURE 5-17   Random Range.

text-based coding into the drag-and-drop interface by using the **random_range** function. It *returns a non-predictable number between the first value specified and the second.*

Remember that our room is 1024 pixels wide. GameMaker: Studio assigns the top left corner of the room the coordinate (0,0). With our dimensions, the upper right corner of the room would be assigned (1024,0). We want our pea instances to appear at any point along the x-axis between x:0 and x:1024, so in the box beside **X**, highlighted in Figure 5-17, enter the function as **random_range (0, 1024)**. The y value of the top of the room is also 0, and the bottom-edge y value is 768, reflecting the height of our room, so for Y enter **random_range (0,768)**. Save and test.

Note that it is common to mistype some part of the function, which will cause an error during compiling. The error window will announce the exact issue. Typically students use brackets instead of parentheses or miss a letter in random_range. Simply close the error window and return to the **Create Instance** action in objectPea's **Create** event to correct the function.

Once the test window opens successfully, you may find that some of the instances stick to the edges and seem to vibrate. This is because we told pea instances that they could generate close to the room edges, but we also told them that if they are on the edge of the room to reverse direction. If an instance generates touching the room boundary it will continue to reverse, then reverse again, moving toward the room and out of the room, but never moving significantly from the boundary. We can fix this with a few simple changes.

Center Sprite Origin

First, close the test window, and then go to **spritePea**. As shown in Figure 5-18, select the **Center** button, and notice how the values in the **Origin** boxes change. The default in GameMaker: Studio is to place sprites by the upper-left corner of the sprite's bounding box, so if a sprite assigned to an objectPea

FIGURE 5-18   Center Origin.

instance spawns at (0,767), only the top row of pixels of the sprite would be in the room, and the rest would be below the bottom edge. By placing the sprite by its center, now half of the sprite would be in the room, and half would be out, so our problem is half solved.

To solve the other half, click **OK** to close the spritePea **Properties** window, and then reopen **objectPea**.

Return to the **Create** event, and then open the **Create Instance** action. Since our sprite is 50 pixels wide by 50 pixels high, the center of the sprite is 25 pixels on each side. This means that if the objectPea instance generates at least 25 pixels inside of each room boundary the entire sprite would be within the room. To do this, we'll shrink our range for each axis, adding 25 to the minimum number of each and subtracting 25 from the maximum number for each. The new X function should read **random_range(25,999)**, and the new y function should read **random_range(25,743)**. Save and test. The pea instances should now all move freely about the room.

Game Maker Grimm Step 5: Player-Controlled Object

We now have plenty of peas to squash, but no way to squash them. We need to create an object that the player can control.

Load Sprite

Start by creating a new sprite. Name it **spriteBoot**. This time, we'll upload an existing image file for the sprite rather than creating an image in the editor. Select **Load Sprite** and navigate to the location of **Bootprint.png**. Select the file and click **Open**. Click the **Center** button under **Origin**.

Keyboard Controls

Create a new object, and name it **objectBoot**. Assign **spriteBoot** from the dropdown list. We'll control a single instance of objectBoot using the keyboard. Add a **Key Press** event, and from the dropdown list choose either **Left** or, from the **Letters** submenu, choose **A**. Add a **Move Fixed** action to the event and choose the middle-left arrow. Set the speed to **8**. Follow the same process to add **Key Press** events for **Right**, **Up**, and **Down** or **D**, **W**, and **S**. Assign a **Move Fixed** action to each using the appropriate direction arrow.

We've now told **objectBoot** how to move when each key is pressed, but we haven't told it when to stop moving. To address this, add a **Keyboard** event, and select **No Key** as the trigger. As shown in Figure 5-19, drag a **Move Fixed** block into the actions area and select the stop square. We don't need to set a speed.

Place an instance in the room by going to **roomFloor**, clicking the **Objects** tab, and then selecting **objectBoot** from the dropdown list. Left-click in the room to place the instance. Save and test. You should now be able to move the objectBoot

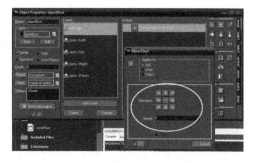

FIGURE 5-19   Keyboard Controls.

instance print up, down, left, and right, but nothing happens when the boot passes over a pea. Close the test window, and let's program that now.

Collision

Reopen the **objectBoot** properties window. Add a new **Event**. Select **Collision**, and then from the dropdown list, select the object with which the boot will collide, **objectPea**. Ask the students what should happen each time the

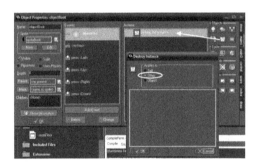

objectBoot instance collides with an **objectPea** instance. There will be a variety of answers, but the two most crucial to the game function are to remove the instance of **objectPea** from the room and to earn points. For the first, go to the **Main1** tab and drag the recycle can icon into actions to **Destroy the Instance**, as shown in Figure 5-20.

FIGURE 5-20   Destroy Instance.

The **Destroy Instance** window offers three options. Since the **Collision** event is in **objectBoot**, leaving the option **Applies to Self** checked would destroy the instance of the boot involved in the collision. We want the action **Destroy the Instance** to apply to the **Other** instance involved in the collision, the **objectPea** instance.

To gain points from the Collision event, go to the **Score** tab. Drag over the first block in the Score section, **Set Score**. Students may decide how many points players should receive each time they stop pea instances. Type this number into the **New Score**

FIGURE 5-21   Set Score Relative to Current Value.

box. Discuss with students what they think the score will be the first time the objectBoot instance collides with an objectPea instance, and then what the score will be after the second time. In the example shown in Figure 5-21, the new score value is **10**. So the score would reset to 10 the first time, and then reset to 10 the second time, and so on. . . . What we want is to increase the score each time. By checking the **Relative** box, each collision will reset the score relative to the current value of score, adding 10 on top of the stored value. Save and test.

The pea instances should now disappear when they collide with the boot print, but we can't see our score. That is because we've programmed the value of the score variable to change, but we haven't programmed a way to display the value.

Game Maker Grimm Step 6: Object Score

In Scratch we created a variable named score, but in GameMaker: Studio, **score** is a built-in, global variable. It is not, however, automatically visible to the player. We'll address that in this section. **Create a new object**. Name it **objectScore**. We will not assign it a sprite.

Add a **Create** event. From the **Score** tab, select **Set Score**. This will set the score as soon as objectScore spawns at the beginning of the game, so we want to set it to **0**, and it is not relative because this time we *do* want to completely reset the score to zero. Click **OK**.

Add another event. This one will be **Draw** and then **Draw** again. From the **Score** tab, select the third icon in the Score area, **Draw Score**. The X and Y values are preset to 0 and 0, which will cause the Score to draw itself in the upper-left corner. Students may customize the location of the Score in the room by adjusting these values. For instance, to place the Score in the bottom center of the room, enter X: 512 and Y: 750, as shown in Figure 5-22. If y is set to the bottom boundary's y value of 768, the score will draw itself below the room, but a value of 750 leaves enough space to draw the score inbounds.

The **Caption** may also be customized. Though the variable will still be called **Score** in the code, the caption that appears on the screen may be changed in this box to **Squashed** or some other appropriate term. Click **OK** to close the window and **OK** again to close objectScore's **Properties** window.

For objectScore to draw itself, we need to place an instance of it in the room. Return to **roomFloor** and add **objectScore** anywhere in the room. A blue circle with a question mark will appear when the object is placed because there is not an assigned sprite. No matter where this stand-in sprite is placed, it will actually generate at the coordinates we gave it in the **Draw Score** action. Save and test. The score should be visible, as in Figure 5-23, and it should increase each time the bootprint collides with a pea. Allow students to continue to test, i.e., play their games, while helping anyone having trouble.

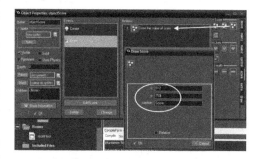

FIGURE 5-22   Draw Score.

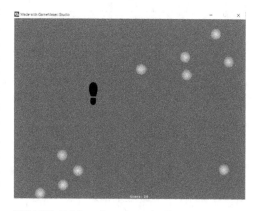

FIGURE 5-23   Game with Score.

Game Maker Grimm Step 7: Time Limit

The fundamentals of the game are now in place, however there is no way for the player to win or lose because there is unlimited time. There are many ways to address this. We'll start with a simple way, and then explore a more complex, but more effective approach. To begin, make a new object and call it **objectTime**.

Alarms

Add a **Create** event. From the **Main2** tab, select the topmost icon, **Set Alarm**.

Steps

When we created **roomFloor** in Step 2, we adjusted some options in the **Settings** tab, but we left the default room speed set to **30**. The speed of the room refers to how many times the room refreshes itself per second. Another way to think of speed is like a film reel. Ours would have 30 frames per second. Each of these frames is a **step**.

Setting an Alarm

Setting an alarm creates a trigger event after the game has run through a designated number of steps. In the example in Figure 5-24, the **Number of Steps** in **Alarm 0** is set to **600**. Ask the students how many seconds would pass before this alarm activates. They can solve this by dividing 600 by the 30 steps per second to reach a conclusion that the alarm is set for 20 seconds into the game. Allow students to set their own time length, but encourage them to keep it under a minute to make it easier to test. If an alarm is set to 9,000 steps, the programmer will need to wait 5 minutes to see if the alarm works properly!

FIGURE 5-24   Set Alarm.

Using an Alarm Event

We've set the time limit for our alarm, but we haven't said what should happen when that time is reached. For instance, an alarm clock typically makes some sort of noise when the set time arrives. To use our alarm, we'll create an **Alarm** event for **Alarm 0**, and then go to **Main2** to assign the action **Display Message**. As shown in Figure 5-25, type a message such as **Time's Up!** to greet players as a pop-up when the alarm goes off. Click **OK** to close the window, and then

OK to close the object properties window.

Return to **roomFloor** to place **objectTime** in the room. It will not be visible to players, as we have not asked it to draw itself. Save and test. A pop-up message, like the one in Figure 5-25, should appear at the designated time.

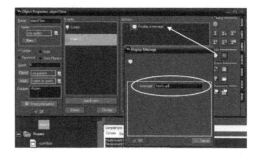

FIGURE 5-25   Display Message.

Win or Lose Rooms

As you and the students probably noticed during the test, the pop-up window temporarily stops the game, and indicates that it should be over, but when the player clicks **OK**, the game resumes. One way to end the game and show the player whether he won or lost is to use additional rooms. Create two new rooms, one called **RoomWin** and one called **RoomLose**. Select a different background color for each.

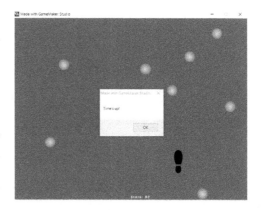

FIGURE 5-26   Game with Pop-Up Message.

Return to **objectTime**. Go to the **Alarm 0** event. Right-click on the **Display Message** action and then chose **Delete**. Go to the **Control** tab. Drag a **Test Instance Count** into the actions area. For players to win the game, they'll need to squash all 12 peas, so when the alarm timer goes off the number of instances of **objectPea** should be **Smaller Than 1** or **Equal to 0**. Change the settings to those in Figure 5-27, and then click **OK**.

FIGURE 5-27   Test Instance Count.

If this test is true, then the player should be directed to the winning room. Go to **Main1** and select the bottom-right block, **Go to Different Room**. From the dropdown menu, select **RoomWin**, as shown in Figure 5-28.

Repeat these steps for **RoomLose**, but remember that the number of instances of **objectPea** will be **Larger Than 0**. The order of the actions is

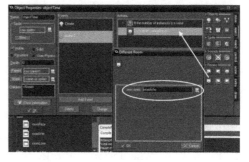

FIGURE 5-28   Go to Different Room.

FIGURE 5-29   Alarm 0 Action List.

critical, as they will be executed in order, so be sure to stack test then room, test then room, as shown in Figure 5-29. When **Alarm 0** event is activated the first test will run. If the objectPea instances are less than 1, the player will go to **RoomWin**, and if not, the program will continue to the next block and test to see if the **objectPea** instances are greater than 1. If they are, the player will be sent to **RoomLose**. One of these two conditions must be true, so the player must be sent to one of the rooms. Save and test.

Game Maker Grimm Step 8: Restart or End Game

Currently the color of the room reached indicates whether a player won or lost, but there's no greeting or option to replay the game and try again. In this step we'll add both.

Achievement Greetings

Create a new sprite called **SpriteWin**. Click **Edit Sprite** and then the **Create a New Sprite** icon. Set the sprite to the size of the room, **1024** pixels wide by **768** pixels high. Use the text tool to create a greeting for players who win. It is often easiest to create a new text box for each line of text. As

FIGURE 5-30   Create SpriteWin.

indicated in Figure 5-30, add an additional line of text asking players if they wish to play again, and indicate the keys to press for yes or no are **Y** and **N**. Click the **Green Checkmark** to save changes to the **Image Editor** and again to the **Sprite Editor**. Returning to the **Sprite Properties** window, select **Center**, and then click **OK** to save the sprite. Follow the same steps to create **SpriteLose**.

Restart or End Game

Create a new object called **objectWin**, and assign **SpriteWin** to it. This action will close the window in which the game runs. Add a **Keyboard** event for the letter Y. As indicated in Figure 5-31, go to the **Main2** tab and select the **Restart Game** action. This action will take the player back to **roomFloor** and reset the objects to their starting positions and variables to their starting values. Add another **Keyboard** event, this time for the letter **N**. As indicated in Figure 5-32, return to the **Main2** tab to select the **End Game** action. Repeat these steps to create **objectLose**.

Place **objectWin** in **RoomWin**. Drag the object to center it, or right-click on it and select **Change Position**. Since the sprite is centered, and it is the same size as the room, we can use the coordinates of the center of the room **(512,384)** to perfectly align objectWin within the boundaries of RoomWin. Follow the same steps to place **objectLose** in **RoomLose**. Save and test. When the alarm goes off at the set time, a win screen like that in Figure 5-33 or a lose screen like the one shown in Figure 5-34 should appear. Make sure to allow yourself to lose once to make sure that a keystroke of Y from that screen would restart the game. Lose a second time and select N to make sure the window closes. Play two more times to test that both options also work for the players who win.

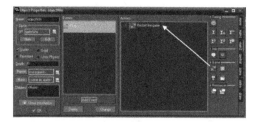

FIGURE 5-31   Restart Game.

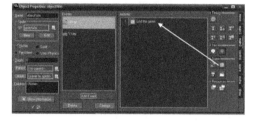

FIGURE 5-32   End Game.

FIGURE 5-33   Win Screen.

Game Maker Grimm Step 9: Upload Background

If there's extra time in class, give students the opportunity to personalize their games by adding a custom background. We'll walk through the steps using **StoneTiles.png**, the background provided for download. Have students use this file as an example, and then if time remains, invite them to search and download their own images. Remember to direct students toward image sources such as Pixelbay.com or OpenClipArt.org, from which properly licensed content may be obtained.

To add a custom background, first find the **Backgrounds** folder in the **Resource Tree**. Right-click on

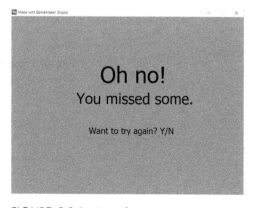

FIGURE 5-34   Lose Screen.

FIGURE 5-35   Load Background to Room.

the folder to select **Create Background**. Name the new resource **backgroundStone**. Just as we did for spriteBoot, select **Load Background**. Navigate to the location of **Stone Tiles.png**, and select **Open**. Once the image loads into the **Background Properties** window, click **OK**.

Open **roomFloor**. Click on the **Backgrounds** tab. About halfway down the window, click the dropdown icon to select **backgroundStone**. The image will automatically tile, repeating in each direction to fill the room. Save and test.

Game Maker Grimm Step 10: Save Game as Executable

Now that students have created their first game with GameMaker: Studio, they may wish to play it at home or to share with friends. Of course, potential players could install GameMaker: Studio and run the game as we have been doing, but if they only want to play it, there's a simpler solution. Students can save their games as an executable file that they can simply open and play. To do this, they will need to go to **File** and then **Create Application**. When the file explorer window opens, they should choose **Single Runtime Executable** from the dropdown options under **Save as Type**. Of course, students who do install GameMaker: Studio at home will have the opportunity to make many more games, including the more complex maze game in the next chapter.

6

Game Maker Grimmer

In the previous chapter we explored the basic structure of the GameMaker: Studio programming environment. We learned how to create and manipulate key elements such as sprites, objects, and rooms. In this chapter, we'll learn how to add Health, display Time, and create animated sprites.

GAME MAKER GRIMMER: PREPARATION

This activity is based on another story from *Grimm's Fairy Tales*, "Hansel and Gretel."

Game Maker Grimmer: Materials Needed

The materials needed do not vary greatly from those used in the previous chapter. Students will need copies of the handout, downloadable from the link in the Appendix, and the instructor will need a projector and screen. Students will need computers with GameMaker: Studio 1.4 installed. Once again, if they wish to keep and edit their games, students will need a way to transfer their projects, such as with a portable USB drive.

For this activity, students will need access to the following electronic files, all of which may be accessed via the website listed in the Appendix:

Tree.png
WoodcutterHouse.png
GingerbreadHouse.png
HanselFront.png or GretelFront.png
HanselBack.png or GretelBack.png
HanselRight.png or GretelRight.png
HanselLeft.png or GretelLeft.png
BrotherComeAndDanceWithMe.mp3

Finally, the full "Hansel and Gretel" story is part of *Grimm's Fairy Tales*, so free digital access to the story is easily acquired from Project Gutenberg, Apple iBooks, Overdrive, and numerous other digital sources.

Game Maker Grimmer: Outcomes

Participants understand how to create animation effects through manipulation of sprite strips.

Participants gain skill working with text-based coding.

Participants learn how to generate visual representations of objects through code.

Participants further develop computational thinking skills.

GAME MAKER GRIMMER: GUIDE

In the tale, a woodcutter and his wife fall upon hard times, and finally have so little food left that they decide to lead their two children, Hansel and Gretel, into the woods and abandon them there. Hansel, aware of their plans, packs his pockets with pebbles, so that he can drop one periodically to mark their path. The next evening, after they are abandoned, the children are able to follow the pebble trail back home, much to their father's delight and their stepmother's chagrin.

After some time has passed, once again their family finds themselves on the verge of starvation. The children learn that their parents once again plan to abandon them, but this time, the door is locked, so Hansel cannot gather pebbles the night before. Instead, he is forced to mark the path with crumbs of bread from his last piece, which of course scatter and are eaten by birds.

Hansel and Gretel wander through the woods trying to get home, but end up, famously, at the witch's gingerbread house. Most people know this part of the story, but many may not realize that after escaping, Hansel and Gretel still had to find their way back home, through a woods that they had never successfully navigated without guidance. Navigation reappears as a theme throughout the story, so for this activity we'll use the story to inspire a maze game.

Players will navigate Hansel or Gretel from one location, through the woods, to the other. Decompose this as a group. What subproblems need to be addressed to create the overall game? Some responses might be:

Create the maze.

Program Hansel and Gretel as controllable objects.

Set and manipulate Health and Time variables.

Define winning and losing triggers.

Add sound and visual effects.

End the game.

Game Maker Grimmer Step 1: Create the Maze

Follow the steps in the previous chapter to open a **New Project** in Game-Maker: Studio. Make sure to have students put their name in their titles and save their projects to easily accessible locations such as the Desktop, assigned server folders, or a flash drive.

Create roomWoods

Right-click on the Rooms folder and create a new room called **roomWoods**. Leave the default **Settings** set to Width **1024** and Height **768**. From the **Backgrounds** tab, choose a **Color** for the forest floor. This color will cover the room for now. Click the **Green Checkmark** to save the changes.

Create Starting and Ending Objects

We need to create a point of origin to the maze, the woodcutter's house, and a destination, the witch's gingerbread house. Create **sprite-WoodcutterHouse** and **spriteGingerbreadHouse**. Load the appropriate image to each, and make sure to **Center** the origin of both, as shown FIGURE 6-1 Create Maze Sprite List and Settings.

in Figure 6-1. Create **objectWoodcutterHouse** and **objectGingerbreadHouse**, assigning the appropriate sprite to each. Save the project to protect progress so far.

See the Forest for the Trees

To create the forest maze we'll create numerous instances of a tree object. Before we can place the trees effectively, however, we need to know their dimensions, so start by creating **spriteTree**. From the Sprite Properties window, select **Load Sprite**, and navigate to the **Tree.png** file. Make sure to **Center** the origin of the sprite before closing the Sprite Properties window. Figure 6-1 reflects the three sprites that should be in the Resource Tree thus far. Create **objectTree,** and assign this sprite to it before closing the window.

Reopen **roomWoods**. Notice the **Minimap** at the bottom left corner of the Room window. It reflects which part of the room is being shown in the main viewing window. Depending on the size of the monitor in use, students may need to use the **Minimap** to select the center of the background, and then use the **Zoom Out** tool in the top toolbar to see the entire room. We'll want to see the entire room as we place the objects.

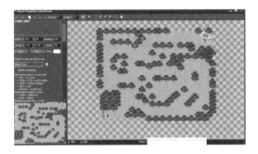

FIGURE 6-2   RoomWoods Maze.

From the **Objects** tab, select **objectWoodcutterHouse**, and place it at the desired starting location. Typically, English language readers would expect to find this on the left hand side, as we would expect the storyline, the game, to move from left to right. Next, place the **objectGingerbreadHouse** at the final destination, typically on the right side of the room. Objects typically snap to the grid when placed. To place the object without snapping, hold down the **Alt** key while clicking.

Select **objectTree**. Left-click to place the instances of the trees throughout the room in such a way as to create a maze. Creating a challenging maze can be more difficult than one might think. Encourage students to research images of mazes for inspiration. As shown in Figure 6-2, since the **objectTree** instances won't be moving, they may be placed on the room edges without fear, and it is possible to create several false trails. Give students a few minutes to create a basic maze, and assure them that they can always come back and edit it to make it easier or harder after testing. Save and test to see how the room will look when loaded.

Game Maker Grimmer Step 2: Playable Character

Now that we have the forest maze, we need a character to guide from one end to the other. In this section we'll add either **Hansel** or **Gretel.** The Hansel sprites are used in the example, but the same steps will work with the Gretel sprites available for download. We'll use multiple sprites to animate the playable character.

Working with Sprite Sheets

When we animated sprites in Scratch, we did so by switching between costumes to create the illusion of movement. Thus far in GameMaker, we've only assigned a single image to each sprite. Now, we'll create animated sprites by using multiple images. A **sprite sheet** is a *collection of images, each representing a different physical expression, merged into one document.* Sprite sheets share characteristics of a flipbook, in which each page depicts a figure with subtle changes that when seen in continuum at a fast past appear to make the figure move. Sprite sheets were commonly used in old-school 2D gaming graphics, and are still used today, even in 3D game platforms for things such as buttons and controls.

GameMaker: Studio uses a similar resource called a **Sprite Strip**. Figure 6-3 shows an example sprite strip for Hansel. In this very basic strip, we see Hansel moving backward with his right foot and then his left. The next two images depict him moving to his right, then the next two indicate forward and the last two to the left. Sprite sheets or strips often contain a plethora of images with significantly more detail, but for our purposes, these few images will serve to create an illusion of movement.

FIGURE 6-3   Hansel Sprite Strip.

If we were to create a sprite from this strip, GameMaker: Studio would default to showing each of these images in progression, making Hansel appear to move backward, right, forward, then left repeatedly. We only want two of these images to show per movement, so we'll create a different sprite for each direction's sprite strip.

Create a new sprite called **sprite-HanselBack**. Choose the **Edit Sprite** button. In the Sprite Editor window choose **File-Create Sprite from Strip**. Navigate to the **HanselBack.png** image. In the **Loading a Strip Image** window, shown in Figure 6-4, indicate the **Number of Images in the Strip**, in this case, **2**. Enter **2 Images Per Row**. The **Image Width** indicates the breadth of each indi-

FIGURE 6-4   Create Sprite from Strip.

vidual section, in this case **32** pixels. The **Image Height** is **42** pixels. These dimensions indicate the points at which the sprite strip should segment into individual images like the costumes in Scratch. Notice that the frames around the images adjust as these numbers change. Click **OK**.

Two distinct images, **Image 0** and **Image 1** should now display in the Sprite Editor window. Click the green checkmark to confirm. In the Sprite Properties window there appears to be only one image assigned to the sprite, but notice that below the Edit Sprite button, text indicates that there are 2 subimages. As highlighted in Figure 6-5, click the green arrow beside **Show** to flip between the two

FIGURE 6-5   Show Subimage.

subimages in the viewing pane. **Cente**r the sprite and click **OK**.

Use the same steps and dimensions to create **spriteHanselFront**, **sprite-HanselRight**, and **spriteHanselLeft**. The settings from the previous sprite strip will remain in each new **Loading a Strip Image** window, so they do not need to be retyped; simply confirm them by clicking OK. Make sure to **Center** each sprite.

Change Object Depth

Create **objectHansel**, but do not initially assign any of the Hansel sprites. Change the **Depth** to **–10** as indicated in Figure 6-6. This will place objectHansel

FIGURE 6-6   Set Depth.

in front of the other objects, such as objectWoodcutterHouse or objectGingerbreadHouse. In Scratch, we used the Go Back () Layers block to stack objects on top of the stage and rearrange their order. In GameMaker: Studio, a negative depth value brings an object closer to the viewer, while a positive depth value pushes it further back.

Change Sprite

Create a **KeyPress** event for the **Left** key. Ask the students which two actions should happen when the left key is pressed. The first is one that we used in the last chapter. From the Move tab, drag the **Move Fixed** icon in to the **Actions** area. Naturally, the **Direction** should be the same as the direction of the **KeyPress** event, **Left** in this case. Since the sprites moving in this game are significantly smaller than the last, we'll set the **Speed** to a smaller, slower value, **3**.

The second action that should happen when a directional key is pressed is that the sprite should switch to that direction's sprite strip. From the **Main 1** tab, add the first icon in the sprite section, **Change Sprite**. As shown in Figure 6-7, choose **spriteHanselLeft** from the dropdown menu to indicate the

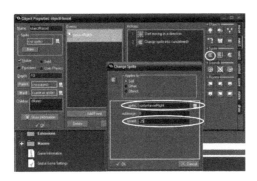

FIGURE 6-7   Change Sprite.

sprite to which the object should change. The **subimage** number may be left at **0** as Image 0 is the first in the array of images in the strip. Finally, set the **Speed** to **.25**. The **image speed** *refers to the rate, in steps, at which the instance cycles through the sub-images.* An image speed of 1 changes the sub-image each step. With the default speed of the room set to 30, this would mean that the sub-image would change 30 times per second. An animation of this speed would be difficult for the human eye to distinguish into distinct motions. With an image speed of .25, each subimage will remain for four steps, slowing down the animation appearance significantly. Once students see the instance of objectHansel moving about the maze, they may choose to come back and change the animation speed. Complete the steps above for each direction **KeyPress Left: Right**, **Up**, and **Down**.

Starting Image

Because the object does not have an assigned sprite, we need to tell it which sprite should display when an instance first generates, such as the beginning of the game. Otherwise, Hansel will be invisible until we press a directional key. Add a **Create** event. Once again, move the **Change Sprite** block into the actions area. Choose the starting sprite for objectHansel, for instance **sprite-HanselFront**. Choose the preferred **Subimage (0 or 1)**, and then set the **Speed** to **0**. This static subimage will serve as the sprite until a directional key is pressed. Place an instance of objectHansel at the starting position in **room-Woods**. Save and test.

Stop Animation without Changing Sprite

In the previous test the instance of objectHansel should switch costume and direction with each directional key press, but there's no way to stop him once he starts moving. Just as in our previous game, we also need to tell the object what to do when no key is activated. Add a **Keyboard** event and select **No Key**. For the action, use a **Move Fixed** block with the **stop square** selected at a **Speed** of **0**. The speed in the move fixed block indicates the rate at which the sprite traverses space. This means that although the instance will be stopped in its trajectory, the previous animation will still be active, so the instance of objectHansel will appear to walk in place. Save and test to see this in action.

To make Hansel appear to stop walking, but not change the direction he is facing, we need to change the image speed, but *not* the sprite. The block that we've been using requires us to do both, so we'll add a little custom code to get around this impediment. Open **objectHansel** again. From the **Control** tab, select the first icon in the Code section, **Execute Code**. GameMaker: Studio has a built in variable named **image_speed**. All we need to do is reset its value. As shown in Figure 6-8, type the following line into the code editor.

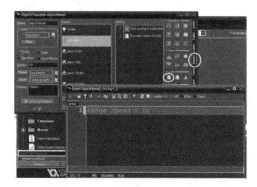

```
image_speed = 0;
```

Click the **green checkmark** to save the code and close the window. Click **OK** and save and test again. Now, when a directional key is pressed, the variable image_speed will set to .25, but when no key is pressed, it will reset to 0, stopping the animation.

FIGURE 6-8   Execute a Piece of Code.

Game Maker Grimmer Step 3: Health

Currently, we can navigate Hansel through the maze, but there is no consequence for veering off of the path, so that players may simply navigate directly from one house to the other without consequence. We'll change this now by introducing a new, popularly requested element, health.

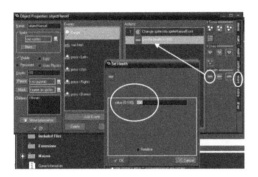

FIGURE 6-9   Starting Value of Health.

Set Starting Value of Health

Reopen **objectHansel** and select the **Create** event. From the **Score** tab, select the first icon in the Health area, **Set Health**. Like Score, Health is a built-in variable in GameMaker: Studio. As shown in Figure 6-9, this block will coexist with the previously assigned Change Sprite action. The order of the actions does not matter significantly in this case, as they'll happen close enough to simultaneously as to not affect the game. To give the playable character full health when it spawns, set the value to **100,** and click **OK**.

FIGURE 6-10   Set Health Relative to Previous Value.

Deduct Health on Collision

Add a **Collision** with **objectTree** event. Ask students which action and setting we should use to subtract from the value of health. Just as in when working with Set Score, we'll place a negative value in the **Set Health** action and check the **Relative** box, so that the collision causes a reduction in the previous value of Health, rather than resetting Health to the designated value.

Draw Health

Finally, we need a way for the game player to track her health. We'll accomplish this by creating a health bar. Start by creating **objectHealth**. Do not assign a sprite. Set the **Depth** to **–20** to make sure that it always appears above other objects. Add a new event. Select **Draw** and then **Draw**. From the Score tab, add the third block in the Health area, **Draw Health**.

As shown in Figure 6-11, we need to set four coordinates for the health bar. The first coordinate, x1, indicates how far from the left boundary the health bar will start. For instance, in the example, the code **view_xview[0]+25** indicates the left edge of the health bar will be 25 pixels from the left edge of the room. Copy this code and paste it into the x2 box. Update the coordinate value to 125, so that x2=**view_xview[0]+**

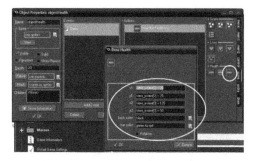

FIGURE 6-11   Draw Health Bar.

125. This code determines the placement of the right edge of the health bar. In this example, the right edge of the health bar will be 125 pixels from the left edge of the room. The health bar, therefore, will be 100 pixels wide, so that each horizontal pixel of the health bar represents one point.

Next, enter the y values. The first y value determines where the top of the health bar will be in relation to the top of the room, and the second reflects the distance of the bottom of the health bar from the top of the room. Set **y1** to **view_yview[0]+25**. Set y2 to **view_yview[0]+125**.

Finally, design the appearance of the health bar. The **Back Color** indicates which solid color, if any, will sit behind the bar color, becoming visible as health disappears. The **Bar Color** default is green to red, so that the color grows increasingly warmer as health dissipates. Students may also choose white to black, or a single color. Click **OK** to save the options, and then place an instance of objectHealth in **roomWoods**. Save and test. The health bar should slide away to the left when objectHansel runs into each instance of objectTree.

Adjust Health Loss Rate

Because the value of health is lowered every thirtieth of a second that the collision continues to occur, health may drop too rapidly to give players a fair chance. Ask students how they think they could adjust this. One way would be to return to the collision event in objectHansel, and change the Set Health value to **.5** or another decimal number.

Game Maker Grimmer Step 4: Timer

In our game so far we can see when health runs out, but the game continues to run. In this step, we'll create a timer, and use it, combined with Health to determine a player's outcome. Before we dig into the timer code, we need to create **roomWin** and **roomLose**, just as we did for the Twelve Huntsmen. For now, simply create the rooms and assign a unique **Background Color** to each.

Create Timer

Start by creating **objectTimer**, and give it a **Create** event. We'll use this event to set the starting number of seconds and to trigger the beginning of a count down. From the **Control** tab, add **Execute Code** into the actions area. First, we need to create a global variable called seconds. Just as in Scratch, global variables could be read and changed by any sprite, in GameMaker: Studio **global variables** *can be read, changed, and used by all object instances at any time.* To define a global variable, place the prefix *global* followed by a period prior to the variable name. This method will need to be used each time the variable is used in the code. Add the following into the first line to set the timer to one minute, or 60 seconds:

FIGURE 6-12   Create Timer.

```
global.seconds = 60;
```

Next, we need to create a global variable called *count_down* and set it to true. Do so with the following line:

```
global.count_down = true;
```

We'll use this variable in an if/then statement in our next bit of code.

Countdown Timer

We've set how many seconds we want in the game, and we've set count_ down to true, but we haven't yet coded how the count down will happen. To do this we need to create a new **Step-Step Event**. Remind students that a Step-Step event reoccurs at the room speed, in this case, 30 times per second, so it is somewhat similar to a Forever loop in Scratch. The actions in the Step-Step event happen over and over while the game is running.

Once again add the action **Execute Code**. We'll start by testing if the value of *count_down* is equal to *true*. Note that as you type the first line of the statement, indicated below in bold, the variable must be represented exactly as it was when created. For instance, *global.countDown* is a different variable than *global.countdown* or *global.count_down*.

```
if (global.count_down = true)
```

Below this line, we need to indicate what should happen if this test is true. In Scratch we would put this information in the mouth of the if/then block. In

GameMaker Language (GML), it goes between brackets. Add the brackets to the code and skip a line between. It should now read:

```
if (global.count_down == true)
{

}
```

If *global.count_down* is true, which we know it is because we made it true in the create event, we want to decrease the value of *global.seconds*. Remind students that this will be happening 30 times a second because the if/then statement is inside of a step event. If we count down by 1 each step, the value of global.seconds will be 0 in 2 seconds. To avoid this, we'll subtract 1 divided by the value of the room's speed, in this case, 30. Since room_speed is a built in variable, we can simply type **room_speed** into the code. By using the variable name, we won't need to update our code later if we decide to change the speed of the room because the value will automatically update. Update the code by adding the line between the brackets:

```
if (global.count_down = true)
{
global.seconds = 1/room_speed;
}
```

Sometimes the typing and syntax involved with text-based coding feels overwhelming to new programmers, but remind students that the logical process is the same as that which we used in Scratch. Figure 6-13 translates what we just did in GML into Scratch.

FIGURE 6-13 Countdown Time Scratch Translation.

Test Health and Time

We'll continue working in this **Execute Code** action. Add another **If/Then** statement to the previous code. It is helpful to skip a line between sections.

```
if (global.count_down == true)
{
global.seconds -= 1/room_speed;
}

if ()
{

}
```

In the parentheses of the first new if/then statement we'll test if global.seconds is less than one or if health is less than one. If either time or health has run out, the condition will be true. Remember that Health, styled as *health* in GML, is a built-in variable, so we didn't need to define it in the same way as global.seconds and global.count_down. We'll use the Boolean operator *or* to combine the variable checks.

```
if (global.count_down == true)
{
global.seconds -= 1/room_speed;
}

if (global.seconds <1) or (health <1)
{
}
```

Finally, we need to add the action to take if either condition is true. We'll use the function **room_goto (),** which is the same as the icon we used in the Twelve Huntsmen: Go to Different Room. Update the script with the function, designating the destination room between the parentheses. Figure 6-14 shows the final, full code to start the timer and check the variables. Figure 6-15 translates the same code into Scratch for comparison. After updating the code, save and test the game.

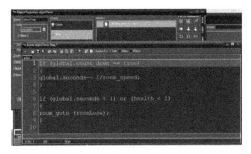

FIGURE 6-14 Countdown Time and Test Variables.

```
if (global.count_down == true)
{
global.seconds -= 1/room_speed;
}

if (global.seconds <1) or
(health <1)
{
room_goto (roomLose);
}
```

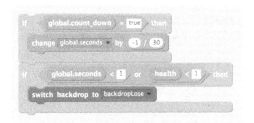

FIGURE 6-15 Full Code Scratch Translation.

Draw Time

We used the Draw event to create a visual representation of the health remaining. Now, we'll use it to create a visual representation of the time remaining. Open **objectTime** and add a **Draw-Draw** event. Once again, add the action **Execute Code**.

The first line of code will set the color to use for the drawing by using the **draw_set_color** function. A list of built-in color constants is available from the "Color and Blending" section of the

GameMaker: Studio Web Online Help System. A direct link to that article is available in the References section of this book. Several of the color terms may be easily guessed using standard syntax, for instance, c_red, c_orange, c_yellow, c_green, c_blue, c_purple, and c_black produce the expected results. The example shown in Figure 6-16 calls a more specific hue: lime green. Start the code with the following line, replacing the color as desired:

FIGURE 6-16   Draw Timer.

```
draw_set_color (c_lime)
```

The second line of code includes the coordinates at which the value of variable *global.seconds* will be drawn. Our health bar's right edge is 125 pixels from the left edge, so setting the **x value** in the code below to **150** will place the timer to the right of the health bar with a 25-pixel separation. The health bar starts 25 pixels down from the top of the room, and continues to 50 pixels down from the top. By setting the **y value** to **37.5** in the example code below, we'll center the timer vertically to the health bar.

```
draw_text (150, 37.5, (global.seconds));
```

Game Maker Grimmer Step 5: Win with Collision

Right now, players of our game lose if they run out of time or if they run out of health, but they will always run out of time because we have no way to stop the clock when Hansel reaches the Gingerbread House. Thus, players will always lose. One simple solution is to Open **objectHansel** and create a **Collision** event with **objectGingerbread** House. From the Main1 tab, drag in a **Go to Room** block and set it to **roomWin**. Save and test. Make sure to test each possibility. Allow time to run out before reaching the Gingerbread house, but save some health. The room should switch to **roomLose**. Also try running out of health before time is up. Again, the room should switch roomLose. Finally, navigate Hansel safely to the Gingerbread house in time while maintaining health. The room should finally switch to roomWin!

Game Maker Grimmer Step 6: Sounds

Let's put the finishing touches on our project by adding sound effects. Game-Maker: Studio accepts either .mp3 or .wav sound files. As always, make sure to guide students through obtaining properly licensed files. The sound effect used in the first example that follows comes from Zapsplat.com, a website that makes numerous, high-quality sound effects available for free for commercial and non-commercial purposes. They may be incorporated into a game, presentation, movie, or other projects that is shared publicly. The standard license, however, does not allow for redistribution of the downloaded sound effects, so the file used in the example is *not* available from the resource link in the Appendix. Students will need to go to the site directly to download their own. Instructors might also choose to download a file onto each computer prior to class. This may be a good option for those working with youth, as Zapsplat .com requires users to create a free account with a valid email address in order to download files. Instructors and students may also prefer to record their own sound effects using other devices and software.

Create a Sound Effect

In this section, we'll add a sound to alert players that **objectHansel** is touching an **objectTree** instance. The sound used in the example is that of footsteps in the forest, with twigs breaking and leaves rustling. Students might also choose a wood chop sound or a more modern alarm sound.

Our first step, after downloading or otherwise acquiring a sound file, is to bring that file into the GameMaker: Studio project's resource tree. Right-click on the **Sound** folder or click the speaker shaped **Create Sound** icon in the toolbar. In the **Sound Properties** window, name the new resource, continuing to use the convention of using the resource type as a prefix, as shown in Figure 6-18 with the example **SoundTwigs**. Click the folder icon to **Load the Sound from a File**. Open the saved sound file, and then click **OK** to close the window.

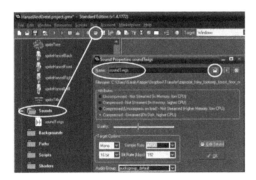

FIGURE 6-17   Create Sound.

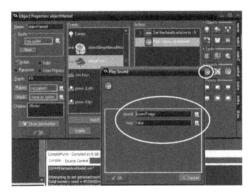

FIGURE 6-18   Play Sound on Collision.

We'll now add a **Play Sound** action to an event that we've already programmed. Challenge students to try to figure out where and how to add the sound, based on what they know so far. They'll open **objectHansel**, navigate to the **Collision** event with **objectTree**, and then from the **Main1** tab, add the **Play Sound** action. As shown in Figure 6-18, make sure to select the appropriate sound from the dropdown list, and set the **Loop** to **False**. The loop in this case would be a forever loop, so that the collision would trigger the sound to start, but the loop would keep it repeating even after the Hansel and the Tree are no longer colliding. By setting the loop to false the sound will only play once per step while the collision is true. Save and test the game.

In the test, the sound likely repeated more than desired. The collision event triggers the sound to play at each step of the collision, 30 times per second, so the sound files overlap each other creating a distortion. The strategy we employed works well if one of the instances is destroyed upon collision, such as in a shooting game, so it's good for students to keep it in mind as they design and create their own games. For this game, however, we'll need to use a different method with some custom coding. Reopen **objectHansel**, and delete the **Play Sound** action from the **Collision-Tree** event.

Play Sound at the Beginning of a Collision

Open the **Create** event in **objectHansel**. From the **Control** tab, add an **Execute Code** block. When the instance of objectHansel spawns, at the beginning of the game, the code will run, defining a custom variable. As shown in Figure 6-19, type the name of the new variable, **readySound,** into the code editor, and then define it as **true**. Click the green check mark to save and close.

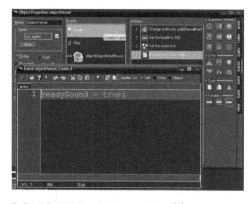

```
readySound = true;
```

FIGURE 6-19   Create a Variable.

Staying in objectHansel, create a new **Step-Step** event. Assign an **Execute Code** action. Begin with an **If-Then-Else** statement.

```
if ()
{
}
else
{
}
```

Next we'll set the condition to test, which is if the instance of objectHansel is colliding with an instance of objectTree. We'll use the **place_meeting (x, y, obj)** function. This function *checks for a collision between the host object and another object at particular coordinates*. Add it into the code, leaving x and y to represent the object's current x and y values, and naming the other object in the collision. Make sure to type the name of the other object correctly. The software often prompts users with the names of defined resources as they type. The appropriate resource may be inserted by clicking on the option from the list.

```
if (place_meeting(x, y, objectTree))
{
}
else
{
}
```

If the collision condition is true, then we'll run another test to see if the variable **readySound** equals true. We know that it will be true initially because of our code in the **Create** event. So the first time Hansel runs into a tree, the collision event will be true and readySound will be true, so the code in the bracket below the **if (readySound)** statement will run. That code will do two things: play soundTwigs and change readySound to false. Update the code with the following:

```
if (place_meeting(x, y, objectTree))
{
   if (readySound)
   {audio_play_sound(soundTwigs, 10, false);
   readySound = false;
   }
}
else
{
}
```

The **audio_play_sound (index, priority, loop)** function *runs the selected audio file.* The first argument, index, indicates the sound to be played. The second argument, priority, determines if this sound should be played over other sounds. Lower priority sounds will stop if a sound with a higher priority is also playing. Finally the loop argument should be set to **True** or **False** to indicate if the sound should repeat or not.

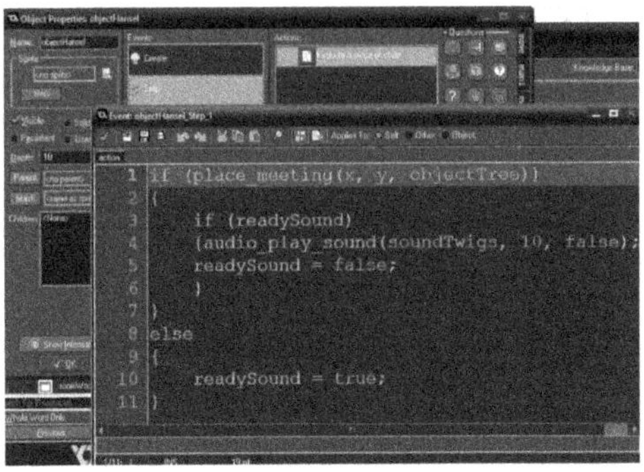

In our code, the sound will play, and then **readySound** will switch to false. This means that though the collision if statement might still be true if Hansel remains touching the tree a step later, the second needed condition to play the sound, ready-Sound equals true, is not. We'll use the **else** section to reset readySound to true. Once Hansel is no longer colliding with a tree, the sound will be ready to play again when triggered by another collision. Update the code as shown in the following coding and in Figure 6-20. Once the code is updated, save and test. The sound should only play at the initial tree contact.

FIGURE 6-20 If Collision and True Then Play and Set to False, Else True.

```
if (place_meeting(x, y, objectTree))
{
  if (readySound)
  {audio_play_sound(soundTwigs, 10, false);
  readySound = false;
  }
}
else
{
  readySound = true;
}
```

Play Background Music

At times we may just want music to play throughout the game, or while in a certain room. We can do this by simply placing a **Play Sound** action in a **Create** event of an object in the appropriate room. The audio file provided, **BrotherComeAndDanceWithMe.mp3**, contains the melody of a song from the nineteenth-century opera *Hänsel Und Gretel* by Engelbert Humperdinck. It's a very upbeat, bright little tune, so let's place it in **roomWin.**

First, we need to create **soundBrotherDance** and upload the file to it, as we did when creating soundTwigs. Next, create **objectWin**, and a **Create** event. As shown in Figure 6-21, select the same **Play Sound** action that we used previously, but change the selected file to **soundBrotherDance** and set the **Loop** to **True**. Place **objectWin** in **roomWin**. Save and test. The music should start playing when the player wins and repeat until the window is closed.

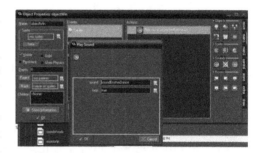

FIGURE 6-21   Loop Sound.

Game Maker Grimmer Step 7: Room Upgrades

Now that the critical functions of the game have all been addressed, students can use their strengthened skills to customize their games. Many will likely want to add spriteWin and spriteLose to the appropriate rooms as we did in the Twelve Huntsmen game, adding in keyboard events to replay or close the game.

Title Screen

If students use image or sound files that require attribution, such as downloaded effects from Zapslat.com, they'll need to add a note somewhere in the game. A title screen or splash screen is a great way to do this. Brainstorm

FIGURE 6-22 Title Screen Example.

with students about what information might go on the title screen, such as the game name, the game designer's name, contributors, attributions, instructions for how to play, and more.

Create a new sprite called **spriteTitle**. In the sprite editor, set the dimensions to the same as the room, 1024 by 768. Use the **Text** tool to add information. Instruct viewers which key to press to start the game. In the example in Figure 6-22, users would press **Enter** to begin.

Create **objectTitle**, and assign **spriteTitle** to it. Add a **Keyboard** event for the appropriate key. Add a **Go to Room** action and select **roomWoods**. Because the code to start the time lives in objectTimer, and the only instance of that object is in roomWoods, the time won't start until the room generates, after the player pushes the start key.

Click and drag **roomTitle** to the top of the rooms list in the resource tree. It will now appear first when the game runs. Add an instance of **objectTitle** to roomTitle. Save and test. The title screen should appear first, and then disappear when the key is struck.

Level Up with Rooms

So far, players win by navigating Hansel to the gingerbread house, but we know that in the story, this is only part of his journey. After he and Gretel have their adventure, they must find their way home. We can complete the story line by adding another level to our game.

Since many of the elements will be the same, we can simply right-click on **roomWoods** and select **Duplicate**. Open the new room and name it **roomLevel2**. Delete **objectWoodcutterHouse** and **objectGingerbreadHouse** from the room, but *not* the resource tree. We still need them for level 1 in roomWoods.

In the first level the collision between objectHansel and objectGingerbreadHouse triggered a change in rooms. We need to update this so that the player now goes to **roomLevel2** instead of **roomWin.** Go to **objectHansel**. Open the collision event with **objectGingerbreadHouse**, and change the **Different Room** parameter to **roomLevel2**. Save and test.

Now, when objectHansel collides with objectGingerbreadHouse, the player should be taken to roomLevel2. At this point the maze is identical, but there are no houses, so there is nothing with which objectHansel can collide to trigger the switch to roomWin. We'll address that now.

Duplicate **objectWoodcutterHouse** and **objectGingerbreadHouse**, and name them **objectWoodcutter2** and **objectGingerbread2,** respectively. Open objectGingerbread2 and add a **Create** event. From the **Move** tab, select a **Jump to Position** action. This **Applies to objectHansel**. Set the **x position** to **10** and the **y position** to **–10**. These settings, shown in Figure 6-23 will place the objectHansel instance at the front door of the objectGingerbread2 at the start of level two. Why did we need to create a new gingerbread house object for level 2? Discuss with the students that if we had placed the Jump to Position action in object-GingerbreadHouse, the instance of objectHansel would, at the launch of the room, go immediately to the gin-

FIGURE 6-23   Jump to Position.

gerbread house, and that collision would now cause roomLevel2 to launch, causing objectHansel to jump again to objectGingerbread house, an endless cycle that wouldn't allow players to actually move or play.

Likewise, we needed to create a duplicate woodcutter's house, because in level 2, we want Hansel's collision with it to trigger a change to roomWin. Open **objectWoodcutter2**. Add a collision event with **objectHansel**, and set the action to **Go to Different Room—roomWin**.

Return to **roomLevel2**. Place an instance of **objectWoodcutter2** at the destination point and an instance of **objectGingerbread2** at the starting point. Rearrange the **objectTree** instances to give players a different, more challenging maze. Save and test. Now, when players reach the gingerbread house, level 2 should start, and players will get fresh health and time to make their way back. When they reach the woodcutter house, they will win.

Following the same steps, students may add multiple levels, and incorporate more sprites and objects to add different obstacles, such as ponds, rock formations, and more. GameMaker: Studio's robust online community provides peer-to-peer support as users dig deeper into coding with the GameMaker Language. As we move forward with more text-based coding, students will begin to recognize patterns between programming languages.

7

Intro to Python

According to Python's creator Guido van Rossum, he began developing the programming language over Christmas break in 1989 and released it to the world in 1991. Since then Python use continues to grow rapidly, due in large part to its readability and comparatively natural syntax. It consistently ranks in the top ten of the TIOBE Programming Community Index, standing in fifth place and rising as of October, 2017. In their 2017 rankings IEEE Spectrum listed Python as number one.

Of course, opinions about the best programming languages are subjective, and depend a great deal on the intentions of the user. Where Python really shines is in the classroom, as users who are still learning to build computational thinking skills find themselves less hindered by overly complicated syntax. The Raspberry Pi® single-board computer, designed to help beginners learn to code, uses Python as its main programming language; indeed, it was built to do so. Yet, Python's applications extend well beyond the classroom. The online community Reddit is built on Python, and it is one of the seven languages supported by the Google App Engine.

Though the games we create with Python will be less visually spectacular than those we created in Scratch and GameMaker: Studio, what makes learning Python equally or more exciting is that students are learning a programming language used in the real world by professional programmers. Knowledge of Python can help them create apps, learn other languages, succeed in college programming courses, and find work as programmers. As an instructor, make sure to emphasize to students that this is only the first of many text-based languages that they will explore, and each will get easier to learn as they transfer knowledge from one to the other.

INTRO TO PYTHON: PREPARATION

The Python Software Foundation oversees continuing advancement of open-source technology related to the Python programming language. Visit their website at www.python.org to keep up with latest news, read inspirational success stories of how Python is being used in numerous fields, and, most importantly for us, download Python. The website also includes a helpful Beginner's Guide, FAQs, and numerous supportive resources.

Download the latest stable version of Python 3 for your operating system. Python is free, so if you are prompted for payment, make sure you are in the right place. The Python download will include a free program called IDLE (Integrated DeveLopment Environment) There are numerous integrated development environments, typically referred to as IDEs, but IDLE was specifically created for working with Python. This program includes a text editor with syntax highlighting, auto completion, and other features that make it easier to correctly type and format code. It also includes a Python shell in which programs will run. The shell provides syntax highlighting to make it easier to locate mistakes—and there will be mistakes.

Intro to Python: Materials Needed and Set-up

The only materials needed for this activity are computers with Python 3 installed, copies of the printable handout from the link in the Appendix, and a projector for the instructor.

Once again, it is ideal to set up the student computers so that the instructor can see their screens. Students typically require a fair amount of help troubleshooting when first using text-based languages, so consider assigning students into troubleshooting partners or teams.

Intro to Python: Outcomes

Participants will transfer and build upon computational thinking skills and coding vocabulary gained in previous activities.

Participants will develop familiarity working with integrated development environments.

Participants will augment their ability to troubleshoot errors.

Participants will gain knowledge of Python syntax and terminology.

INTRO TO PYTHON: PYTHON ORIENTATION

Run the **Python IDLE.** The Python shell should launch, displaying the Python version and copyright information. The top line in the window should indicate that you are using a version of **Python 3,** rather than Python 2. Click the **File** menu at the top, and select **New File.** Throughout our work with Python we'll keep these two types of windows open. The new file that we just created is an editor window. The **editor** is *used to create, edit, and save Python programs.* The original window that opened is the **shell,** which *is used to run python programs.*

Python Orientation: Write and Run a Program

Let's see the editor and shell in action. Enter the following code in the editor:

```
print ("Hello World!")
```

This program uses the **print()** function which simply *displays the content between the brackets in the shell*. The content in this case is a **string**, *a sequence of characters*. Strings must be opened with a single or double quotation mark and closed with the same type of punctuation. The quotations will not print when the program runs.

The program must be saved before it can run. Return to the **File** menu and choose **Save As**. Name the file **HelloWorld.py**. Make sure to keep the .py extension, so that the shell will recognize the file as a Python file. Go to the **Run** menu and select **Run Module** to run the program in the shell window. The message should appear without quote marks. Congratulations! You've just written your first Python program!

Python Orientation: Errors

Of course, it's possible that your first program did not run smoothly, and, even if it did, it's almost certain that you'll run into an error message at some point. While this can be frustrating, Python IDLE tries to help users easily diagnose and fix mistakes.

EOL Error

For instance, if we tried to run the code shown in Figure 7-1, we would get the pop-up message, "EOL while scanning string literal," and then the line with the error would be highlighted in the editor window. An EOL, or **End of Line error** means that *Python reached the end of a line while still in a string.* Typically this is caused by not properly surrounding the string with quotes. In the example in Figure 7-1, the final quotation is missing. The same error message and highlight would appear if the programmer used a combination of single and double quotations such as ("Hello World!').

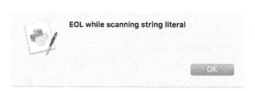

Name Error

Another common error will show up in the shell. A **Name Error** means that *Python does not recognize the function or variable name used in the program*. For instance, in Figure 7-2

FIGURE 7-1   EOL Error and Highlight.

FIGURE 7-2   Name Error.

a Name Error appears because the coder typed "pint" instead of "print." Print is a recognized function. Pint is not. The coder can address this by simply returning to the HelloWorld.py file in the editor and fixing the typo.

Our program so far only has one line, but as we create more complex programs with multiple lines of code, finding the error can become more difficult. Fortunately, there's a tool to help. Right-click on the line named in the error message. In Figure 7-2, this is line 2. Select **Go to File/Line**. The editor window should open with the offending line highlighted in grey. Keep in mind that sometimes the typo causing the error is actually a line above or below the line highlighted.

Syntax Error

An **Invalid Syntax** error message means that *Python does not know how to interpret a line.* This is one of the most common error messages because it can be caused by a simple typo, using the minus symbol instead of an underscore,

FIGURE 7-3   Invalid Syntax.

confusing upper or lower case letters, or using different types of brackets. It can also be caused by improper use of functions. In Figure 7-3 the error message results from incorrectly defining a variable.

Coders of all ages and skill levels encounter errors regularly. The important thing is not to always code perfectly the first time, but to be able to resiliently identify and learn from mistakes. Encourage students to go through the following checklist to address errors before asking for help from the instructor.

- Read the error message. It often tells you exactly what is wrong.
- Look for red.
- Look for grey using file/line.
- Check spelling.
- Check spacing.
- Confirm single or double quotes.
- Check your code line by line against the instructions.
- Ask a peer to check your code.

With these practices in mind, let's dig into coding with Python by making our first game.

INTRO TO PYTHON: GUESS THE NUMBER

Students are often a bit intimidated when starting out with a text-based programming language. Help them gain traction by reminding them that Scratch and GameMaker: Studio employ many of the same principles used in Python. Indeed, Scratch is designed to introduce coding concepts, so students may be surprised by how much they already know. Throughout this section, we'll use figures translating the code between Python and Scratch to help students make connections. In fact, we'll be creating the same basic game that we made in the Cat Got Your Number? activity in Chapter 2. Open a new file. Save it as **GuessTheNumber.py.**

Guess the Number Step 1: Variables and Functions

Just as we did in the Cat Got Your Number? game, we'll ask players to try to guess a secret number between 1 and 20. We'll want to limit the number of guesses the player may take. The first step in that process is to create a variable called **guessesTaken.**

Variables

To define a variable in Python, simply type the desired name of the variable followed by the equal sign and then the starting value. We'll create a variable called **guessesTaken** and assign it a value of **0**. Type the following into the editor window.

```
guessesTaken = 0
```

Variables can also contain strings. Define a variable called **myName** and assign it your name or someone else's. Remember that strings need to be surrounded by quotation marks. Figure 7-4 shows how defining variables in Python compares with doing so in Scratch.

```
myName = "Sarah"
```

Save and run the program. Nothing may seem to happen, but remember that we didn't say to print anything. In Scratch, created variables are displayed by default on the stage. In Python we can call the

FIGURE 7-4   Define Variables.

value of a variable by typing the variable name into the shell at the prompt and clicking enter. Try calling the values for both variables as shown in Figure 7-4.

Functions

Python, like other programming languages, makes use of **functions**, *bits of code designed to perform a specific task that can be called in a larger program*. There are numerous functions prebuilt into Python. Users can call them to add particular functionality to their programs without having to recreate the wheel. For instance, in the Python Orientation activity, we used the print() function to make the string "Hello World" appear on the screen. Making strings appear on the screen is a pretty common goal, so it follows that all of the individual lines of code required to do so are gathered into an easily reusable function called print(). Functions are essentially a shortcut. We don't need to know how they work exactly. We just need to understand what they do and how to write them.

Input ()

The **input()** function in Python *stops the flow of the program until the user enters a response and submits it with the return key*. We'll use this function to gather the player's name. In the editor, replace the value assigned to myName with the input() function to assign the player's response to that variable.

```
myName = input ()
```

Save and test. In the shell, type a new name, as shown in Figure 7-5 and then hit enter. The name should now be stored in myName. Call the new value by typing myName into the shell at the prompt.

Though this code works, it is a bit confusing. The player would not necessarily know what to enter. Fortunately, the input() function includes an optional prompt string parameter. Update the program in the editor by adding a prompt question in the parentheses. Save and test. The user should be greeted with guidance now.

FIGURE 7-5   Input Equals myName.

```
myName = input ("What is your
name?")
```

Concatenate

Let's add to this code by greeting the player by name. To do this we need to **concatenate,** or combine, a string with the variable myName. Add a print() function. As shown in Figure 7-6, place the greeting string in the print parameter as normal, but add a space before the closing quotation mark. Otherwise, the name will print right next to the greeting. Instead of "Hello Anne" we would see "HelloAnne." Type the plus sign and then the variable name. Save and test.

```
print ("Hello" + myName)
```

FIGURE 7-6   Concatenate String and Variable.png.

Guess the Number Step 2: Random Number

Each time the game is played, we want the secret number to be a different, randomly selected number. To generate a random number we need to import a Python module. **Modules** are *source files that contain reusable code elements such as functions, classes and global variables.* We use modules to keep our program files clean and manageable and to save our selves a lot of work! For instance, we'll import the random module, which is a file that comes with the installation of Python. The file random.py contains hundreds of lines of code that make up a number of pseudo-random number generator functions. We'll be using the function **random.randint (a,b)** which *returns an integer that is greater than or equal to a and less than or equal to b.*

Modules typically import quickly, but not necessarily instantaneously, so the best practice is to place the import statement at the beginning of the program file. Click to the left of the current first line and tap enter or return on the keyboard twice to create some white space. In the first line type:

```
import random
```

Next, we'll use the random. randint(a,b) function to generate a

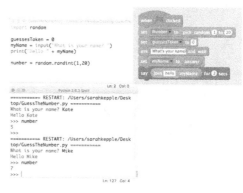

FIGURE 7-7   Generate Random Number. png.

pseudo-random number and assign that value to a variable called number using the following code:

```
number = random.randint(1,20)
```

As shown in Figure 7-7, run the program a few times in the shell. Each time you call the value of number it should be different.

Guess the Number Step 3: Take a Guess

Now that we have a random number for players to try to guess we need to prompt them to do so and evaluate their answers. Add a line at the bottom of the code to explain the game.

```
print ("I'm thinking of number between 1 and 20")
```

Once again, we'll use the input() function to gather a response from the player and assign it to a variable.

```
guess = input ("Take a guess")
```

Int() Function

Even though the player will likely type a number in response, that number is stored in the variable guess as a string. So, if the player's guess was 7, and we called the value of guess in the shell it would print it with quotes just like other strings. When we call guessesTaken there are no quotes because Python recognizes its value as an integer. An **integer** is *a whole number (without decimals)*. We need guess to be understood to be an integer in order to compare it to number. To do this we'll use the int() function which converts a number into an integer. Place this line under the "Take a guess" line.

```
guess = int(guess)
```

If Statements

Simple if statements in Python read very much like plain English. The condition is laid out, and then the command to execute if the condition is true is entered underneath. Just as in Scratch, if the condition is false, the command is skipped. Make sure to use the tab key to indent the command for each statement. Python relies on the indention in tandem with the colon before the indentation to group sections together. Notice that to check that two variables have the same value, we'll use a double equal sign. The single equal sign is an assignment operator (guessesTaken = 0 or myName = "Sarah"), whereas the double equal operator compares.

```
if guess < number:
   print ("Your guess is too low.")

if guess > number:
   print ("Your guess is too high.")

if guess == number:
   print ("That's it!")
```

The example code above uses double quotes to surround strings. If you've been using single quotes, you may run into an issue with the last print command. If entered as print ('That's it!'), only the word "that" would be read as the string because the apostrophe is understood as a closing quotation mark. To avoid this, either use double quotes around a string containing a single quotation or use a backslash to indicate to escape, or ignore, the following character as part of the code.

```
print ("That's it!" or 'That\'s it!')
```

As shown in Figure 7-8, you may wish to temporarily add a command to print the random number prior to guessing. By doing so, the tester knows which numbers to enter to test each "if" statement. Add the following line below the random.randint(1,20) function and then save and test.

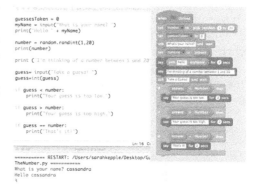

```
print (number)
```

Guess the Number Step 4: Loop and Interruption

FIGURE 7-8 Compare Variable Values.

Just as when we tested the Cat Got Your Number? game after adding the "If () Then" statements, you may have noticed that our program as it stands now will only test the number once. To give the player multiple guesses we need to create a loop.

While Loop

In Scratch, we needed an if () then, else combined with a forever() loop to give the player another guess as long as guessesTaken was less than five. In Python, we can accomplish this with a while loop. A **while** loop *runs the commands it contains as long as a condition is true*. Add the while loop above the print("Take a guess") line. As you'll recall, the colon indicates that an indentation is coming, that commands live inside of the conditional statement, to be executed if true. Indent each of the lines from print ("Take a guess") through if guess == number.

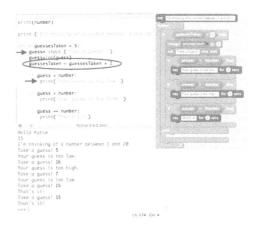

```
print(number)

print ('I'm thinking of a number between 1 and 20')

while guessesTaken < 5:
    guess= input ('Take a guess!')
    guess=int(guess)
    guessesTaken = guessesTaken + 1

    guess < number:
        print('Your guess is too low')

    guess > number:
        print('Your guess is too high')

    guess == number:
        print('That's it!')

                                    Python 3.6.3 Shell
Hello Kyrie
15
I'm thinking of a number between 1 and 20
Take a guess! 5
Your guess is too low.
Take a guess! 16
Your guess is too high.
Take a guess! 7
Your guess is too low.
Take a guess! 15
That's it!
Take a guess! 15
That's it!
>>>
                                                Ln: 274  Col: 4
```

FIGURE 7-9   While guessesTaken Is Less Than Five.

Make sure to indent the print lines inside of each if guess statement as shown in Figure 7-9.

```
while guessesTaken < 5:
```

Each time the player takes a guess, we need to add one to the value of guessesTaken. Add the following line below guess = int(guess)

```
guessesTaken = guessesTaken + 1
```

The full while loop code should look like that in Figure 7-9. Compare your program and then save and test.

Break

As you and your students likely noticed while testing your programs, and as you can see in Figure 7-9's shell window, currently a player may guess the correct number and then be prompted to guess again because there are still guesses remaining. To fix this we'll use a **break** statement, which *terminates the current loop and resumes at the next line after the loop*. Replace the print line under if guess == number with a break statement and then save and test.

```
if guess == number:
    break
```

```
*GuessTheNumber.py - /Users/sarahkepple/Desktop/GuessTheNumber.py (3.6.3)*
import random

guessesTaken = 0
myName = input('What is your name?')
print('Hello ' + myName)

number = random.randint(1,20)

print ('I'm thinking of a number between 1 and 20')

while guessesTaken < 5:
    guess= input ('Take a guess!')
    guess=int(guess)
    guessesTaken = guessesTaken + 1

    if guess < number:
        print("Your guess is too low")

    if guess > number:
        print("Your guess is too high")

    if guess == number:
        break

if guess == number:
    guessesTaken = str(guessesTaken)
    print ('That's it!' + myName + ', you guessed my number in \
        ' + guessesTaken + ' guesses!')

if guess != number:
    number=str(number)
    print('Nope. The number I was thinking of was ' + number)
                                                Ln: 9  Col: 0
```

FIGURE 7-10   Guess the Number Full Program.

Guess the Number Step 5: Closing the Game

With the added break statement, the loop now ends when the player either guesses the correct number or runs out of guesses. Because there is no code after the loop, the game itself ends rather abruptly. Let's add winning and losing messages. We'll use "if" statements to test which message to display. Type the following flush with the left edge of the window, as these loops will be outside of the "while" loop. Notice that we'll use a new operator, **!=**, which means *not equal to*. Save and then test.

```
if guess == number:
    print ("That's it")
```

```
if guess != number:
   print ("Nope.")
```

This code works. The player should learn whether he won or lost, but we can make it a little more elegant by using variables. In the winning message we'll call the player by name and use the guessesTaken variable to display how quickly they got the correct number. To do this, we need to convert the variables that are storing integers into strings so they can be concatenated into the appropriate print message. Just as the int() function to converts a string to an integer, the **str()** function *converts an integer to a string.* Notice the **backslash (\)** in the code below and in Figure 7-10. This slash allows us to wrap the string onto another line so that the complete code is visible in a smaller window.

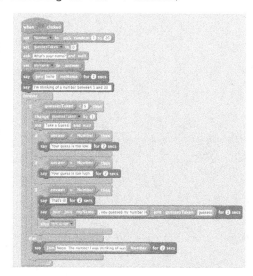

FIGURE 7-11   Guess the Number Full Shell.

```
if guess == number:
   guessesTaken = str(guessesTaken)
   print ("That's it!" + myName +",you guessed my number in" \
   + guessesTaken + "guesses!")

if guess != number:
   number = str(number)
   print("Nope. The number I was thinking of was" + number)
```

Save and test the updated program. Make sure to test for both winning and losing as shown in Figure 7-11. Discuss Figure 7-12, the full program translation in Scratch, with students. How did coding this program in Python compare to coding it in Scratch?

As students gain comfort working with Python they may find it just as easy or easier to navigate than Scratch, but they are typically anxious to find a way to incorporate graphics. In the next chapter we'll explore how to make this happen with an additional resource called Pygame as we continue to develop knowledge of Python.

FIGURE 7-12   Guess the Number Full Scratch Comparison.

8

Pygame

In the previous chapter we created a simple text only game using the built-in functions print() and input() to communicate between the player and the program. This type of game uses a **command line interface**, or CLI, *which prompts and waits for user feedback via the keyboard before responding*. This becomes a bit of a challenge for creating games that continue to run as a user plays. For example, in contrast to our Guess the Number project, in our Game-Maker: Grimm game, we controlled the bootprint with the keyboard, but the rest of the game continued to run, the peas continued to bounce even if no key was pressed.

To create Python games that continue to run without user input and that look more like the games to which we've become accustomed, we'll need to install pygame. **Pygame** is *a free and open source programming language library for creating multimedia projects in Python*. There are numerous Python libraries, and each contains a collection of modules. For example, the random module that we used in our Guess the Number game is included in Python's standard library that is installed automatically with Python. To use other libraries we need to install them separately.

PYGAME: PREPARATION

The best way to install pygame varies depending on the user's operating system and settings, but all approaches will typically require administrator access, which means you'll most likely need assistance from your organization's IT department. Visit the Getting Started page of www.pygame.org to find instructions. The resource link in the Appendix includes additional tips. Though the actual download and install of pygame typically takes only a few minutes, there can be a few complications. Make sure to plan ahead to give yourself or your IT folks enough time to overcome any obstacles.

Pygame: Materials Needed

Participants will need computers with Python 3 and pygame installed, and each will benefit from a copy of the handout. Instructors will want a projector and a copy of the handout. Additionally, the activities in this chapter are based on J. M. Barrie's classic work *Peter Pan*, originally published in novel form as *Peter and Wendy*, so instructors may wish to provide students with copies of the text. Note that in most countries outside of the United Kingdom, copies of the public domain novel are freely available from a wide variety of sources including Project Gutenberg, Apple iBooks, and Overdrive. The play version, *Peter Pan, or the Boy Who Never Grew Up*, remains under copyright at the time of this writing, and of course the Disney animated version and other adaptations retain their own copyrights. Make sure to check the terms of use of the version you intend to use before distributing to the class. Make sure that students have access to the TinkerBell.png file. It will need to be in the same folder that stores the Python files. After installing pygame, you may also wish to download and run the sample code available, like the TinkerBell.png file from the resources link in the Appendix.

Pygame: Outcomes

Participants will expand upon computational thinking skills and coding vocabulary.

Participants will develop familiarity with pygame functions.

Participants will augment knowledge of standard Python functions.

TINKER BELL TRAPPED: GUIDE

Our first pygame activity will be based on the events of the third chapter in *Peter Pan*, "Come Away, Come Away!" in which Peter flies into the nursery in pursuit of his shadow. When he is unable to reunite with it as expected, he wakes Wendy with his crying and the two begin to talk. Tinker Bell the fairy, of course, accompanies Peter, and falls victim to his reckless pursuit of his shadow when she is accidentally shut into a chest of drawers. In this first activity, we'll create a window, representing the chest, and code Tinker Bell to fly around.

Tinker Bell Trapped Step 1: Import and Initialize

Open Python IDLE and create a new file. Save it as **TinkerBell.py**. As we learned in the previous chapter, it is a best practice to import any modules to be used later in the game at the beginning of the program. On the first line add the following line, which is an abbreviated way to import two different modules.

```
import pygame, sys
```

The pygame module provides us with most of the additional functionality that we'll need, and the sys module will close the game when the player exits. Before we can do much with pygame, however, we need to initialize the module. To do this, add the following line.

```
pygame.init()
```

These two lines of code begin almost every pygame you'll write or encounter.

Tinker Bell Trapped Step 2: Set up the Window

In our command line interface game Guess the Number, the user played directly in the shell. Now that we have pygame imported and initialized we can create a program with a **graphical user interface** (GUI), a *visual approach to interacting with a computer employed by most modern operating systems that includes windows and icons*. Early adapters of home computers in the 1980s would have been amazed to see modern Microsoft Windows and Apple Operating Systems, as they were still dependent primarily on command line interfaces. Though some of the classic home computers could run games with graphics, sometimes even getting input from a joystick or other game controller, in order to load, they required prompts from the user to be entered into a command line interface.

Today, of course, virtually every home computer is designed to run a GUI. To open a game, users double-click on its icon on the desktop or in the application menu. We can have multiple windows open, scroll through them, click in or out with the mouse or track pad or even interact using a touch screen. Scratch is both a programming language and a visual programming environment that takes advantage of the host computer's GUI to build, interpret and play games. In GameMaker: Studio we saw a bit of a hybrid in which the software, designed for GUI, allowed us to drag and drop programming blocks, click through the resource tree and click to type in lines of code, and then the software compiled the program into a game that could be played in the GUI. Scratch is a programming language and environment intended to educate. GameMaker: Studio is a programming language and a shortcut tool for creating games. Python, on the other hand, is a straightforward programming language, used by professionals around the world. With Python, we're digging deeper behind the scenes, so to create a GUI game we installed gamepy with the appropriate tools, and now we'll use them to create a GUI game window like we had for GameMaker: Studio.

Comments

Computer programmers tend to use certain conventions to make programs easier to read and edit later. One of these conventions is adding **comments**, which are *notes included about the program without affecting functionality*. In Python, comments begin with a pound symbol (commonly known as a hashtag) and extend to the end of the line. Just as a hashtag comment on a social media post may describe what's happening or mark the post for later reference, a comment beginning with the same tag in Python helps the original programmer remember what each segment is supposed to do, communicate to collaborators about the progress on a section or find that part of the code later. In the IDLE, comments turn red when properly marked. Let's use one to indicate a new segment of the code that we'll use to set up the game window. Skip a line to indicate a new segment and then add the following.

```
#set up the window
```

Window Size

To create the window, we'll start by giving it a variable name, in this case **displayWindow**. Next, we'll use the pygame function **display.set_mode()** to create a **Pygame Surface** object which *produces a two-dimensional rectangle*. Since this function comes from the pygame module, we need to use **pygame** as a prefix.

```
#set up the window
gameWindow = pygame.display.set_mode
```

To finish the function, we need to set the dimensions of the rectangle in pixels. Just as in the other languages with which we've worked, these dimensions are set in pixels, width first and then height. Update the code with the dimensions. Remember to place them in their own parentheses.

```
#set up the window
gameWindow = pygame.display.set_mode((640, 480))
```

Window Caption

There won't be anything in our window yet, so let's give it a caption, so we can identify it as ours. Add the Pygame **display.set_caption()** function with an appropriate caption for the game such as "Tinker Bell Trapped."

```
#set up the window
gameWindow = pygame.display.set_mode((640, 480))
pygame.display.set_caption('Tinker Bell Trapped')
```

Tinker Bell Trapped Step 3: Game Loop

Every game that we've made so far, and likely every video game your students will ever make uses the concept of the game loop, central to video game design. The **game loop** *is generally composed of three phases; respond to events, update, and render, which cycle continuously as the game runs.* In

Scratch the When Green Flag Clicked block triggers the beginning of such a cycle and then placing other blocks inside of a Forever loop causes the cycle to continue until a trigger such as clicking the red stop sign breaks the loop. In GameMaker: Studio, running the program causes the game loop to begin. We added events to objects, and those events each had actions that ran if the event condition was true. In both cases the software did a lot of the heavy lifting to set up the overall game loop. In Python, and other text-based languages, we'll create our game loop ourselves. Skip a line and then add a new comment for the game loop section.

```
#game loop
```

Add a while loop. This while loop equates to a Forever loop because it checks to see if True = True.

```
#game loop
while True:
```

For Loop

Inside of the while loop, we'll place a **for** loop which *iterates through a sequence in order*. The for loop is often used to repeat a chunk of code a set number of times. For instance, the following example, which we won't use in our game loop would print "hi" three times. Enter it into the shell to try it yourself.

```
for x in range (0,3):
    print("hi")
```

In our game loop, we'll use the for loop to cycle through the game events. Add the "for" loop to the game loop section.

```
#game loop
while True:
    for event in pygame.event.get():
```

Pygame Event.get()

Each time certain triggers take place, such as pressing a key or clicking the mouse, a pygame event object is created in the pygame library. It may help to think of this as a record or receipt for each action instance. In the for loop we used the **pygame.event.get()** function *which returns a list of event objects that have happened since the last time the function was called*. So, when the game first starts, no events will have happened, but in a few minutes perhaps a key press event has occurred and then a mouse click and then a key press again. The pygame.event.get() function would return a list with the key press as the first event, the mouse click as the second and then key press as the third. On each iteration of the for loop, the variable *event* will be assigned the value of next event object. In the next step we'll use an if statement to see if the event is one that will cause our game to end.

Event Type

Pygame event objects each have a type identifier. We want the game to keep running as long as the type of event is a key press or mouse click, or other such interactive playing types of events, but we want the game to end if the event type is **pygame.QUIT**. We'll add in an if statement to check to see if the type of the event object currently assigned to our variable event (the latest event object) is in fact a pygame.QUIT type of event.

```
#game loop
while True:
    for event in pygame.event.get():
        if event.type == pygame.QUIT:
```

Closing the Game

If it is a quit type of event object, then, of course, we want the game to end. To do this we'll run two functions to close out the game. The first is **pygame.quit()** which *reverses the initialization process, deactivating the pygame library*. Theoretically, this function is automatically called when the Python interpreter shuts down; however, there can be issues with IDLE if it is not explicitly included. The pygame.quit() function doesn't actually quit the program. To do that we'll also need a sys.exit() function. Update the game loop's if statement.

```
#game loop
while True:
    for event in pygame.event.get():
        if event.type == pygame.QUIT:
            pygame.quit()
            sys.exit()
```

Update the Game

We've covered two out of the three parts of a classic game loop. We've initially rendered the game and we've created an if statement to respond to events, but we still need to update the game if there has not been a quit event type. To do this, we'll add a **pygame display.update()** function *which redraws the surface object returned by pygame.display.set_mode()*. This is a bit like a refresh in a browser window. At this point, nothing about our surface object, which we stored in gameWindow has changed, so we won't see a change as the same black window regenerates. Check your full code as follows, and then save and test. A black window should appear with the designated caption. If everything goes well, you should be able to close the window by clicking on the x, but if there are hiccups simply *type* **quit()** to *force the shell to exit the program.*

```
import pygame, sys
pygame.init()

#set up the window
gameWindow = pygame.display.set_mode((640, 480))
pygame.display.set_caption('Tinker Bell Trapped')

#game loop
while True:
    for event in pygame.event.get():
        if event.type == pygame.QUIT:
            pygame.quit()
            sys.exit()

    pygame.display.update()
```

Tinker Bell Trapped Step 4: Frames per Second

When we worked with Game-Maker: Studio, we could set the speed of each room, which equated to steps per second, or how many times the room refreshed per second. In Python speed is equivalent to **frame rate** or **refresh rate**. We can set the frame

FIGURE 8-1   Tinker Bell Game Window.

rate by creating a pygame time.Clock object. We'll assign it the variable game stepClock. Create a new section between the pygame.initi() function and the #set up the window section with the comment # frame rate, and then add the following code.

```
#frame rate
FPS = 30
stepClock = pygame.time.Clock()
```

In GameMaker: Studio the steps start automatically, but when using pygame, we need to use a tick() method at the end of each game loop iteration to advance the clock at the desired Frames per Second (FPS) speed. Add the following code below pygame.display.update(). It should be indented just like the previous line so that it is included in the game loop.

```
step.Clock.tick(FPS)
```

We could test this again, but nothing would appear to change as no matter how fast or slow our window refreshes, it is still just a black window. Compare

```
import pygame, sys
pygame.init()

#frame rate
FPS = 30
stepClock = pygame.time.Clock()

#set up the window
gameWindow = pygame.display.set_mode((640, 480))
pygame.display.set_caption("Tinker Bell Trapped")

#game loop
while True:
    for event in pygame.event.get():
        if event.type == pygame.QUIT:
            pygame.quit()
            sys.exit()

    pygame.display.update()
    stepClock.tick(FPS)
```

FIGURE 8-2   FPS and Window Code.

your full code so far to that in Figure 8-2, and then we'll move on and add an image.

Tinkerbell Trapped Step 5: Loading and Drawing Images

If our game is about Tinker Bell being trapped, then we better add Tinker Bell! If you have not already, make sure the file TinkerBell.png is installed in the same folder as the TinkerBell.py file, the Python file on which you are currently working. Begin with a comment, such as #load image to identify this section, which we'll place between the #frame rate section and the #set up the window section.

Load Image

To load the image, we'll use the Pygame image.load() function. Place the file name of the image in quotes between the parentheses to call it. The pygame.image.load() function creates a surface object that has the image drawn on it. We'll store that surface object in a variable for easy reference. It's most efficient if this variable is something brief such as TinkImg. We'll also create variables to hold the x and y coordinates, and we'll assign them a starting value. As in GameMaker: Studio, the top left corner of the window is (0,0) and the sprite is, by default, placed by its top left corner rather than its center. Update your #load image section code as shown here.

```
#load image
TinkImg = pygame.image.load("TinkerBell.png")
TinkX = 10
TinkY = 10
```

Place Image

We've created a surface object called TinkImg and set variables to describe where we want it to first appear, so now we need **Blit,** to *draw one surface object onto another.* In the game loop, add a line under while true. The blit method first names the host surface object, in this case gameWindow. Attach the suffix .blit and parentheses to finish the method name. Inside the parentheses we'll set the source surface object, which we stored in TinkImg and then the coordinates within the host surface object (gameWindow) where the source surface object should appear. We already assigned these coordinates to our variables TinkX and TinkY. The completed blit method is shown below as well as it's location within the game loop.

```
#game loop
while True:
    gameWindow.blit(TinkImg,
    (TinkX, TinkY))
```

FIGURE 8-3   Blit Image.

Save and then test. Tinker Bell should now appear in the black window as shown in Figure 8-3, and the full code should appear as in Figure 8-4.

Tinker Bell Trapped Step 6: Motion

Tinker Bell probably wouldn't stay in one place when trapped. Let's make her move around the window. Start by creating a new section with the heading #motion directly below and in the whileTrue: loop, above the gameWindow.blit() line we just added. Create some space between the two sections.

When we made sprites move in Scratch we used Change X By to adjust the horizontal location and Change Y By to adjust the vertical location. We'll do the same thing in

```
import pygame, sys
pygame.init()

#frame rate
FPS = 30
stepClock = pygame.time.Clock()

#set up the window
gameWindow = pygame.display.set_mode((640, 480))
pygame.display.set_caption("Tinker Bell Trapped")

#load image
TinkImg = pygame.image.load("TinkerBell.png")
TinkX = 10
TinkY = 10
direction = "right"

#game loop
while True:
    gameWindow.blit(TinkImg, (TinkX, TinkY))

    for event in pygame.event.get():
        if event.type == pygame.QUIT:
            pygame.quit()
            sys.exit()

    pygame.display.update()
    stepClock.tick(FPS)
```

FIGURE 8-4   Load and Blit Image Code.

this Python program. Each step or frame, we'll check the current location of the Tinker Bell sprite, and once it reaches a set threshold we'll change its direction. We'll start this loop with an if statement, but before we can do that, we need to set Tinker Bell's starting direction. Return to the #load image section, and below her starting location add a variable called direction and give it the string value "right."

```
#load image
TinkImg = pygame.image.load("TinkerBell.png")
TinkX = 10
TinkY = 10
direction = "right"
```

Next we'll return to our #motion section, and add our first if statement. We know that this statement will evaluate to true because we set the game to begin with direction set to "right." Since it's true, Tinker Bell will move five pixels to the right each step. Update the #motion section with the code below and then save and test.

```
#game loop
while True:
    #motion
    if direction == "right":
        TinkX += 5
```

Fill Surface

In the test, Tinker Bell certainly moves to the right, but each drawing of her remains visible on the screen, so that she's a bit of a blur. We can fix this by filling the gameWindow, so that each time the blit method redraws Tinker Bell, it does so on top of the filled in window. At the moment, the surface object gameWindow is transparent, so we can see through it to each past Tinker Bell. If we fill gameWindow with color each step, however, we'll only see the latest blit of Tinker Bell. We'll discuss color in more detail in Free Tinker Bell: Step 2. For right now, we simply need to define the color black and use the fill () method to make the gameWindow opaque. In the #set up the window section, define a variable called black.

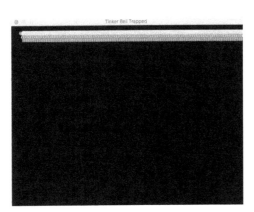

FIGURE 8-5   Tinker Bell Blur.

```
#set up the window
gameWindow = pygame.display.set_mode((640, 480))
pygame.display.set_caption("Tinker Bell Trapped")
black = (0, 0, 0)
```

In the #game loop, add the fill () method below while True:

```
#game loop
while True:
    gameWindow.fill(black)
```

Save and test again. There should only be one Tinker Bell image that moves. The others have been covered over by the fill that happens at the beginning of each frame.

Change Direction

If Tinker Bell is supposed to be trapped, we can't have her exit the right side of the window. Ask students what would need to happen to get her to stop. What triggers her to move each step? If the value of direction continues to be "right" then she'll continue to move five pixels to the right. Let's put in another if statement to test if she's reached the right boundary. Remember that TinkX refers to the left edge of the sprite, so we want her to stop before the left edge reaches the right edge at 640. She's about 30 pixels wide and tall, so we'll subtract 40 from 640 and enter that value, 600, as her right boundary in the second if statement. Add this second if statement below TinkX += 5. If Tinker Bell's x value is equal to 610, we'll stop her by changing the value of direction from "right" to "down" as shown below, and then save and test.

```
#game loop
while True:
   gameWindow.fill(black)
   #motion
   if direction == "right":
     TinkX += 5
     if TinkX == 600:
       direction = "down"
```

Tinker Bell should now stop when she reaches 610 pixels to the right, but she doesn't move down. That's because we didn't tell her what to do if direction = "down". We'll do that now by using an elif statement.

Elif Statement

When we worked with Scratch we used If () Then, Else block to tell sprites to execute the first chunk of code if the statement was true, otherwise, execute the second chunk. Python also has else statements that execute when the if statement evaluates to false, but in that scenario, there can be only one option for true and one option for false. We're going to need to evaluate multiple possibilities. An **else if (elif)** statement *evaluates multiple conditional statements and executes the code within the first one to be true.* Update the #motion code with if and elif statements for the other directions, as shown in Figure 8-6.

Now, each frame, the #motion code will check to see if direction is set to right, if not it will check to see if it is set to down, if not,

```
#game loop
while True:
    gameWindow.fill(black)
    #motion
    if direction == "right":
        TinkX += 5
        if TinkX == 600:
            direction = "down"
    elif direction == "down":
        TinkY += 5
        if TinkY == 440:
            direction = "left"
    elif direction == "left":
        TinkX -= 5
        if TinkX== 10:
            direction = "up"
    elif direction == "up":
        TinkY-= 5
        if TinkY == 10:
            direction = "right"
```

FIGURE 8-6 Motion Code.

```
import pygame, sys
pygame.init()

#frame rate
FPS = 30
stepClock = pygame.time.Clock()

#set up the window
gameWindow = pygame.display.set_mode((640, 480))
pygame.display.set_caption("Tinker Bell Trapped")
black = (0, 0, 0)

#load image
TinkImg = pygame.image.load("TinkerBell.png")
TinkX = 10
TinkY = 10
direction = "right"

#game loop
while True:
    gameWindow.fill(black)
    #motion
    if direction == "right":
        TinkX += 5
        if TinkX == 600:
            direction = "down"
    elif direction == "down":
        TinkY += 5
        if TinkY == 440:
            direction = "left"
    elif direction == "left":
        TinkX -= 5
        if TinkX== 10:
            direction = "up"
    elif direction == "up":
        TinkY-= 5
        if TinkY == 10:
            direction = "right"

    gameWindow.blit(TinkImg, (TinkX, TinkY))

    for event in pygame.event.get():
        if event.type == pygame.QUIT:
            pygame.quit()
            sys.exit()

    pygame.display.update()
    stepClock.tick(FPS)
```

FIGURE 8-7   Tinker Bell Trapped Step Six Code.

it will see if it is set to left, and then finally to up. Each time Tinker Bell reaches the maximum x or y value for that section, the direction will change, keeping her circling around the window. Save and test it out! If you run into trouble, compare your code to that in Figure 8-7.

FREE TINKER BELL: GUIDE

In this activity we'll transform our Tinker Bell Trapped animation into a playable game in which we can guide her to freedom. Encourage students to save a copy of Tinker Bell Trapped, so that they have a backup and can refer back to it as necessary. Open one of the copies and rename it FreeTinkerBell.py. They may also wish to change the window caption accordingly by updating the title string in the pygame.display.set_caption() function.

Free Tinker Bell Step 1: Key Controls

Currently, Tinker Bell begins moving as soon as the game loop begins. To be able to control her ourselves, we need to remove and replace the #Motion section. This is one of the reasons students should make a copy. If they want to automate movement in the future, they can refer back to TinkerBell.py.

Create Sequence of Pressed Keys

Have the students delete only the #motion section from the FreeTinkerBell.py file. In the same location start a new section with the comment #Key Controls. We'll use the **pygame.key.get_pressed()** function which *generates a sequence of Boolean values representing the state of each key on the keyboard.* For instance if the left key was being pressed at the moment the pygame.key.get_pressed() function was called, then it would be listed as true in the sequence. Since we'll place this function in the game loop, the sequence will refresh each frame. Each time it refreshes, we'll store the sequence in a variable called "keys." Remember to indent the line to place it inside the while True loop.

```
#game loop
while True:
    gameWindow.fill(black)
    gameWindow.blit(TinkImg, (TinkX, TinkY))

    #Key Controls
    keys = pygame.key.get_pressed()
```

If Specific Key Pressed

We want to check the key pressed sequence each frame to see if our control keys are listed as true, and if so, we want to move Tinker Bell accordingly. All of the keys in the sequence are represented by key constants. We'll use if statements to look for these constants in the key pressed sequence. Students may use the directional arrows (K_LEFT, K-RIGHT, K_UP, K_DOWN) or wasd (K_w, K_a, K_s, K_d). Each key constant is preceded by the pygame prefix. Let's start with K_LEFT.

```
#Key Controls
keys = pygame.key.get_pressed()
if keys[pygame.K_LEFT]:
```

In the #load image section, create a variable called TinkSpeed. This will store the value of the number of pixels Tinker Bell should move each step that a control key is pressed. For instance, if we want her to move 10 pixels each time a key is pressed, we'll set the speed by adding TinkSpeed equals ten.

```
#load image
TinkImg = pygame.image.load("TinkerBell.png")
TinkX = 10
TinkY = 10
direction = "right"
TinkSpeed = 10
```

Return to the #Key Controls section. When the left key is pressed, we'll subtract the TinkSpeed from Tinker Bell's current x value, which we assigned to TinkX. Update the left key if statement to reflect this.

```
#Key Controls
keys = pygame.key.get_pressed()
if keys[pygame.K_LEFT]:
    TinkX = TinkX - TinkSpeed
```

Students may copy and paste the if block three more times and simply update the keyboard constant, variable and operator to complete the keyboard controls.

Relying on their experience working with coordinates in previous activities, students should be able to problem solve how to add the other directions. Challenge them to do so, and then save and test. If they get stuck, the full key control code is below.

```
#game loop
while True:
  gameWindow.fill(black)
  gameWindow.blit(TinkImg, (TinkX, TinkY))

  #Key Controls
  keys = pygame.key.get_pressed()
  if keys[pygame.K_LEFT]:
    TinkX = TinkX - TinkSpeed
  elif keys[pygame.K_RIGHT]:
    TinkX = TinkX + TinkSpeed
  elif keys[pygame.K_UP]:
    TinkY = TinkY - TinkSpeed
  elif keys[pygame.K_DOWN]:
    TinkY = TinkY + TinkSpeed
```

Keep Tinker Bell in the Window

Currently there is nothing to prevent Tinker Bell from leaving the window, which is a bit of a problem since she's supposed to be trapped. We can fix this by adding an additional if statement to each key pressed statement. We'll test to see if Tinker Bell's current coordinates are within the room before executing the next line that tells her to move. Walk students through creating the first additional if statement for the left key. The left window boundary coordinate is 0, so we want to check that TinkX is greater than 0 as shown below.

```
#Key Controls
keys = pygame.key.get_pressed()
if keys[pygame.K_LEFT]:
  if TinkX >0:
    TinkX = TinkX - TinkSpeed
```

Things get a little more complicated with the right key. The right boundary coordinate is 640, but, because Tinker Bell will be drawn down and to the left of TinkX and TinkY, she needs to stop before TinkX reaches 640. Recall that the Tinker Bell image is about 40 pixels wide, so if we subtract 40 from 640 we'll leave room for her image to draw within the window.

```
#Key Controls
keys = pygame.key.get_pressed()
if keys[pygame.K_LEFT]:
  if TinkX >0:
    TinkX = TinkX - TinkSpeed
```

```
elif keys[pygame.K_RIGHT]:
  if TinkX <600:
    TinkX = TinkX + TinkSpeed
```

Encourage students to use the same thinking process to independently complete the conditional statements for the up and down keys.

```
#Key Controls
keys = pygame.key.get_pressed()
if keys[pygame.K_LEFT]:
  if TinkX >0:
    TinkX = TinkX - TinkSpeed
elif keys[pygame.K_RIGHT]:
  if TinkX <600:
    TinkX = TinkX + TinkSpeed
elif keys[pygame.K_UP]:
  if TinkY >0:
    TinkY = TinkY - TinkSpeed
elif keys[pygame.K_DOWN]:
  if TinkY <440:
    TinkY = TinkY + TinkSpeed
```

Free Tinker Bell Step 2: Draw Obstacles

Let's create some obstacles in the drawer. The player will need to navigate Tinker Bell around them in order to free her.

Rectangle Objects

The **pygame.Rect** object *stores rectangular coordinates.* We can use these stored coordinates to draw the rectangles onto a surface object, call specific coordinates and to check for collisions. Start a new section above the game loop called #rectangle objects. We'll start by creating a long rectangle called rectTop to serve as the lid trapping Tinker Bell. The first value in the parentheses is the starting x position. The second is the starting y position. The third parameter is the width of the rectangle, and the fourth is the height. Add a second rectangle object to run along the bottom of the window as shown below.

```
#rectangle objects
rectTop = pygame.Rect(0,0,640,30)
rectBottom = pygame.Rect(0, 450, 640, 30)
```

Draw Rectangles

If we were to run our program at this point we would not see the rectangles that we created. That is because we have simply stored the coordinates where they'll appear, but we haven't drawn them. We'll want to draw them on top of the gameWindow surface object, so we'll place the code to draw them in the game loop so it generates each step. In the whileTrue loop, under the gameWindow.blit line, add a new segment, #draw obstacles.

We'll use the **pygame.draw.rect()** function which *draws rectangles to a surface*. The first argument in the parentheses is the surface on which the rectangle will be drawn. The second is the color that will fill the rectangle. The third is the rectangle object to be drawn.

```
#game loop
while True:
    gameWindow.fill(black)
    gameWindow.blit(TinkImg, (TinkX, TinkY))

    #draw obstacles
    pygame.draw.rect (gameWindow, green, rectTop) #top
    pygame.draw.rect (gameWindow, green, rectBottom) #bottom
```

Colors

If we were to run the program right now we would receive an error message because we have not yet defined the color green. Students will no doubt be familiar with the color wheel and the three primary colors for mixing paint, red, yellow and blue. If we were painting a green rectangle we could mix blue and green paint together to create our color. Colors on a computer monitor, however, are created with a mix of three primary colors of *light*: red, green, and blue. When red, green, and blue light are mixed together they can create what we think of as white light, but we can also change the intensity of each light color to produce a broad spectrum of colors. To dig further into the science of light colors, refer to the "Color Addition" article on www.physicsclassroom.com.

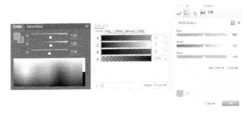

FIGURE 8-8   Photoshop, Inkscape and Word RGB Color Pickers.

Many software applications that support manipulation of graphics, such as Adobe Photoshop, Inkscape, and even Microsoft Word, offer RGB color pickers as shown in Figure 8-8. Users can manipulate tools such as sliders to change the intensity of each light level, or they can manually enter values.

Color	RGB Values
Red	(255, 0, 0)
Orange	(255, 165, 0)
Yellow	(255, 255, 0)
Green	(0, 128, 0)
Blue	(0, 0, 255)
Purple	(128, 0, 128)
White	(255, 255, 255)
Black	(0, 0, 0)

FIGURE 8-9   RGB Color Values Chart.

Pygame also allows us to manually enter color values. The chart in Figure 8-9 lists some common colors. Notice that the value for red is always listed first, then green, then blue. To get pure red, we would enter the values (255, 0, 0), as 255 is the highest level of intensity for a light color and zero is the lowest.

Define Colors

We've already entered the values for black into our code. In the #set up the window section, find the black=(0,0,0) line. Click in front of this line and click enter to create a new #colors section. Add a variable to store the values for green and red. Once these are defined our draw.rect function should work properly. Save and test. There should be green bars on the top and bottom of the screen.

```
#colors
black = (0, 0, 0)
green = (0, 255, 0)
red = (255, 0, 0)
```

Update Boundaries

As you test the game, you may notice that Tinker Bell can fly under the top and bottom bars. To fix this, we'll need to update the if statement values in the #key controls. We set the boundary for the up key to zero as Tinker Bell draws below her TinkY coordinate, but we now want her to draw below the bar, which is 30 pixels high. We set the down key boundary to 440, so that she has room to draw without going out of the room. We'll need to subtract the 30 pixels of the rectangle from that to create the new boundary. Update both values as shown below. Save and then test. Tinker Bell should now be trapped between green bars.

```
elif keys[pygame.K_UP]:
    if TinkY >30:
       TinkY = TinkY - TinkSpeed
elif keys[pygame.K_DOWN]:
    if TinkY <410:
       TinkY = TinkY + TinkSpeed
```

Obstacle Shelves

Now that we know how to create and fill rectangles, let's create a few more to make it slightly harder for Tinker Bell to navigate to the top when the lid opens. Add the coordinates in the #rectangle objects section, and then add the draw functions in the #draw obstacles section in the game loop. Save and then test. There should be three additional green bars.

```
#rectangle objects
rectTop = pygame.Rect(0,0,640,30)
rectBottom = pygame.Rect(0,450,640,30)
rectShelf1 = pygame.Rect(0,330,200,30)
rectShelf2 = pygame.Rect(213,225,200,30)
rectShelf3 = pygame.Rect(426,120,200,30)

#game loop
while True:
  gameWindow.fill(black)
  gameWindow.blit(TinkImg, (TinkX, TinkY))

  #draw obstacles
  TinkBox = pygame.Rect(TinkX, TinkY, 37, 37)
  pygame.draw.rect (gameWindow, green, rectTop) #top
  pygame.draw.rect (gameWindow, green, rectBottom) #bottom
  pygame.draw.rect (gameWindow, green, rectShelf1) #low
  pygame.draw.rect (gameWindow, green, rectShelf2) #mid
  pygame.draw.rect (gameWindow, green, rectShelf3) #high
```

Free Tinker Bell Step 3: Collision

Our obstacles aren't much of an obstacle at the moment since Tinker Bell can fly through them. To address this, we'll first need to create a rectangle object to surround Tinker Bell. In the #draw obstacles section, create a variable called TinkBox. We'll use it to store a pygame.Rect object with the same dimensions as the Tinker Bell image. Unlike the other Rect.objects, we'll create this one in the game loop because we want the rectangle's starting x and y position to be the same as Tinker Bell's in any given frame. As we move Tinker Bell using the commands in the #key controls section, TinkX and TinkY adjust accordingly, so we'll use these variables to create TinkBox.

```
#draw obstacles
pygame.draw.rect (gameWindow, green, rectTop) #top
pygame.draw.rect (gameWindow, green, rectBottom) #bottom
pygame.draw.rect (gameWindow, green, rectShelf1) #low
pygame.draw.rect (gameWindow, green, rectShelf2) #mid
pygame.draw.rect (gameWindow, green, rectShelf3) #high
TinkBox = pygame.Rect(TinkX, TinkY, 37, 37)
```

Remember that we won't see this box because we have not drawn it, but we can still use the coordinates stored in the TinkBox rectangle object to check for a collision. In the game loop, between the #draw obstacles section and the #key controls section, start a #collision section.

Create a List

We'll be checking if TinkBox is colliding with any of the other rectangles in a list. A **list** in Python is simply *a sequence of items, each assigned an index* number *beginning with zero.* For instance, in the list shown in Figure 8-10, fish would have the index of 0, cat an index of 1, and dog an index of 2. Once the list has been created, we can call elements by their index value.

In our newly created #collision section, create a list of all of the rectangles except TinkBox.

```
>>> pets = ["fish", "cat", "dog"]
>>> print(pets)
['fish', 'cat', 'dog']
>>> print(pets[1])
cat
>>> print(pets[2])
dog
>>> print (len(pets))
3
>>>
```

FIGURE 8-10 Pet List.

```
#collision
rectangles = [rectTop, rectBottom, rectShelf1, rectShelf2,
rectShelf3]
```

Check Rectangle Collision

We'll use this list with the pygame **Rect.collidelist()** method, which *tests if a rectangle is colliding with any of those in a list. If so, it reports back the index number of the first collision. If not, it reports back an index of –1.* Add this method to the #collision section.

```
#collision
rectangles = [rectTop, rectBottom, rectShelf1, rectShelf2,
rectShelf3]
collision = TinkBox.collidelist(rectangles)
```

Now, each frame that TinkBox collides with one of the rectangles in the list, *collision* will reset to that rectangle's index. For instance, if TinkBox is colliding with rectShelf1 the value of *collision* will be two.

If Tinker Bell collides with one of the rectangle obstacles, we don't want to stop her upward progress. Return to the #key controls section. In the up key if statement add the condition that collision must be less than 0, and then save and test. Tinker Bell should now have to navigate around the obstacles to make her way to the top.

```
#key controls
keys = pygame.key.get_pressed()
if keys[pygame.K_LEFT]:
   if (TinkX >0):
      TinkX = TinkX - TinkSpeed
elif keys[pygame.K_RIGHT]:
   if (TinkX <600):
      TinkX = TinkX + TinkSpeed
elif keys[pygame.K_UP]:
   if (TinkY >30 and collision <0):
      TinkY = TinkY - TinkSpeed
elif keys[pygame.K_DOWN]:
   if (TinkY <410):
      TinkY = TinkY + TinkSpeed
```

Free Tinker Bell Step 4: Obstacle Animation

Even with the obstacles, it's still not particularly difficult for Tinker Bell to navigate to the top. Let's increase the difficulty by making the obstacles move. In the game loop create a #move obstacles comment below the #draw obstacles comment. One of the benefits of using a pygame.Rect object to create a rectangle is that in addition to being able to use the Rect.collidelist() method, we can also call each attribute of the rectangle, such as the left x value, right x value, and center x value. We'll use this last attribute to check if a particular rectangle's horizontal center has reached or exceeded the window boundaries, and if so, we'll reverse the rectangle's direction.

The top rectangle should now also bounce from left to right, creating a gap, but Tinker Bell can't get through it due to her y value restrictions. To finish our escape route we'll need to adjust our #key controls. Remove TinkY >30 from the up key if statement. Now, Tinker Bell should be blocked if rectTop is in the way, but will otherwise be able to shoot out the top. Save and then test. That's it! You've created your first Python game. Check out the full code below, or from the link available in the Appendix.

```python
import pygame, sys
pygame.init()

#variables
rectChangeX1 = 5
rectChangeX2 = 10
rectChangeX3 = 15
rectChangeXt = 20

#frame rate
FPS = 30
stepClock = pygame.time.Clock()

#set up the window
gameWindow = pygame.display.set_mode((640,480))
pygame.display.set_caption("Free Tinker Bell")
Window = gameWindow.convert_alpha()

#colors
black = (0,0,0)
green = (0,255,0)
red = (255,0,0)

#load image
TinkImg = pygame.image.load("TinkerBell.png")
TinkX = 10
TinkY = 400
TinkSpeed = 10

#rectangle objects
rectTop = pygame.Rect(0,0,500,30)
```

```
rectBottom = pygame.Rect(0,450,640,30)
rectShelf1 = pygame.Rect(0,330,200,30)
rectShelf2 = pygame.Rect(213,225,200,30)
rectShelf3 = pygame.Rect(426,120,200,30)

#game loop
while True:
  gameWindow.fill(black)
  gameWindow.blit(TinkImg, (TinkX, TinkY))
  #draw obstacles
  pygame.draw.rect (gameWindow, green, rectTop) #top
  pygame.draw.rect (gameWindow, green, rectBottom) #bottom
  pygame.draw.rect (gameWindow, green, rectShelf1) #low
  pygame.draw.rect (gameWindow, green, rectShelf2) #mid
  pygame.draw.rect (gameWindow, green, rectShelf3) #high
  TinkBox = pygame.Rect(TinkX, TinkY, 37, 37)

  #move obstacles
  rectShelf1.centerx += rectChangeX1
  if rectShelf1.centerx >650 or rectShelf1.centerx <0:
    rectChangeX1 = rectChangeX1 * -1

  rectShelf2.centerx += rectChangeX2
  if rectShelf2.centerx >650 or rectShelf2.centerx <0:
    rectChangeX2 = rectChangeX2 * -1

  rectShelf3.centerx += rectChangeX3
  if rectShelf3.centerx >650 or rectShelf3.centerx <0:
    rectChangeX3 = rectChangeX3 * -1

  rectTop.centerx += rectChangeXt
  if rectTop.centerx >650 or rectTop.centerx <0:
    rectChangeXt = rectChangeXt * -1

  #collision
  rectangles = [rectTop, rectBottom, rectShelf1, rectShelf2,
  rectShelf3]
  collision = TinkBox.collidelist(rectangles)

  #key controls
  keys = pygame.key.get_pressed()
  if keys[pygame.K_LEFT]:
    if (TinkX >0):
      TinkX = TinkX - TinkSpeed
  elif keys[pygame.K_RIGHT]:
    if (TinkX <600):
      TinkX = TinkX + TinkSpeed
  elif keys[pygame.K_UP]:
    if (collision <0):
      TinkY = TinkY - TinkSpeed
  elif keys[pygame.K_DOWN]:
    if (TinkY <410):
      TinkY = TinkY + TinkSpeed
```

```
for event in pygame.event.get():
  if event.type == pygame.QUIT:
    pygame.quit()
    sys.exit()

pygame.display.update()
stepClock.tick(FPS)
```

9

Web Coding with HTML

One of the great benefits of creating games designed for the web is that they're easy to share. Virtually every computer comes with web browsers such as Microsoft's Internet Edge (formerly Internet Explorer) or Apple's Safari. Many users have already installed Google Chrome or Mozilla Firefox. The games that we'll create for the remainder of the book can be interpreted by these common pieces of software, allowing students to easily share their games with friends. Friends can simply download these games from a flash drive or cloud service, or as an email attachment and play it right in their browsers.

WEB CODING WITH HTML: PREPARATION

Not only is it easy for programmers' friends to play their games using common software, it's also possible to create online games using simple text editing tools such as Apple's TextEdit or Microsoft's Notepad, which are built into their respective operating systems. It is easier, however, to use a tool specifically designed for coding.

Komodo Edit is one such tool. It is a text editor with IDE-like features such as code completion and color-coding, and it supports numerous languages including HTML, JavaScript, and Python. It is available for Windows, Macintosh, and Linux, and, best of all, it is free. Komodo Edit is available for download from ActiveState, which also sells a more robust, full-featured version, Komodo IDE. The free version is sufficient for our work. Go to the resources link in the Appendix to download Komodo Edit or search online.

Web Coding with HTML: Materials Needed

Make sure to install Komodo Edit onto the computers and print out copies of the handout, available from the resource link in the Appendix, for the

143

students prior to class. If installation is not possible, practice using the same built in text editor that the students will use. Note that the images in the handout will look different, but the code will be the same. It will be beneficial for students to have Internet access, but it is possible to complete the activity without it. Even if there is no internet connection students will need a good web browser. Google Chrome or Mozilla Firefox are preferable, but built in browsers such as Safari on Apple or Microsoft Edge on Windows will work. Avoid using Internet Explorer; this default browser on older versions of Windows should be avoided as it is no longer supported by Microsoft and may cause issues. As always, it is helpful to have a projector for the instructor.

We'll once again be using Peter Pan as inspiration, so you may wish to provide copies of J.M. Barrie's book *Peter Pan*, originally published in novel form as *Peter and Wendy*. Note that in most countries outside of the United Kingdom, copies of the public domain novel are freely available from a wide variety of sources including Project Gutenberg, Apple iBooks, and Overdrive.

Students will need access to the following image files, which can be downloaded from the resources link in the Appendix along with a link to view the completed game:

Hook.jpg
JollyRoger.jpg
MaroonersRock.jpg
MermaidLagoon.jpg
Neverland.jpg
PeterPan.png
TheLittleHouse.jpg
Peterpan.png

Web Coding with HTML: Outcomes

Participants will develop understanding of how web languages and browsers interact to create user experience.
Participants will build basic understanding of Hypertext Markup Language (HTML) syntax and terminology.
Participants will grow computational thinking skills.
Participants will expand file management skills.

WEB CODING WITH HTML: GETTING STARTED GUIDE

Students interested in web development, web design, or creating online games will benefit from learning Hypertext Markup Language, commonly referred to as HTML. Unlike the other languages we've learned, HTML is not a programming language, as it does not implement any logic, such as conditional statements, or evaluate expressions, like doing math. **HTML** *is a standardized system to describe text files to web browsers to achieve visual and* *hyperlink effects.* Programmers place data between tags to tell browsers whether that data is a heading, a link, or a paragraph.

Even though HTML isn't a programming language, it is a vital tool for those programming for the web and it is quite useful even for those who aren't. Those who know some basic HTML can customize websites they've built with What You See Is What You Get (WYSIWYG) platforms such as Wix, Wordpress, and Squarespace in ways that those limited to drag-and-drop tools cannot.

Take a look at the source code for any given webpage, and you're bound to see HTML tags, even if the page was created with a WYSIWYG. If you have an Internet connection, try this out with your students. Have them open a web browser such as Chrome or Firefox, and then have them navigate to a favorite website. Right-click on the page and choose **View Page Source**. A new tab will open displaying the text code that the browser is reading to display the webpage to us in the way we are accustomed. On the very first line students should see something like <!doctype html>, which declares to the browser which version of HTML is used within. The rest of the content will be encapsulated between an <html>tag, and a closing tag</html>, indicating that even if JavaScript and CSS are also being used, they're living inside of an HTML file. Websites are typically made up of several webpages, each one of which is an HTML file. For webpages to work, they must be correctly coded from regular text to HTML, so it is still fair to say that students will be coding as they complete this next activity.

Getting Started Step 1: Setting Up an HTML File

Before we begin creating files, we should create a space for them to live. Later in the activity we'll be linking the pages that we create to each other, so we'll want them to live in the same folder. **Have students open the main location to which they'll save**, whether that will be the Desktop, a flash drive, or a server folder. Within that location, have them create a new folder called **HTMLpages**. Close out of this window, but make note of the path to get there.

Open **Komodo Edit**, and choose **New File**. If you are working with a text editor such as TextEdit for Mac, make sure to go in to **Format** and **Make Plain Text.** Komodo Edit automatically launches using plain text.

Document Type

A declaration of the document type should always lead off an HTML file. Past versions of html still float around the Internet, and browsers still read them, but to do so most effectively they need to be notified of which rules to follow. We'll be using HTML5, which uses a non-case sensitive declaration. Type this declaration into the first line of the document:

```
<!doctype html>
```

From the **File** menu, choose **Save As**. Choose **HTMLpages** as the destination folder. The file is a plain text file, ending with the extension .txt. We want to save this document as an html file, so make sure to use the **.html** extension. Name the file **MyFirstWebpage.html** before clicking save.

Now that we've identified the document as an html file, Komodo Edit will provide us with code completion and color-coding to make things a bit easier. We can see this in action when we add the html tags. Click return after the doctype declaration. Komodo Edit will jump the cursor down to line two and automatically indent it. This indentation isn't required in HTML as it is in Python, but it does make it easier to read the code and keep track of blocks. We'll want to use indentations later, but since the html tags that we're about to place will surround the rest of the content, we'll go ahead and backspace to align the cursor with the left border. Begin to type the opening HTML tag as indicated below, and notice that the closing tag should automatically appear. The tags will also change color.

```
<!doctype html>
<html></html>
```

HTML tags are *set groups of characters that indicate what should happen with the content nested between the opening tag and the closing tag.* They begin with the less than symbol and end with the greater than symbol. These symbols are also referred to as angle brackets. There is almost always an opening tag and a closing tag that is similar but includes the forward slash. All of our remaining lines will go between the opening html tag, <html>, and the closing html tag, </html>, so click return/enter a few times to create some space.

Comments

As we've discussed, comments are a way for coders to make notes and exchange information without affecting functionality. In HTML, we can add comments by using the <!— . . . —> tag. The ellipsis represents the comment itself. Note that the exclamation point must be adjacent to the left angle bracket, and that the comment is self contained within the single tag, rather than surrounded by separate opening and closing tags. Let's add a comment to our document. This comment may be indented.

```
<!doctype html>
<html>
   <!—This is a secret message—>
</html>
```

Paragraph

The **paragraph tag** *indicates an element of regular text to print in the browser,* typically with vertical space before and after. Let's add a line using this tag and then save our work.

```
<!doctype html>
<html>
   <!-This is a secret message->
   <p>This is a public message.</p>
</html>
```

Test in Browser

Since HTML documents are created to be read by browsers, we can use a browser to see what our file would look like if it were uploaded to a server and accessed online. **Open a web browser**. Go to **File** then **Open**. In both Chrome and Firefox the shortcut to open a file is Control-O for Windows or Command-O for Mac. Navigate to the **HTMLpages** folder and select the **MyFirstWebpage.html** file, then click **Open**. If all is entered correctly, "This is a public message." should appear by itself in the opened tab. If it does not appear or other text appears then

FIGURE 9-1   MyFirstWebpage Paragraph.

there is an error in the code. Encourage students to work with each other as troubleshooting partners, comparing their code to that in the handout and in Figure 9-1 to identify solutions. Note that the numbers displayed in Komodo Edit and in Figure 9-1 are for reference only while working within the software, and are not part of the saved document.

Encourage students to leave the browser window open with the file loaded. As they make changes to the document, they can simply click the refresh button in the browser to update the file. Students may minimize the browser window for now, or keep it on one side of the screen with Komodo Edit on the other.

Getting Started Step 2: Organizing the Page

An HTML page typically includes two main sections, the head and the body.

Head

The **head** element *contains meta-data about the document.* This metadata, or data about data, may describe the page's title, character set, style, scripts, or other information. The head tags are placed at the top of the page, under the doctype information. We'll place the title element inside of the head.

FIGURE 9-2   Head and Title.

The **title** element *is mandatory and defines the page title.* Let's name our page Webpage 1. Add the title tags as indicated in Figure 9-2. Save and then test by refreshing the file in the browser. The title should appear in the tab.

Body

The **body** *element contains all of the main content of the HTML document.* It is a required element, and there can be only one body section. Delete the comment and paragraph lines, and insert the body tags below the head element.

Headings

The six levels of headings in HTML outline subsections of the document and are used by search engines to index the structure and content of the page. The largest heading, <h1>, indicates the top most content grouping with the smallest, <h6>, representing the least most subgroup. Let's use components of Peter Pan to create an example. We'll use a level one heading to segment the content into two main groupings, characters and locations. We'll further subdivide locations with level two headings for London and Neverland, and we'll subdivide characters into adults and children. Finally, we'll subdivide the children into Darling Siblings and Lost Boys using a level three heading, and we'll break adults into Darling Parents and Pirates. Update the file as shown in Figure 9-3, and then save and test by refreshing the Webpage 1 tab in the browser. The results should look similar to Figure 9-4.

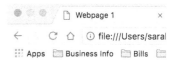

Characters

Children

Darling Siblings

Lost Boys

Adults

Darling Parents

Pirates

Locations

London

Neverland

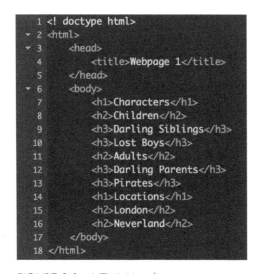

```
 1  <! doctype html>
 2  <html>
 3      <head>
 4          <title>Webpage 1</title>
 5      </head>
 6      <body>
 7          <h1>Characters</h1>
 8          <h2>Children</h2>
 9          <h3>Darling Siblings</h3>
10          <h3>Lost Boys</h3>
11          <h2>Adults</h2>
12          <h3>Darling Parents</h3>
13          <h3>Pirates</h3>
14          <h1>Locations</h1>
15          <h2>London</h2>
16          <h2>Neverland</h2>
17      </body>
18  </html>
```

FIGURE 9-3   HTML Headings.

FIGURE 9-4   Browser Headings.

Formatting

Most formatting on modern websites should be done using **Cascading Style Sheets (CSS)**, *a language used to define how documents written in HTML should look.* There are, however, a few acceptable formatting elements in HTML, such as **bold**, <i>*italic*</i> and <u>underline</u>. Let's experiment with these in our document by playing with the names of the Darling children as shown in Figure 9-5. Notice that the formatting tags in lines 10, 11, and 12 are nested within paragraph tags. Nested tags represent an element within another element. When elements are nested, the last element to open must be the first one to close. Save and test.

Getting Started Step 3: Hyperlinks

Hyperlinks *are clickable connections from one document to another.* Websites are, at their core, multiple html documents, often linking to each other through a main menu on the home page. To add a hyperlink into our document we'll use the <a> tag combined with an href attribute, which clarifies the target destination address. The address is placed within quotes, as shown in

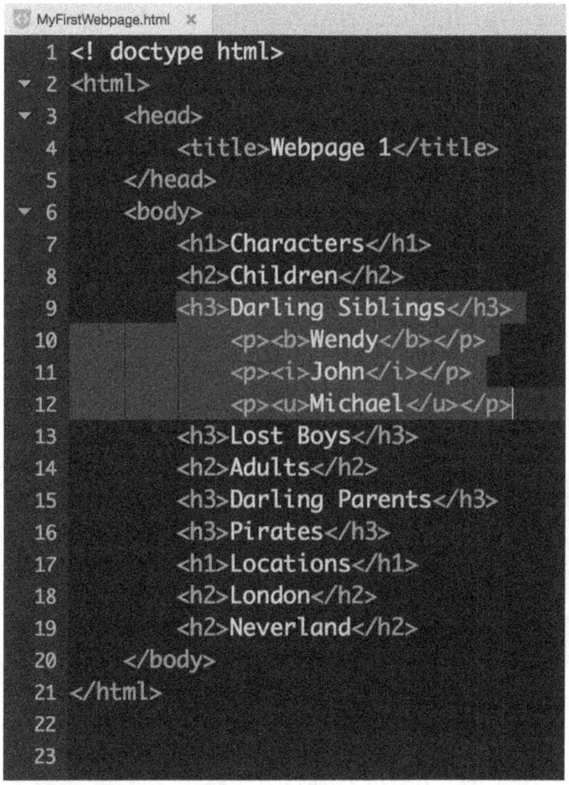

```
MyFirstWebpage.html  ×
 1  <! doctype html>
 2  <html>
 3      <head>
 4          <title>Webpage 1</title>
 5      </head>
 6      <body>
 7          <h1>Characters</h1>
 8          <h2>Children</h2>
 9          <h3>Darling Siblings</h3>
10              <p><b>Wendy</b></p>
11              <p><i>John</i></p>
12              <p><u>Michael</u></p>
13          <h3>Lost Boys</h3>
14          <h2>Adults</h2>
15          <h3>Darling Parents</h3>
16          <h3>Pirates</h3>
17          <h1>Locations</h1>
18          <h2>London</h2>
19          <h2>Neverland</h2>
20      </body>
21  </html>
22
23
```

FIGURE 9-5   Formatted Text.

```
1 <! doctype html>
2 <html>
3    <head>
4        <title>Webpage 1</title>
5    </head>
6    <body>
7        <h1>Characters</h1>
8        <h2>Children</h2>
9        <h3>Darling Siblings</h3>
10           <p><b>Wendy</b></p>
11           <p><i>John</i></p>
12           <p><u>Michael</u></p>
13       <h3>Lost Boys</h3>
14       <h2>Adults</h2>
15       <h3>Darling Parents</h3>
16       <h3>Pirates</h3>
17       <h1>Locations</h1>
18       <h2>London</h2>
19       <h2>Neverland</h2>
20           <p><a href="http://www.gutenberg.org/ebooks/16">Read the Book</a></p>
21   </body>
22 </html>
```

FIGURE 9-6 Hyperlink.

Figure 9-6. Let's add a hyperlink to the Project Gutenberg Peter Pan website. The text placed between the opening a tag and the closing tag will become the visual representation of the link. Save the HTML document and then refresh the browser. The link should work, and students can return to their pages by clicking the back button.

WEB CODING WITH HTML: TEA OR ADVENTURE? GUIDE

In this activity we'll pull together what we've learned so far to create a game based on the fourth chapter in *Peter and Wendy*, "The Flight." As Peter leads the Darling children toward Neverland he asks them if they would like an adventure to start, or if they would rather have their tea first. They're a bit mixed in their responses, as they're both fascinated by and a bit afraid of the mysterious wonders of the island. In our game, players will be asked to choose between options, and will be taken to different pages accordingly. Each choice will impact future available choices.

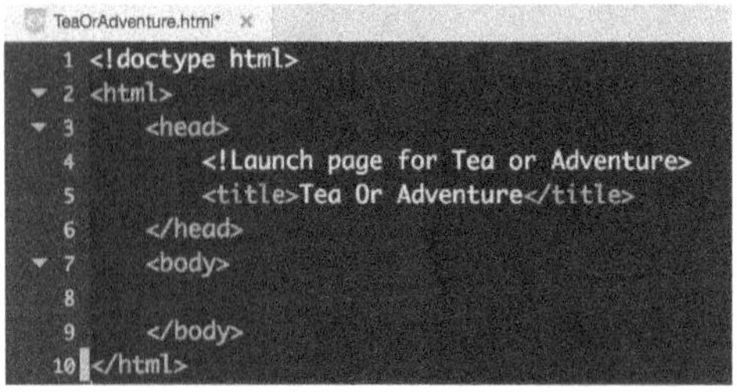

```
1 <!doctype html>
2 <html>
3    <head>
4        <!Launch page for Tea or Adventure>
5        <title>Tea Or Adventure</title>
6    </head>
7    <body>
8
9    </body>
10 </html>
```

FIGURE 9-7 Tea or Adventure? Set Up.

Tea or Adventure? Step 1: Set up Launch File

Create a new document in Komodo by going to **File**, then **New**, and select **New File**. Save the file as **TeaOrAdventure.html**, and place it in the **HTMLpages** folder. Enter the required elements that we learned in the first two steps of Getting Started, and add a comment as shown in Figure 9-7. Save this file, and then open it in the browser. Once again, we can leave this file open in the browser, and simply refresh to see our changes.

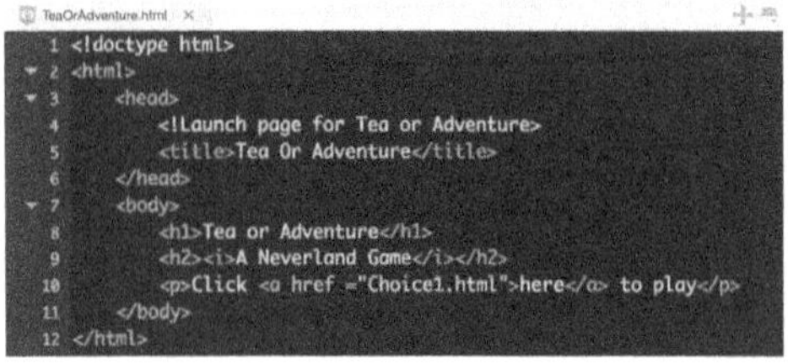

Add text in the body to inform visitors of the purpose of the page, and add a link to the first choice of the game, as shown in Figure 9-8. Students may choose to use different heading tags or formatting options,

```
1 <!doctype html>
2 <html>
3    <head>
4        <!Launch page for Tea or Adventure>
5        <title>Tea Or Adventure</title>
6    </head>
7    <body>
8        <h1>Tea or Adventure</h1>
9        <h2><i>A Neverland Game</i></h2>
10           <p>Click <a href ="Choice1.html">here</a> to play</p>
11   </body>
12 </html>
```

FIGURE 9-8 Click to Play.

but they must include a link to **Choice1.html**. Notice that this link address looks a little different than a typical website address. That is because we're not linking to a page housed online, but rather to a local document. If you save the document and test the link it won't work yet because we haven't created Choice1.html.

Tea or Adventure? Step 2: Choice1 Page

Create a new file in Komodo called **Choice1.html**, and make sure to save it in the HTMLpages folder. The browser will automatically look for the linked file in the same location as the current file, so keeping all of the choice pages in the same folder will save us some effort. If they all lived in different folders we would need to type out the path to each one.

Define Change

Complete the required set up for an HTML page. Copy and paste lines eight and nine from the TeaOrAdventure.html file into the body of **Choice1.html** to place a consistent heading on each page of the game. To separate this information from the information that will change on each choice page, we'll use a **<hr>** tag, which *is used to separate content or define a thematic change within an HTML page*. It is an open tag, meaning there is no end tag. In the past, this tag was used to create a horizontal line across the page, but in HTML5, this is not an explicit purpose of this tag as formatting is to be accomplished through CSS. Most browsers will, however, still draw the line, which suits our purposes here. In a page with CSS, the <hr> tag might trigger a change in background color, font, or other visual cue. Add this tag below the heading two tag.

Add Line Break

Add a heading three element with text along the lines of "Your First Choice." After this, we'll use a **
** tag, which *adds a line break*. This functions a bit like a soft return in word processing, which jumps the cursor down to the next horizontal line of text without breaking formatting or starting a new paragraph. This will have the effect of giving us a little more space before adding an empty paragraph element as shown in Figure 9-10. Save and test. Make sure that everything is working properly. In the browser, the link from **TeaOrAdventure.html** should now open **Choice1.html**. Compare your browser results to those in Figure 9-10.

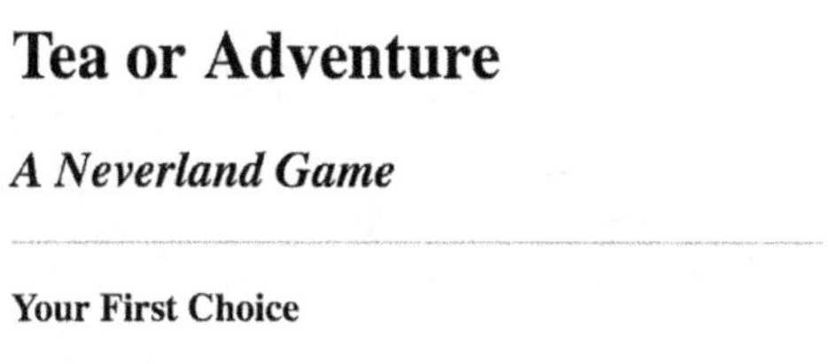

Tea or Adventure

A Neverland Game

Your First Choice

FIGURE 9-9   Choice Template Browser.

ChoiceTemplate.html

```
<!doctype html>
<html>
    <head>
        <title>Choice1</title>
    </head>
    <body>
        <h1>Tea or Adventure</h1>
        <h2><i>A Neverland Game</i></h2>
        <hr>
        <h3>Your First Choice</h3>
        <br>
        <p></p>
    </body>
</html>
```

FIGURE 9-10 Choice Template HTML.

Create a Template

We'll be creating numerous choice pages, so let's make our lives easier by not having to type all of this set up over and over again. Go to **File** and **Save As**. Rename the file **ChoiceTemplate.html**, and make sure to save it to the HTML pages folder. This will create a copy of the Choice1 .html file that we can use as a template to start each of the other new pages. The renaming process will close Choice1.html in Komodo Edit, and open **ChoiceTemplate.html**, but don't worry; Choice1.html is still in the HTMLpages folder. We'll go back to it in just a bit. For now, let's create the other pages that we'll need. Go to **File** and **Save As** to rename the next file **ChoiceTea.html**. Follow the same process to create **Adventure.html**, **Mermaids .html**, and **Pirates.html**.

Complete Choice1 Text

In Komodo Edit, go to **File**, **Open**, and then select **Choice1.html** from the **HTMLpages** folder. We need to give players their first choice. Between the paragraph tags, have students explain the situation using the following sentence or invite them to phrase it their own way.

> *<p>As you fly into Neverland,*
> *you're excited to explore,*
> *but you're also hungry.*</p>

Choice1.html

```
<!doctype html>
<html>
    <head>
        <title>Choice1</title>
    </head>
    <body>
        <h1>Tea or Adventure</h1>
        <h2><i>A Neverland Game</i></h2>
        <hr>
        <h3>Your First Choice</h3>
        <br>
        <p>As you fly into Neverland,
        you're excited to explore,
        but you're also hungry.</p>
        <br>
        <h3>Which will you do first?</h3>
        <h4>A. Have your tea.</h4>
        <br>
        <h4>B. Go on an adventure.</h4>
    </body>
</html>
```

FIGURE 9-11 Choice1 HTML.

In this example, also shown in Figure 9-11, there is a line break after each comma. This will be ignored in the browser, but makes the coded text easier to read in Komodo Edit.

Add an empty **
** line, and then ask the first question, "*Which will you do first?*" In the example in Figure 9-11, an **<h3>** tag emphasizes the question. List the options, "*Have your tea*," or, "*Go on an adventure.*" Students may choose to format these options however they choose. Save and then refresh Choice1.html in the browser.

Complete Choice1 Links

We want the player to click on her choice, so we need to add links to each. Using what they learned about hyperlinks in Getting Started: Step 3, students choose a particular word in the phrase to become the link, or choose the entire phrase as shown in Figure 9-12. Save, and then test both links. They should open their respective pages, although the content in them will be limited to the template content at the moment.

```
1  <!doctype html>
2  <html>
3      <head>
4          <title>Choice1</title>
5      </head>
6      <body>
7          <h1>Tea or Adventure</h1>
8          <h2><i>A Neverland Game</i></h2>
9          <hr>
10         <h3>Your First Choice</h3>
11         <br>
12         <p>As you fly into Neverland,
13         you're excited to explore,
14         but you're also hungry.</p>
15         <br>
16         <h3>Which will you do first?</h3>
17         <h4><a href ="ChoiceTea.html">
18         A. Have your tea.</a></h4>
19         <br>
20         <h4><a href = "ChoiceAdventure.html">
21         B. Go on an adventure.
22         </a></h4>
23     </body>
24  </html>
```

FIGURE 9-12   Choice One HTML with Hyperlinks.

Tea or Adventure? Step 3: Update Choice Pages

We have pages created for each possible choice, so now we simply need to update them with the appropriate content.

Adventure

Open the **ChoiceAdventure.html** file in Komodo Edit. Change the title on line 4 to "Adventure" or allow students to choose a relevant title for the page. Add a description in the empty paragraph element such as, "Off to your first adventure!" Add a question such as, "Where will you go?" Offer the options "Mermaid Lagoon" and "The Jolly Roger" Link each option to its appropriate page, as shown in Figure 9-13. Save, and then view Adventure.html in the browser, either by opening the file, or by clicking the link in the Choice1.html file. The links to **ChoiceMermaids.html** and **ChoicePirates.html** should now work.

```
1  <!doctype html>
2  <html>
3      <head>
4          <title>Adventure</title>
5      </head>
6      <body>
7          <h1>Tea or Adventure</h1>
8          <h2><i>A Neverland Game</i></h2>
9          <hr>
10         <h3>Your First Choice</h3>
11         <br>
12         <p>Off to your first adventure! </p>
13         <br>
14         <h3>Where will you go?</h3>
15         <h4><a href ="ChoiceMermaids.html">
16         A. Mermaid Lagoon.</a></h4>
17         <br>
18         <h4><a href = "ChoicePirates.html">
19         B. The Jolly Roger.
20         </a></h4>
21     </body>
22  </html>
```

Mermaid Lagoon

Open the **ChoiceMermaids.html** file in Komodo Edit. Again, update the title in line 4 to reflect the choice

FIGURE 9-13   Choice Adventure.

FIGURE 9-14   Choice Mermaids HTML.

FIGURE 9-15   Choice Pirates HTML.

FIGURE 9-16   Choice Tea HTML.

made, such as "Mermaid Lagoon." Update the heading on line 9 to describe the adventure, and then fill in the story in the paragraph element. There are actually two different adventures that happen in *Peter and Wendy*, "Chapter 8: The Mermaids' Lagoon," so students could paraphrase either, link to the chapter in an online account, or create their own fan fiction account. The example in Figure 9-14 summarizes the first adventure in the chapter. Save and then test by opening **ChoiceMermaids.html** in the browser.

Jolly Roger

Open the **ChoicePirates.html** file in Komodo Edit, and update both the title in line 4 and the heading in line 10. The adventure shown in the paragraph element in Figure 9-15 is from "Chapter 15: Hook or Me This Time."

Tea

Open **ChoiceTea.html** in Komodo Edit. Follow the same steps as the other files to update the title, heading and paragraph elements. The story summary in Figure 9-16 is taken from "Chapter 6: The Little House."

Tea or Adventure? Step 4: Add Images

Let's jazz up our game with some images. The original illustrations for Peter and Wendy are also in public domain. To add an image we'll use the **<img/> tag**, which has one attribute, the source. Images are not stored in an

HTML file. Rather, they are linked, so just as when we linked to another page, we'll type the location of the image in quotations after the src attribute and an equal sign, as shown in Figure 9-17. Save, and then test, comparing your browser results for **ChoiceTea.html** with those in Figure 9-18.

Using the same process, add the **Hook.jpg** image to the **ChoicePirates.html** page, and add the **Marooners Rock.jpg** to the **ChoiceMermaids.html** page.

```
1  <!doctype html>
2  <html>
3      <head>
4          <title>Tea</title>
5      </head>
6      <body>
7          <h1>Tea or Adventure</h1>
8          <h2><i>A Neverland Game</i></h2>
9          <hr>
10         <h3>Have Your Tea</h3>
11         <br>
12         <p>You decided to have tea first, so you fly
13         straight toward the Lost Boys' home. Unfortunately,
14         jealous Tinkerbell tricks Toodles into shooting you!
15         Thankfully, you'll be alright. While you recover,
16         the boys build a little house around you and Peter
17         keeps watch outside.
18         </p>
19         <img src ="TheLittleHouse.jpg"/>
20     </body>
21 </html>
```

FIGURE 9-17   Add Image.

Add Images as Hyperlinks

Not only can we link *to* images in HTML, but we can link *from* images to other files. Open **ChoiceAdventure.html**. In the example in Figure 9-19, the **<img/>** tag is placed inside of the **<a>** tag for each option, along with the text for that option, so that the player could click on the text or the picture. Add linked images to both options. Save and then test, comparing to the

Tea or Adventure

A Neverland Game

Have Your Tea

You decided to have tea first, so you fly straight toward the Lost Boys' home. Unfortunately, jealous Tinkerbell tricks Toodles into shooting you! Thankfully, you'll be alright. While you recover, the boys build a little house around you and Peter keeps watch outside.

FIGURE 9-18   Tea Image in Browser.

```
1  <!doctype html>
2  <html>
3      <head>
4          <title>Adventure</title>
5      </head>
6      <body>
7          <h1>Tea or Adventure</h1>
8          <h2><i>A Neverland Game</i></h2>
9          <hr>
10         <h3>Your First Choice</h3>
11         <br>
12         <p>Off to your first adventure! </p>
13         <br>
14         <h3>Where will you go?</h3>
15         <h4><a href ="ChoiceMermaids.html">
16         A. Mermaid Lagoon.
17         <br>
18         <img src= "MermaidLagoon.jpg"/></a></h4>
19         <br>
20         <h4><a href = "ChoicePirates.html">
21         B. The Jolly Roger.
22         <br>
23         <img src= "JollyRoger.jpg"/></a></h4>
24     </body>
25 </html>
```

FIGURE 9-19   Adventure   Images   as Hyperlinks.

Tea or Adventure

A Neverland Game

Your First Choice

Off to your first adventure!

Where will you go?

A. Mermaid Lagoon.

B. The Jolly Roger.

FIGURE 9-20
Adventure Images in Browser

browser results shown in Figure 9-20. Following the same steps add **Neverland.jpg** to the opening page, **TeaOrAdventure.html**, and link it to **Choice1.html**.

Add Replay Image

In the browser, reopen the very first page of the game, **TeaOrAdventure.html**, and play through each choice. Each page should now link together to create a playable story. When users reach the end of a particular storyline, they can click the back button several times to go back to the beginning and try again, but it would be best if they had a cleaner way to return to the start of the game.

Let's add an illustration, **PeterPan.png**, to the end pages and link it to the starting page, **TeaOrAdventure.html**. In this case, we'll link only the image. In the example in Figure 9-21, a **<h6>** tag is used on line 18 of **ChoiceMermaids .html** to give the instruction to, "Click Peter Pan to Return

```
ChoiceMermaids.html ×
 1  <!doctype html>
 2  <html>
 3      <head>
 4          <title>Mermaid Lagoon</title>
 5      </head>
 6      <body>
 7          <h1>Tea or Adventure</h1>
 8          <h2><i>A Neverland Game</i></h2>
 9          <hr>
10          <h3>Adventure in Mermaid Lagoon</h3>
11          <br>
12          <p>Captain Hook and his pirate band
13          have captured Tiger Lily, and are stranding her
14          on Marooners rock. You imitate Captain Hook's voice
15          and trick his men into letting her go!</p>
16          <img src ="MaroonersRock.jpg"/>
17          <br>
18          <h6>Click Peter Pan to Return to Neverland!
19          <a href ="TeaOrAdventure.html">
20          <img src ="PeterPan.png"/></a></h6>
21      </body>
22  </html>
23
```

FIGURE 9-21   Return to Start Image Link HTML.

to Neverland!" Close the heading on the other side of the image to keep everything on the same line in the browser. Line 19 contains the link to the start of the game, and it closes around the image source on line 20. Once you've successfully saved and tested this, and seen results similar to those in Figure 9-22, copy and paste the relevant lines into **Choice-Tea.html** and **ChoicePirates.html**.

Players can now work their way through the various choices, see images as they go, and click on a link to return them to the beginning. Compared to the games we created in GameMaker: Studio and Scratch, this one is pretty rudimentary in its play and graphics, but we truly made it from scratch this time. We can, however, create more interactive games by incorporating JavaScript. We'll do that in the next chapter.

Adventure in Mermaid Lagoon

Captain Hook and his pirate band have captured Tiger Lily, and are stranding her on Marooners rock. You imitate Captain Hook's voice and trick his men into letting her go!

Click Peter Pan to Return to Neverland!

FIGURE 9-22   Return to Start Image Link Browser.

10

Web Coding with JavaScript

In the previous chapter we explored HTML, one of the three languages fundamental to web development. One of the others is JavaScript. HTML is used to define webpage content, whereas JavaScript determines the behavior of webpages. JavaScript is the fundamental programming language of the Internet. If you've used web applications like Chrome, Firefox and Microsoft Edge, Gmail, Facebook, or Twitter, then you've used JavaScript. It is an absolute must for students who are interested in web development.

WEB CODING WITH JAVASCRIPT: PREPARATION

One of the benefits of working with JavaScript is that interpreters are built into every major web browser; so new users can start messing around with it immediately without installing anything new. Coders can work directly in the JavaScript console initially, and then use a text editor to create programs. Komodo Edit, the text editor that we installed in the previous chapter to create HTML files, also works well to create JavaScript files.

Web Coding with JavaScript: Materials Needed

Installation of Komodo Edit onto student computers prior to class is preferable, but activities may be done with a built-in text editor, such as Apple's TextEdit or Microsoft's Notepad. Students will need a browser such as Chrome or Firefox, and they'll each need a copy of the handout available from the appendix. The game is based on "Rumpelstiltskin" from *Grimm's Fairy Tales*, so you may wish to read the story aloud, or direct students to free, public domain copies. Students will need access to the file **rumpel.png**, and an example file of the game, TheNameOfTheQueen.html is also available to download.

Web Coding with JavaScript: Outcomes

Participants will augment knowledge of HTML elements and incorporate them with JavaScript.

Participants will increase general coding vocabulary and recognize patterns across languages.

Participants will build understanding of JavaScript functions, methods, properties, and syntax.

Participants will expand computational thinking skills.

GETTING STARTED WITH JAVASCRIPT: GUIDE

Let's start out by working in the JavaScript console, which is similar to the shell interface that we used in Python. The console can carry out entered JavaScript expressions. Open a browser such as Chrome or Firefox. Windows users can open the console in **Chrome** by pushing **CTRL**, **SHIFT,** and **J**. Macintosh users should use the keys **COMMAND, OPTION,** and **J**. For Firefox, use the Windows keys **COMMAND, SHIFT,** and **K** or the Macintosh combination **COMMAND, OPTION,** and **K**.

Getting Started with JavaScript Step 1: Variables

As you and your students have no doubt gathered after proceeding through the previous lessons, variables are an important part of most programming languages, and JavaScript is no exception.

Define and Call Variable

In Python, we could simply type the name of the variable we wanted to create and then use an equal sign to assign a value. In JavaScript, the variable statement begins with **var**. Some coders like to preface variables with the word my, which can be helpful to remind them that the name is user derived. Let's create a variable called myScore and assign it the value of 0. At the console prompt simply type: **var myScore=0**, and click enter to store the value. As shown in Figure 10-1, we can now call the value of myScore by typing the variable name in the console and tapping enter.

```
> var myScore =0
<· undefined
> myScore
<· 0
```

FIGURE 10-1   Define and Call Variable.

Reassign Variables

Once a variable is created, we can reassign what it contains without using **var**. In JavaScript we don't have to declare the data type the variable will contain, and we can change it from a string to a number and back again if we want to do so. Try saving a string into myScore. Just as in Python, single or double quotation marks will work, but they must match. As shown in Figure 10-2, call the reassigned variable, and then place a number in it again.

```
> myScore = "awesome"
<· "awesome"
> myScore
<· "awesome"
> myScore = 0
<· 0
> myScore
<· 0
```

Changing Variable Values

FIGURE 10-2   Reassign Variable.

There are multiple ways to change the numeric value of variables. Let's explore three different ways to get the same results.

Incrementing and Decrementing

To **increment** or *increase the value of a variable by one*, we can use the ++ operator. To **decrement** or *decrease the value by one* we can use the – –(two minus signs) operator. Try it, as shown in Figure 10-3.

Plus Equals and Minus Equals

If we want to change the value of score by more than one, we can do so more efficiently by using the += or –= operators, as shown in Figure 10-4.

```
> myScore
<· 0
> ++myScore
<· 1
> ++myScore
<· 2
> --myScore
<· 1
> --myScore
<· 0
> --myScore
<· -1
```

```
> myScore +=4
<· 3
> myScore-=5
<· -2
> myScore =0
<· 0
> myScore +=20
<· 20
> myScore-=5
<· 15
```

FIGURE 10-3   Increment and Decrement.

FIGURE 10-4   Plus Equals and Minus Equals.

```
>  myScore=0
<  0
>  myScore=myScore+3
<  3
>  myScore=myScore−12
<  −9
```

FIGURE 10-5   Change Variable by Variable.

Variable Equals Variable

+/− Finally, we can use a variable to reassign its own value, as shown in Figure 10-5.

Getting Started with JavaScript Step 2: Arrays

We use variables all of the time in coding to store a single, changeable value, but sometimes you may need to store more than one value and call it on demand. An **array** *is variable that can store multiple, indexed values*. For instance, we could create an array to store the names of the lost boys by entering the following;

```
var lostBoysArray = ["Tootles", "Nibs", "Slightly", "Curly", "The
Twins"]
```

```
>  var lostBoysArray = ["Tootles", "Nibs", "Slightly", "Curly", "The Twins"]
<  undefined
>  lostBoysArray [1]
<  "Nibs"
>  lostBoysArray [2]
<  "Slightly"
>  lostBoysArray[0]
<  "Tootles"
```

FIGURE 10-6   Fill and Call an Array.

Each element in the array is assigned an index number, beginning with zero. We can call an element by typing the array name followed by the index number in brackets, as shown in Figure 10-6. Notice that because the indexing is zero based, *Nibs* is assigned the index of *1* rather than *Tootles*.

THE NAME OF THE QUEEN: GUIDE

The game we'll make to explore JavaScript is based on the story "Rumpelstiltskin" in which the miller brags erroneously to the king that his daughter can spin straw into gold. The king whisks the girl away to his castle, where he locks her in a chamber and orders her to spin all of the straw within into gold by morning if she values her life. The girl is beside herself, but as she laments her predicament, a strange little man appears and offers to help for the price of her necklace, which she gladly trades. Unfortunately, in the morning the king's greed grows when he sees the spun gold, and he demands that she repeat the performance. That evening, the girl trades her ring to the little man. On the third day, the king once again demands a night of spinning, but adds that if she completes it this time, she will be his wife. Unfortunately, she has nothing left to give the little man, and so she agrees to give him her first child. Later, when she becomes queen and gives birth, she is horrified to remember this bargain. The little man gives her three days to guess his name, and if she does, she may keep her child.

Students will likely be somewhat familiar with this tale, but what they may not realize is that, though the story's plot revolves around guessing

Rumpelstiltskin's name, he is the only character whose name the reader ever learns. The girl is referred to only as the miller's daughter or the queen. In our game, we'll turn the tables, and ask players to guess her name.

The Name of the Queen Step 1: Create the File Structure

We've been working directly in the console, but to create a program using JavaScript, we'll need to open a text editor such as Komodo Edit. Do this now and create a new file. Our JavaScript code will live inside of an html document, so follow the steps we used in Step 1 of Chapter 9 to create a basic html page with a doctype declaration, head, and body. Save it as **TheNameOfTheQueen .html** inside of a new folder. Let's call this folder **JSfiles**. Place the **rumple. png** image in the folder as well. It is often simplest if this is located on the desktop during class, but it could also be in a student's server folder or on a flash drive.

The Name of the Queen Step 2: HTML Elements

Remember that JavaScript controls how a page functions, but HTML provides the content. Before we get going with our scripts, we need to create some content to manipulate.

ID Attribute

Add four paragraph lines in the body. As shown in Figure 10-7, we'll add an id attribute inside each of the opening paragraph tags. The **id attribute** *specifies a unique name for an html element.* Later, we'll use these ids to manipulate their corresponding elements. Enter a prompt such as, "The queen guessed my name, but can you guess hers?" between the first paragraph tags. In the example, an additional direction "Choose a letter," is given after a <br> tag to place it on a new line. The line break is optional, as is any additional formatting, but players will need to know to enter a single letter. The other paragraph elements may be left blank, or filled with a space as in the example. Save and test. The results should resemble Figure 10-8.

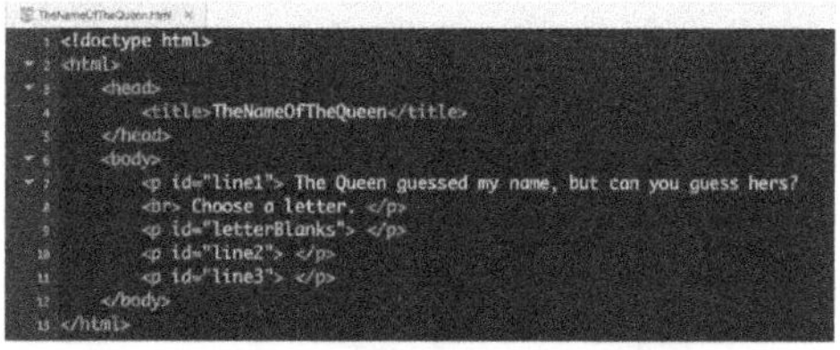

FIGURE 10-7   Paragraph IDs HTML.

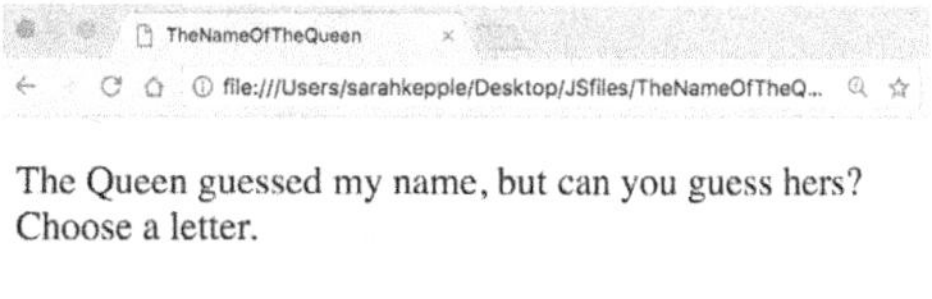

The Queen guessed my name, but can you guess hers?
Choose a letter.

FIGURE 10-8   Paragraph Lines in Browser.

Input

Since we asked the player for a letter, we better give her a place to type it. The HTML **input** element *specifies a field in which the user can enter data*. We'll use two of these. The first will create a text box in which the player will enter her guess. The second will create a button to submit that guess. Under the paragraph lines, add two input tags with the following attributes.

```
<input id = "guess" type = "text" value = ""/>
<input type = "button" value = "Submit" onclick = "letterGuess();"/>
```

The **id** attribute in the first line *allows JavaScript to pull the data entered*, just as we did in Scratch and Python. The **type** attribute *specifies the input object to be created*, in this case a text box with cursor. The **value** *attribute defines the default content to display*. In the second line, the type attribute indicates that a button object will be created, and the value attribute assigns the word *Submit* as the default text on the button. The **onclick** attribute *launches the designated sequence when the button is activated*. In this case, it will trigger the JavaScript function letterGuess(), which we'll create shortly. Finally, let's jazz this up a bit by adding an image. As we did in Chapter Nine, use the <img src=""/> tag to add the **rumpel.png** image. Figure 10-9 shows the input and image lines in context of the larger HTML file. Save and test in the browser. Though the results should appear like Figure 10-10, note that the button will not actually trigger anything yet because we haven't created the script to run yet. We'll start working with JavaScript next.

FIGURE 10-9   Input and Image HTML.

FIGURE 10-10   Input and Image in Browser.

The Name of the Queen Step 3: Set-up

The JavaScript code will live within the HTML tags <script> </script>. Place these after the HTML elements of the previous step. To get started, we need to create an array of possible queen names for the player to guess. You may wish to have students research German names that would have been popular when the Brothers Grimm were writing. Alternatively, you may let them choose or provide a list of German names. As we did in the Getting Started with

JavaScript activity, we'll create the array by assigning the array a variable and then filling it.

```
<script>
    var names = ["liesl", "gretl", "marta", "brigitta", "louisa"]
</script>
```

Math Methods

Each time the page is refreshed, we want the player to guess one of these names, selected at random. To do this we'll use the **Math.random()** method which *returns a non-predictable floating-point, or decimal number between 0 and 1*. We'll multiply this fraction by the number of entries in the names array by using length property in **names.length**, so if the number Math.random number returned is .34 and we multiply that times the number of elements in the names array (5), we would get 1.7. We'll then use the **Math.floor()** method to *round the number down to the nearest integer*. All of this would produce the number 1. We'll use this randomly generated number to call the element with the index value of [1]. In this example, that would be Gretl. This result will change each time the following script runs, so we want to create a variable called **SecretName** to store the value. Add the code below as shown in Figure 10-11.

FIGURE 10-11   Array Math Script.

```
var secretName = names[Math.floor(Math.random() * names.length)]
```

Answer Array

With so many names in the world, we'll need to give players a bit of a hint. In a traditional hangman game, the game maker draws blank lines to indicate the number of letters in the name. Each time the player guesses a letter correctly, the game maker fills in the appropriate blank. We'll use this common practice for our game too. We'll start by creating a variable to store a blank array.

```
var answerArray = []
```

We want to fill the answerArray with the number of blanks of the secretName. That value will change depending on which word our random code selects, so we'll use the length property. When used with an array, as in the previous

FIGURE 10-12   Answer Array Script.

step, the **length** property *sets or returns the number of elements in an array, but when used with a string it returns the number of characters in the string.* In this case we'll be using it to find the length of the string inside of secretName, so our code will be **secretName.length**. We'll place this inside of a **for** loop. The loop will start by creating a variable called **n**. It will then check to see if the value of is less than the number of characters in secretName, and if so, it will increment **n** until that is no longer true. The code inside of the loop will then fill the blank answerArray with an **n** quantity of blanks. Update the code as shown below and in Figure 10-12, which zooms in on just the script section of the overall TheNameOfTheQueen .html file.

```
for (var n = 0; n<secretName.length;i++){
   answerArray[n] = "_"
}
```

Get Element by ID

For the final step of our set up, we'll want to display the answer-Array blanks on the screen. To do this we'll use the **getElementById()** method which *returns the assigned HTML element*, in our case, the "letterBlanks" paragraph element. We'll combine this method with the **innerHTML** property, *which sets or returns the HTML content of the element.* We initially left letterBlanks empty, but now we'll fill it with the blanks of answerArray. Add the line shown in Figure 10-13. Save and test. When the browser is refreshed, the blank lines representing each letter of one of the words should display, as shown in the close up in Figure 10-14. Note, that quantity of blanks will vary for each student, each time the page is refreshed.

FIGURE 10-13   getElementById Script.

The Queen guessed my name, but can you guess hers? Choose a letter.

Submit

FIGURE 10-14   getElementById Browser.

The Name of the Queen Step 4: Check and Report

Currently, a player could type a letter into the text box, but nothing happens when she clicks submit. Recall that when we created the button input in the HTML section, we set it to launch the function letterGuess(). A **function** is simply *a block of code intended to perform a particular task*. JavaScript, like Python, includes many built-in functions, but both languages also allow users to create their own functions. In this step, we'll create the function letterGuess() which will check if the letter guessed is in the secretName, and, if so, return the letter in place of the appropriate blank.

Define the Function

Functions are defined by the function keyword. In a function declaration, this keyword is followed by the user-defined name of the function, parentheses to hold potential parameters, and curly brackets to hold the code to be executed when the function is called. Below the last line in the script, add the function letterGuess() declaration.

```
function letterGuess(){
}
```

Retrieve Guess

If we want to check the player's guess, the first thing we'll need to do is retrieve the value entered. When we created the text box input, we gave it the id "guess." The value was initially empty, but once our player types into the box, the value changes. When the player clicks submit we'll retrieve this updated value by using the **getElementById()** method and assigning the value to a new variable called **playerGuess**. Add that statement inside of the letterGuess() function.

```
function letterGuess(){
   var playerGuess = document.getElementById("guess")
}
```

Test and Update Loop

Next, we'll add a **for** loop. In the parameters of the for loop, we'll create a variable called **L** as in "letter" and set it's initial value to **0**. Then, we'll give the condition to test, which is if **L** is less than the number of characters in the secretName, increment **L**. So, if the secretName is "gretl", which has five characters, the for loop will run five times. Add the following line under the var playerGuess line.

```
for (var L = 0; L<secretName.length; L++){
}
```

The code that will run five times will of course be placed between the curly brackets after the for statement. This code will be an **if statement** that checks to see if the L character of secretName is equal to the value of the playerGuess. So if the secretName is "gretl" and the playerGuess is "e", then the if statement will be true the third time that the loop runs. Add the if statement into the for loop.

```
for (var L = 0; L<secretName.length; L++){
   if (secretName[L] === playerGuess.value) {
   }
}
```

When the if statement is true, the code between its brackets will run. That code will replace the underscore at the appropriate index number in the answerArray with the character of the playerGuess. So, with our gretl example, the for loop would run the first time, and the if statement would find that the secretName index value of 0 is not equal to the playerGuess of e, but is instead equal to g. The loop would run again, and again the if statement would be false as the index of 1 is equal to r, not the playerGuess of e. The third time the loop runs and checks the index of 2, the if statement would be true, as the character in the number two index position of *gretl* is *e*. The code in the if statement bracket will then call up the answerArray index of 2 and replace the underscore with *e*. Remind students that although e is the third letter in gretl, it is the index position of 2, because array indexes begin at 0. Add the code to update the answerArray index position as shown here.

```
for (var L = 0; L<secretName.length; L++){
   if (secretName[L] === playerGuess.value) {
      answerArray[L] = playerGuess.value
}
```

Report Correct Letter

Finally, we want to show players their progress. To do so, we'll update the letterBlanks html paragraph element. We can simply copy and paste the same getElementById line that we used prior to starting the letterGuess() function. As shown in Figure 10-15, make sure to place this line outside of the for loop brackets, but inside the function letterGuess() brackets. After completing this step, save and test. As shown in Figure 10-16, after guessing a correct letter, that letter should appear in place of the appropriate blank or blanks. Remember that the for loop continues to run after the first match, so if a player

FIGURE 10-15   Check and Report Correct Letter Script.

guesses a letter that appears more than once in the same word, all instances will fill in.

The Queen guessed my name, but can you guess hers? Choose a letter.

The Name of the Queen
Step 5: Respond if Correct

FIGURE 10-16   Check and Report Correct Letter Browser.

Let's add an acknowledgment when the player solves the puzzle by guessing all of the letters. To do so, we'll need to check to see if there are any blanks remaining each time the player guesses a correct letter, so to start we'll create a variable called **LetterDashes** to store the number of initial blanks. We'll place the declaration statement above the letterGuess() function. Challenge students to use what we've already explored to figure out how to assign LetterDashes a value that corresponds to the number of characters in the secretName. If they need a hint, refer them to the length property introduced in Step 3. They should come up with the following statement.

```
var LetterDashes = secretName.length
```

Next, we want to decrement LetterDashes for each correct letter guessed. To do this, we'll add a line at the end of the if statement.

```
for (var L = 0; L<secretName.length; L++){
    if (secretName[L] === playerGuess.value) {
        answerArray[L] = playerGuess.value
        LetterDashes—
    }
```

Finally, we need to add a second if statement inside of the first. Each time the player guesses a correct letter, this if statement will check to see if LetterDashes is less than 1, and if so, it will congratulate the player by updating the text in the HTML paragraph element identified as "line 3." Update the script as reflected in Figure 10-17, and then save and test. Note that the backslash in the congratulations string in line 36 simply allows us to wrap the text to fit in the window. When each correct letter is guessed, the response should resemble Figure 10-18.

While testing, students may notice that if a player accidentally submits a correct letter that has previously been submitted, it throws off this new bit of code. For instance, if the secretName is gretl, and the player guesses g, r, e, t, and then t again, the congratulations message appears, even though the name isn't solved with the final letter l. This happens because the if statement that decrements LetterDashes still evaluates

FIGURE 10-17   Congratulate Player Script.

The Queen guessed my name, but can you guess hers? Choose a letter.

g r e t l

Good job! It was gretl

t   Submit

FIGURE 10-18   Congratulate Player Browser.

to true if *t* is guessed twice, since *t* is in secretName. To solve this, we need to add another condition to the if statement to check that the letter is not already in the answerArray.

And

By this point, students will likely recognize that every programming language we've studied has built in logical operators such as and, or, and not. In JavaScript, the operator for **and** is two ampersands, **&&**. We'll place these between the two different conditions that need to evaluate to true in the first if statement, so place secretName[L] === playerGuess.value inside of its own parentheses.

```
if ((secretName[L] === playerGuess.value) &&)
```

Not Equal

For the second condition we'll use the **not equal to** comparison operator, !=. Add the additional condition inside its own parentheses, as shown in Figure 10-19. Save and test. Now, if a player guesses a previously guessed letter, the if statement will evaluate to false, so that LetterDashes remains at the same value and will only decrement when the player guesses a new correct letter.

FIGURE 10-19   And Not Equal to Answer Array (L) Script.

The Name of the Queen Step 6: Limit Guesses and End Game

Our game is almost complete, but we need to add a way for players to fail. Currently, they could simply guess their way through the whole alphabet! Let's address this by limiting the number of guesses available, and adding a loop to check and respond to the number of guesses.

Set Variable Guess Number

Add a variable called guessesLeft above the letterGuess() function. We could assign this a finite value such as "10," but since the name lengths vary, that would mean that the player who gets Gretl as the secretName can guess several more incorrect letters than the player who gets Brigitta. Instead, we can once again use our length property to set the initial number of guesses to the number of characters in secretName plus a defined cushion.

```
var guessesLeft = secretName.length + 3
```

Each time the player takes a guess, we need to decrement guessesLeft, so add a line doing so inside of the function letterGuess(), but before for loop, as shown in Figure 10-20.

Place for Loop Inside of If

FIGURE 10-20   Declare and Decrement guessesLeft Script.

Each time the letterGuess() function runs, we want to test if there are guesses remaining. If so, we want to execute the for loop, and if not, we want to alert the player that they have lost. To do this, we need to add an if statement and an else statement. Copy and paste the for loop into the if statement as shown in Figure 10-21. For clarity, indent the if statements inside of the for loop as shown.

FIGURE 10-21   If guessesLeft >−1 Execute For Loop Script.

Update User Feedback

As shown in Figure 10-21, we'll also want to move the letterBlanks line inside of the if guessesLeft >−1 statement, but outside of the for loop. Below that, we'll add an additional statement to show the player how many guesses remain. This statement, on line 44 in Figure 10-21 inserts the value of guessesLeft into an HTML paragraph element called "guessNumber." Make sure to return to the top of the file and create a paragraph element with the appropriate id as shown in Figure 10-22, and then save and test. The number of guesses remaining should appear and decrease after each guess, and the letter insertion should end when guessesLeft reaches zero.

Else End Game

Add an else statement as shown in Figure 10-23. The code inside will run if the player does not solve the riddle in the given number of guesses. Students may customize the losing message. This message will appear

FIGURE 10-22   Add guessNumber HTML.

FIGURE 10-23   Else Player Loses Script.

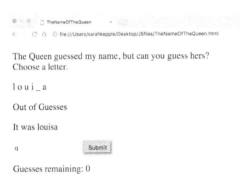

FIGURE 10-24   Else Player Loses Browser.

FIGURE 10-25   Full Code for the Name of the Queen.

after the player submits a letter with zero guessesLeft as shown in Figure 10-24. That's it! Compare your full code to that in Figure 10-25, or download the HTML file from the resources link in the appendix.

WHERE TO GO FROM HERE

After completing all of the coding activities in this book you and your students may be wondering, "What's next?" There are many possibilities. We've taken an art class approach to exploring coding, dabbling in different languages as a teacher might guide students through different media, all the while building underlying skill and learning overarching concepts.

You and your students may find that you prefer a particular language and want to dig deeper. A great way to do this is to give students a particular project. Challenge them to use what they've learned in that language to try to create their own games. You can give them a specific task, such as creating a (cartoon violence only) first person shooter, or designing a game based on a favorite story. Take a few club sessions to do this, helping them transfer their skills to solve problems in similar ways and discovering new strategies through research. You'll find resources to help you on your way in the bibliography.

Students may also be itching to explore new languages or concepts. For instance, students interested in web development or design may wish to learn how to incorporate CSS or learn SQL. Students interested in app creation might wish to build on their Python knowledge with Django or get started with Ruby and Ruby on Rails. Those who prefer visual programming languages like Scratch and GameMaker: Studio, can take their games and their skills to the next level with Alice, Carnegie Mellon's free programming environment for creating 3D animations and games. Finally, those students who have caught the bug and want to become gaming system developers will probably want to take a look at C++, C#, or Unity. There are numerous online and print resources for all of these languages and tools. As you've hopefully discovered throughout these activities, each language learned will make it easier to tackle the next, and adventures await those who are willing to try.

Appendix

To access the online resources go to
http://www.sarahkepple.com/books/teachingcoding
and enter the password:

GameOn!

Glossary

algorithm—A set of step-by-step instructions to solve a problem or perform a task.

array—A variable that can store multiple, indexed values.

Boolean—Presents a condition that can either be true or false.

break statement—Terminates the current loop and resumes at the next line after the loop.

camel case (stylized CamelCase)—The practice of capitalizing the first letter of each new word or abbreviation in a compound file name.

Cascading Style Sheets (CSS)—A language used to define how documents written in HTML should look.

coding—The term now commonly used to describe playful experimentations with computer programs or creating code.

command line interface (CLI)—Prompts and waits for user feedback via the keyboard before responding.

comments—Notes included about the program without affecting functionality.

computational thinking—The logical process of identifying and breaking down problems and analyzing the components to create a solution.

concatenate—To combine a string.

decrement—Decrease the value of a variable by one.

else if statement—Evaluates multiple conditional statements and executes the code within the first one to be true.

events—Trigger scripts to begin.

for loop—Iterates through a sequence in order.

functions—A block of code intended to perform a particular task.

game loop—Generally composed of three phases; respond to events, update, and render, which cycle continuously as the game runs.

GameMaker: Studio—A game creation system blending drag-and-drop visual coding with text-based GameMaker Language coding.

GameMaker: Studio create event—Triggers its assigned actions as soon as an instance of the object exists in the room.

GameMaker: Studio image speed—The rate, in steps, at which the instance cycles through the sub-images of a sprite.

GameMaker: Studio intersect boundary event—Triggers actions when the sprite overlaps with the edges of the room.

GameMaker: Studio object—May contain actions and events, be assigned a sprite, and serve as a template for multiple instances of itself.

GameMaker: Studio place_meeting (x, y, obj) function—Checks for a collision between the host object and another object at particular coordinates.

GameMaker: Studio random_range—Returns a nonpredictable number between the first value specified and the second.

GameMaker: Studio steps—The number of frames per second in a room.

global variables—Can be read, changed, and used by all object instances at any time.

graphical user interface (GUI)—A visual approach to interacting with a computer that includes windows and icons; employed by most modern operating systems.

HTML <a> tag—Creates a hyperlink to the address stored in the href attribute.

HTML <br> tag—Adds a line break.

HTML <hr> tag—Used to separate content or define a thematic change within an HTML page.

HTML <img/> tag—Links an image into a document.

HTML body element—Contains all of the main content of the HTML document.

HTML head element—Contains metadata about the document.

HTML Headings—Outline subsections of the document and are used by search engines to index the structure and content of the page.

HTML id attribute—Specifies a unique name for an html element and allows JavaScript to pull the data entered.

HTML input element—Specifies a field in which the user can enter data.

HTML onclick attribute—Launches the designated sequence when the button is activated.

HTML <p> tag—Indicates an element of regular text to print in the browser.

HTML tags—Set groups of characters that indicate what should happen with the content nested between the opening tag and the closing tag.

HTML title element—A mandatory component that defines the page title.

HTML type attribute—Specifies the input object to be created.

HTML value attribute—Defines the default content to display.

hyperlinks—Clickable connections from one document to another.

HyperText Markup Language (HTML)—A standardized system to describe text files to web browsers to achieve visual and hyperlink effects.

increment—Increase the value of a variable by one.

JavaScript—A programming language that determines the behavior of webpages.

JavaScript getElementById() method—Returns the assigned HTML element.

JavaScript innerHTML property—Sets or returns the HTML content of the element.

JavaScript length property—Sets or returns the number of elements in an array, but when used with a string it returns the number of characters in the string.

JavaScript Math.floor() method—Rounds the number down to the nearest integer.

JavaScript Math.random() method—Returns a non-predictable floating point, or decimal number between 0 and 1.

JavaScript var—The keyword used to declare a variable.

modules—Source files that contain reusable code elements such as functions, classes, and global variables.

program—A set of detailed instructions.

programming—Refers to the logic, the crafting of the instructions.

pygame—A free and open source programming language library for creating multimedia projects in Python.

pygame blit—Draws one surface object onto another.

pygame display.update() function—Redraws the surface object returned by pygame.display.set_mode().

pygame draw.rect() function—Draws rectangles to a surface.

pygame event.get() function—Returns a list of event objects that have happened since the last time the function was called.

pygame key.get_pressed() function—Generates a sequence of Boolean values representing the state of each key on the keyboard.

pygame quit()—Reverses the initialization process, deactivating the pygame library.

pygame Rect object—Stores rectangular coordinates.

pygame Rect.collidelist() method—Tests if a rectangle is colliding with any of those in a list. If so, it reports back the index number of the first collision. If not, it reports back an index of –1.

Pygame surface object—Produces a two-dimensional rectangle.

Python—A multipurpose, text-based programming language.

Python end of line error—Python reached the end of a line while still in a string.

Python IDLE editor—Used to create, edit, and save Python programs.

Python IDLE shell—Used to run Python programs.

Python input() function—Stops the flow of the program until the user enters a response and submits it with the return key.

Python invalid syntax error—Python does not know how to interpret a line.

Python list—A sequence of items, each assigned an index number beginning with 0.

Python name error—Python does not recognize the function or variable name used in the program.

Python print() function—Displays the content between the brackets in the shell.

Python quit() function—Forces the shell to exit the program.

Python random.randint (a,b)—Returns an integer that is greater than or equal to a and less than or equal to b.

Python str() function—Converts an integer to a string.

Scratch—A visual programming language and online community designed to teach kids to code.

Scratch () and () block—Checks that two conditions are both true.

Scratch answer block—A sensing block, in that it can absorb information and a reporting block because it stores that information for potential use in other parts of the script.

Scratch ask () and wait block—Gives the user a prompt and launches an input box.

Scratch block palette—Contains bits of code that snap together to form scripts.

Scratch create clone of (myself) block—May be used to create a copy of the sprite in which it is located or it may create a copy of a different sprite.

Scratch forever block—Causes the blocks it contains to loop continuously from the time the program starts until the time it ends or the script is interrupted.

Scratch global variable—Can be read and changed by any sprite.

Scratch go back () layers block—Changes the assigned depth value of a sprite.

Scratch go to x () y () block—Moves the block to indicated Cartesian coordinates.

Scratch hide block—Renders the sprite invisible to the viewer without deleting it.

Scratch if () then, else block—Checks its Boolean condition, and if it is true, it activates the code held inside the first C, but if the condition is false, it activates the code inside the second C.

Scratch join () () block—Concatenates, or merges, two values together.

Scratch play sound () block—Plays the selected audio while the remaining script continues to run.

Scratch play sound () until done block—Pauses the remaining subsequent script blocks until the audio file finishes playing.

Scratch say () for () secs block—Adds a speech bubble to the sprite with the designated text for the indicated amount of time.

Scratch set size to () % block—Shrinks or grows the sprite from its original size depending on the number indicated.

Scratch show block—Renders the sprite visible to the viewer.

Scratch sprite library—A collection of sprites including some with multiple costumes.

Scratch sprites—Visual elements that we can program and control.

Scratch start as a clone block—Activates each newly created clone. It is a Hat block, which means that it is intended to start a new script.

Scratch switch costume to () block—Used to jump to a specific costume rather than the next one in consecutive order.

Scratch touching block—Sensing block that detects if a sprite's boundaries are overlapping with those of another element and reports back a Boolean value of true or false.

Scratch x position block—Reports the current horizontal coordinate of a sprite.

sprite sheet—A collection of images, each representing a different physical expression, merged into one document.

sprites—Standalone graphical elements that can move or be manipulated among other graphical elements.

string—A sequence of characters.

syntax—The standard arrangement of components in a certain language to create shared meaning.

variable—Is a changeable value assigned to a letter, word, or symbol.

when green flag clicked block—Launches the program when the user initiates a mouse down on the green flag above the stage panel.

while loop—Runs the commands it contains as long as a condition is true.

References

Braun, Linda and Marijke Visser. "Ready to Code: Connecting Youth to CS Opportunity Through Libraries." Office for Information Technology Policy. January, 2017. Accessed November 13, 2017. http://www.ala.org/advocacy/sites/ala.org.advocacy/files/content/pp/Ready_To_Code_Report_FINAL.pdf

Cass, Stephen. "The 2017 Top Programming Languages." Institute of Electrical and Electronics Engineer (IEEE) Spectrum: Technology, Engineering, and Science News. July 18, 2017. Accessed October 20, 2017. https://spectrum.ieee.org/computing/software/the-2017-top-programming-languages

"Color Addition." The Physics Classroom. Accessed October 29, 2017. http://www.physicsclassroom.com/class/light/Lesson-2/Color-Addition

"Colour And Blending." GameMaker: Studio Web Online Help System. 2013. Accessed October 14, 2017. http://docs.yoyogames.com/source/dadiospice/002_reference/drawing/color%20and%20blending/index.html

Common Core State Standards Initiative. 2014. "Note on Range and Content of Student Speaking and Listening." Accessed February 16, 2017. http://www.corestandards.org/ELA-Literacy/CCRA/SL/

"Computer and Information Technology Occupations." Occupational Outlook Handbook. October 24, 2017. Accessed November 13, 2017. https://www.bls.gov/ooh/computer-and-information-technology/home.html

Computer History Museum. "Exhibition: Personal Computers: The Homebrew Computer Club." 2015. Accessed November 15, 2017. http://www.computerhistory.org/revolution/personal-computers/17/312

Creative Commons. Accessed October 02, 2017. https://creativecommons.org/

"English Language Arts Standards: Anchor Standards: Literacy." Common Core State Standards Initiative. Accessed November 13, 2017. http://www.corestandards.org/ELA-Literacy/CCRA/L/

"English Language Arts Standards: Anchor Standards: Speaking and Listening." Common Core State Standards Initiative. Accessed November 13, 2017. http://www.corestandards.org/ELA-Literacy/CCRA/L/

183

"Free eBooks." Project Gutenberg. August 19, 2017. Accessed October 07, 2017. https://www.gutenberg.org/wiki/Main_Page

"Grant Funding for Computer Science & Computational Thinking Programs." YALSA Blog. June 28, 2017. Accessed November 13, 2017. http://yalsa.ala .org/blog/2017/06/28/grant-funding-for-computer-science-computational -thinking-programs/

Hoffman, Judy, John Carlo, and Denise M. Davis. "Executive Summary: Public Library Funding & Technology Access Study 2011–2012." Digital supplement of American Libraries magazine. Summer 2012. Accessed February 10, 2017. http://www.ala.org/research/sites/ala.org.research/files/content/initiatives /plftas/2011_2012/plftas12_execsummary.pdf

Hutchison, Amy, Larysa Nadolny, and Anne Estapa. 2016. "Using Coding Apps to Support Literacy Instruction and Develop Coding Literacy." The Reading Teacher, 69(5), 493–503.

Kipling, Rudyard, Don Daily, and Elizabeth Encarnacion. The Jungle Book. The Classic Edition, Kennebunkport: Cider Mill Press, 2014.

Lunovox. "Sprite de Fada (Fairy)." OpenGameArt.org. July 18, 2011. Accessed October 23, 2017. https://opengameart.org/content/sprite-de-fada-fairy

Office, U.S. Copyright. "More Information on Fair Use: U.S. Copyright Office." Copyright September 2017. Accessed October 02, 2017. https://www.copyright .gov/fair-use/more-info.html

Open Cleveland. 2017. Accessed November 15, 2017. http://www.opencleveland.org

Pew Research Center. May 2016. "News Use Across Social Media Platforms 2016."

Resnick, Mitch. "Mitch Resnick." Mitch Resnick: Speaker: TED.com. TED, January 2013. Accessed February 16, 2017.

Resnick, Mitchel. "Learn to Code, Code to Learn." EdSurge. May 8, 2013. Accessed November 13, 2017. https://www.edsurge.com/news/2013-05-08-learn-to -code-code-to-learn

"Searching for Computer Science: Access and Barriers in U.S. K–12 Education." Landscape of K–12 Computer Science Education in the U.S. August 1, 2015. Accessed October 21, 2017. http://services.google.com/fh/files/misc/searching -for-computer-science_report.pdf

Smith, Aaron. "Searching for Work in the Digital Era." Pew Research Center: Internet, Science & Tech. N.p., 19 Nov. 2015. Web. Accessed Feb. 15, 2017. http:// www.pewinternet.org/2015/11/19/searching-for-work-in-the-digital-era/

Thong, Michelle. "Hack Nights Are a Civic Good." Code for America Blog-Medium. June 13, 2017. Accessed November 15, 2017. https://medium.com/code-for -america/hack-nights-are-a-civic-good-86986cc7f0d3

"TIOBE Index for October 2017." TIOBE Index: TIOBE—The Software Quality Company. Accessed October 20, 2017. https://www.tiobe.com/tiobe-index/

Truss, Lynn. 2006. Eats, Shoots & Leaves: Why, Commas Really Do Make a Difference! New York: G.P. Putnam's Sons.

"Tynker: Coding for Kids." *Parents: Frequently Asked Questions.* Tynker.com. 2017. Accessed March 25, 2017. https://www.tynker.com/parents/

Van Rossum, Guido. "Why was Python Created in the First Place?" General Python FAQ. Accessed October 20, 2017. https://docs.python.org/3/faq/general .html#why-was-python-created-in-the-first-place

ZapSplat—Download free sound effects. Accessed October 12, 2017. https://www .zapsplat.com/

Annotated Bibliography

Alice. Carnegie Mellon University. 2017. Accessed November 20, 2017. http://www
.alice.org/

> Alice is an initiative of Carnegie Mellon University which offers 3D anima-
> tion software, tutorials, educator resources, and more on this official web-
> site. Alice 3 transitions from the original framework into Java.

Code Combat. 2017. Accessed November 20, 2017. https://codecombat.com/

> Code Combat offers fun multiplayer games that are played by writing real
> code, such as Python or Javascript. Instructors can set up "clans" to monitor
> student progress. Note that while there are many free lessons, and teachers
> get free subscriptions for evaluation purposes, there are premium subscrip-
> tions that cost money.

Codecademy. 2017. Accessed November 20, 2017. https://www.codecademy.com/

> Codecademy offers free, online, interactive tutorials for just about every
> major programming language. Users can create free accounts to track their
> progress through modules. This is a great resource for coding enthusiasts or
> instructors to learn independently, or it can be used as part of a class or club.

CodinGame 2017. Accessed November 20, 2017. https://www.codingame.com/start

> CodinGame offers users a huge selection of programming languages from
> which to choose. Users can create a free account or continue without one to
> debug games with the help of tutorials, a viewer and console output window.
> CodinGame is most appropriate for teens and adults who are already famil-
> iar with general coding concepts. It's a great way for those who've had an
> introduction to a programming language to advance their skills.

Google's Python Class. Google Developers. December 13, 2012. Accessed November 20, 2017. https://developers.google.com/edu/python/?hl=en

> Google's Python Class is a free online course to help those with some coding experience learn and use Python. It includes written and video modules that are appropriate for teens or adults looking for a self-paced learning system, or for a coding club instructor to teach herself.

Marji, Majed. *Learn to Program with Scratch: A Visual Introduction to Programming with Games, Art, Science, and Math.* San Francisco, CA: No Starch Press, 2014.

> This book written by an electrical engineer and technically reviewed by a creative-computing educator explains just about everything there is to know about Scratch, and also bigger ideas that are transferrable to other programming environments. Colored illustrations help break up the large amount of text. At 261 pages, this is a resource best suited to teens and adults, although adults who serve children will find activities that they can use with their groups.

McComb, Gordon. *The Gamer's Guide to Coding.* Toronto: Sterling Publishing, 2017.

> Well-designed visuals make it easy to follow McComb's instructions and explanations. Though the book's primary focus is JavaScript, it also digs deeper into HTML and CSS than most other resources, and the activities are designed specifically for those interested in creating games.

McCue, Camille. *Coding for Kids for Dummies.* Hoboken, NJ: John Wiley & Sons, 2015.

> Though the book's title indicates that it's for kids, this book is less child-friendly than the Vorerman and Woodcock book for parents. However, it introduces a unique tool called MicroWorlds Ex which uses natural language for commands and combines sequential and event-driven programming. The major drawback to MicroWorlds Ex or MWEX is that it is not free like Scratch and GameMaker.

Payne, Bryson. *Teach Your Kids to Code: A Parent-friendly Guide to Python Programming.* San Francisco, CA: No Starch Press, 2015.

> This is one of several how-to-code books in a series from No Starch Press. Like the Marji book on Scratch, graphics and color-delineated code examples help break up the text, which is aimed toward an adult audience, but does not assume preliminary expertise and is accessible for tweens and teens.

Rohde, Michael. *GameMaker Studio for Dummies.* Online-Ausg. ed. Hoboken, NJ: Wiley, 2014.

> Like many of the "For Dummies" series of instructional books, the writing is friendly and conversational, and the instruction starts at the very beginning with how to drag and drop elements into the interface to create a game. It gradually expands to include how to use GameMaker's text-based coding language.

Strom, Chris. *3D Game Programming for Kids.* Pragmatic Bookshelf, 2013.

> Strom gets readers going right away with a slick and free interface of his own invention, the ICE Code Editor, which allows users to code directly in a

browser and create 3D animations and games, learning JavaScript along the way.

Sweigart, Al. *Making Games with Python & Pygame*. Published by the Author. 2012.

Al Sweigart generously publishes all of his beginner friendly coding books under a creative-commons license. They can be purchased in print form, but he also makes them available for free online at http://inventwithpython .com/. His writing is casual and friendly, and he coaches readers from the ground up while still keeping things interesting for those with a little experience. On the website, check out his other books on Python and Scratch.

Vorderman, Carol, and Jon Woodcock. *Help Your Kids with Computer Coding: A Unique Step-by-Step Visual Guide, from Binary Code to Building Games*. New York, NY: Dorling Kindersley Limited, 2014.

Like many DK books, this manual is well organized with colorful graphics and pictures. The text begins with a basic introduction to computer coding, moves into how to program with Scratch, then advances to Python and then ends with brief sections on internal computer components and programming careers.

W3Schools, 2017. November 20, 2017. http://www.w3schools.com/

W3Schools offers free online tutorials for almost everything that has to do with coding for the web. Subjects include HTML, CSS, JavaScript, PHP, SQL, and JQuery.

Index

About the Author

SARAH KEPPLE, MLIS, is owner of and chief learning strategist at Gigalearn, LLC, where she uses her experience in school and public libraries to help transform community technology learning. She has presented on participatory technology learning for the American Library Association, American Association of School Librarians, Library Information Technology Association, Public Library Association, Young Adult Library Services Association, Toy Library Association, and eTech Ohio conference, and she publishes via her blog www.sarahkepple .com. The author of Libraries Unlimited's *Library Robotics: Technology and English Language Arts Activities for Ages 8–24*, Kepple holds a bachelor of fine arts degree from Kent State University as well as a master's degree in library and information science from Drexel University. She is a Treu-Mart Youth Development Fellow through Case Western Reserve University.

www.ingramcontent.com/pod-product-compliance
Lightning Source LLC
LaVergne TN
LVHW062314060326

832902LV00013B/2205